GEO-ECONOMIC SURVEY OF LAKSHADWEEP

About the Author

Prof. B.N. Sinha is the retired Professor and Head, Department of Geography of the Utkal University, Bhubaneswar. He was also the Professor and Head of Geography, of the Karnataka University, Dharwar. Currently he is the Visiting Professor, Department of Earth Sciences, Manipur University, Imphal. He is the author of sixteen books and about 85 papers, published in national and international journals. He was not only the Honorary Editor of the Indian Council of Geographers for about a decade but also Secretary of the Eastern Geographical Society, Bhubaneswar.

He is the past President of Deccan Geographical Society, Osmania University, Hyderabad; Indian Council of Geographers and now he is the President of Eastern Geographical Society. He was a member of the Panel in Geography of the University Grants Commission and a member of the Geology and Geography Section of the Indian Science Congress for two terms.

As a Visiting Professor, under the Senior Fulbright Heys Exchange Programme to the U.S.A. during 1973-74, he has lectured in many American and Canadian Universities from coast to coast. He has successfully guided several scholars leading to their doctoral degree both in Karnataka and Utkal Universities. He is one of the leading researchers in geography in India.

GEO-ECONOMIC SURVEY OF LAKSHADWEEP

B.N. SINHA
President
National Institute of Theoretical and Applied Research
Bhubaneswar
and
Former Professor of Geography
Utkal University, Bhubaneswar

CONCEPT PUBLISHING COMPANY, NEW DELHI 110059

ISBN 81-7022-503-5

First Published 1994

Published and Printed by
Ashok Kumar Mittal
Concept Publishing Company
A/15-16, Commercial Block, Mohan Garden
NEW DELHI-110059 (India)

Lasertypeset by
Printing Express
H-13, Bali Nagar
NEW DELHI-110015

PREFACE

The idea of studying Lakshadweep and Minicoy Islands was first mooted when myself and Prof. Oomen were together in the United States as Visiting Professors under Exchange Programme during 1973-74. After we returned to India, I followed it up and submitted a research proposal to the U.G.C. where I conceived not only of making it a collaborative inter-disciplinary research but also inter-University in character. The obvious choice was the three disciplines; Geography, Geology and Economics and I was lucky to have friends who could agree to the proposal to be the Co-directors.

Prof. Naganna, the then Prof. and Head, Department of Geology, Bangalore University, Bangalore and Prof. Oomen, Prof. and Head, Department of Economics, John Mathai Institute, Calicut University, Trichur agreed to work as Co-directors with me. I chose them not only because they are experts of repute in their fields of specialisation but also Prof. Oomen was a man from Kerala and Malayalam was his mother tongue while Prof. Naganna was a Kanadika and his mother tongue was Kannad. These two languages are widely spoken and understood in the Lakshadweep Islands. Thus, they and their researchers acted as local guides of the students of Geography of the Utkal University whose mother tongue was Oriya. Dr. D.K. Singh, the then Reader, now Professor, of this Department helped the students of Geography in field investigations. I acted as the Co-ordinator-cum-Principal Investigator of the entire project.

Research Investigators were recruited from these three fields and from three places, Bhubaneswar, Bangalore and Trichur. P.G. Students of Geography also helped in field investigations in the Lakshadweep Islands.

The first problem I had to face was to coordinate these three departments located at three different places while the field of research was located in the Lakshadweep Islands.

In 1977, going to Lakshadweep was a tough job since sailings to Lakshadweep were very limited and the commercial ships were old and obsolete and that too again the sailings were only confined to a few months during winter and completely absent during the turbulent South-West monsoon period. I had to approach Late Jagajivan Ram, the then Union Minister of Defence, to get Indian Navy's help to transport the first batch of researchers to Lakshadweep to which he readily agreed and directed the Indian Navy to transport us to Kavaratti, the capital of Lakshadweep Islands from Cochin. A history was created in the Indian Navy as we were the first batch of civilians to be transported by the Indian Navy by I.N.S. Kaveri and from Kavaratti to Cochin by I.N.S. Brahmaputra. We are thankful to the Indian Navy for their unique help rendered to us in ferrying us from Cochin to Kavaratti and back. Thereafter, many trips have been undertaken by the researchers who spent many months in the islands.

I am sorry that this project took about more than a decade due to many unforeseen and unavoidable circumstances. The most important problem arose when Prof. Oomen left for Middle East for several years and after his return also he could not be of much help due to his own research problems. Prof. Naganna also remained busy in his work and his active involvement in the academic administration of the Bangalore University when he became the Rector. I too also became involved in the University administration when I became the Member of the Syndicate for six long years and in other personal research projects. Visiting Lakshadweep became also problematic as it was included in the inner-line of the Indian Territory.

However, this delay in finalising the report was a blessing in disguise. In the 1980s, a large number of other researchers, Government Departments of the Union Territory, were engaged in research on the Islands. To name one was the "Futurology Workshop on Identification of S & T inputs towards long-range Socio-economic Prospective on Lakshadweep Island" workshop held at Trivandrum in July 1986, where a lot of materials which hitherto were not available came to light. The 1981 Census was also available after mid-1980s. All these documents became invaluable assets in finalising the Geo-economic Survey Report of the Lakshadweep Islands.

I am glad that the report has come up well and is being published by Concept Publishing Company, New Delhi and as it will be like a Bible on the Islands where all the aspects from A to Z have touched upon.

I will be failing in my duty if I do not thank the U.G.C. who funded the research project. I am also thankful to a band of dedicated researchers who were employed in the project. My thanks are specially due to Prof. S.N. Tripathy, Professor and Head, Department of Geography, Utkal University, for all that he has done in this research project. My thanks are also due to Shri P. Padhi, Lecturer, Centre of Regional Studies, who has meticulously gone through the report many times and has made necessary changes wherever it is desirable. My thanks are also due to Shri P. Pattnaik, Research Investigator, Centre of Regional Studies who has assisted me and Shri Padhi in finalising the project report. In this connection, the two young researchers to be thanked are: Shri A.K. Sinha and Shri D. Chotaray who have completed the Cartographic works meticulously without whose help, the maps could not have taken shapes. The finishing touches were given by Shri H. Nayak, Senior Steno, Centre of Regional Studies who has made the draft typing of the research report. I am also grateful to Shri S.N. Behera, Typist of the Department of Geography who could type neatly in the electronic type-writer of the Department without whose help, this would not have been possible.

I am thankful to the University authorities for kindly allowing me to undertake this research problem. I will consider my labour fruitful, if this report is of any help to the researchers of the country and abroad.

B.N. Sinha
Co-ordinator-Cum-Principal Investigator,
Geo-economic Survey of Lakshadweep

[illegible] M. [illegible] Tripathy, Professor and Head, Department of Geography, [illegible] University, [illegible] the Research [illegible] the research project. [illegible] my [illegible] [illegible], Senior [illegible] Centre of Regional Studies, who [illegible] meticulously went through the report [illegible] and [illegible] necessary changes wherever it is desirable. My thanks are also due to [illegible] Research Investigator, Centre of Regional Studies, who [illegible] in [illegible] the [illegible] two young researchers to be [illegible] Chaudary who [illegible] [illegible], without whose help the maps [illegible] the [illegible] [illegible] Senior [illegible] of Regional Studies [illegible] the [illegible] report [illegible] Department of Geography who [illegible] [illegible] of the Department without whose help this would not have been possible.

[illegible] kindly [illegible] [illegible] [illegible] [illegible] [illegible] of the [illegible]

[illegible]

Co-ordinator Cum Principal Investigator

[illegible] Survey [illegible]

CONTENTS

LIST OF TABLES

LIST OF FIGURES

BASIC BASE

1

INTRODUCTION

The Origin of the Name

The early classical geographers and Arab travellers were referring the entire archipelago consisting of both Lakshadweep and Maldives by 'Divis' or 'Dibajaat'.[1] In the records of a Dutch Company the islands are referred as Laccadives (Lakshadweep). J. V. Stein Van Gollensesse in A. D. 1743 referred it as 'Lekker-Diva' in the Memorandum on Administration of the Malabar Coast.[2] In British records it was referred to as 'Laccadives' but it was not popular as the local people called themselves as inhabitants of 'Divis' till recently.

The colloquial term 'Laccadives' is derived from 'Lakshadweep' which means as 'hundred thousand island'. The Union Territory was called as 'Laccadive, Minicoy and Amindivi islands' till recently. The Union Territory was officially known as Lakshadweep only on 1st November, 1973 from it's anglicised name 'Laccadives'.

The 'Amindivi' is the collective name used for 'Amini' group of islands. There is no ancient source for the name 'Amindivi or Amini Divi'. The local people call it 'Amini Island'. They first embraced Islam. The island might have been named as 'Amini" [3] by the Arabs as Prophet Himself was known as 'Al-Amin'. The Minicoy, the southern most island, is known as 'Malik' to Minicoyans and Maladivians. 'Malik' is an Arabic word for 'King'. Because of the beauty of the islands the name Malik (King – King of Islands) might have been used. Now it is known as 'Minicoy', through phonetic deviations.

The word 'Lakha' in Sanskrit as well as in Malayalam might have been derived from the root 'lag' as that which is attached or fixed, means 'a mark or sign especially a mark to aim art'. These islands lie in the direct trade route between Malabar-Africa and Arabia and were used as a land-mark for the early navigators during the sailing-ship-days which probably is the reason why this is called as 'Lakshadweep'.

Lakshadweep with an area of 32 sq. km. and a population of 40.2

thousand as per 1981 Census, has assumed greater importance now than ever before in the light of the establishing a Naval Base at Dicogo Garcia in the Indian Ocean by the United States of America. The growing menace of the Pakistan and Chinese Naval Forces in the Indian Ocean have also added importance to these islands. Further our offshore hydrocarbon resources in the E.E.Z. in the Bombay Highs, naval establishment at Cochin, Goa and Mazagon Docks at Bombay which need to be protected from enemy attack at the time of emergency. The national and international shipping route which passes through nine Degree Channel can be better protected from Lakshadweep Islands. From these military and defence point of view, a geo-economic study of Lakshadweep assumed a great national importance. It is important now to know the terrain, its people, the economic potentialities, since, at the time of any emergency, Lakshadweep will be *our first line of defence in the Arabian Sea.*

This research project is a collaborative research concerning three Universities and three disciplines such as the Department of Geography, Utkal University, Bhubaneswar; Department of Geology, Bangalore University, Bangalore, and Department of Economics, Calicut University, Trichur. Each of these Departments was responsible for the specified aspects of the study as indicated in the following paragraphs and at the end, the findings have been coordinated and finalised by me as the Co-ordinator.

The project aimed at making a comprehensive study of the islands embracing the terrain, its people and the economic bases with expertise available in these three different departments like Geography, Geology and Economics of the three Universities.

A Brief Over-view of Work Already done on Lakshadweep Islands

Not much work has been done till end of seventies on these off-shore islands excepting the availability of some topographical maps prepared by the Survey of India. Very little literature is available on these islands which amounts to almost nil. In the eighties emphasis has been laid on these islands. Apart from our survey a workshop on "Futurology Workshop on Identification of S & T Inputs towards Long Range Socio-economic Perspective of Lakshadweep Islands" has been organised at Trivandrum in July 1986 has brought these islands to lime light.

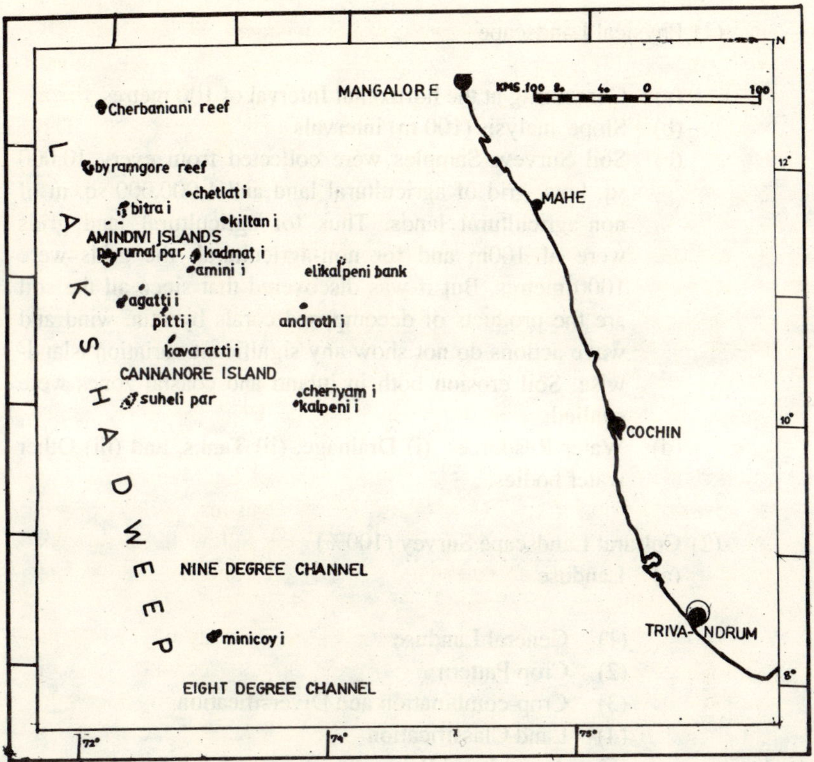

FIG. 1.1: Location of Lakshadweep Islands

Hypothesis

The present research is an area study and hence the question of testing a hypothesis does not arise. As regards the questionnaire, it was designed to suit the local needs which are entirely different from those of the main land. Extensive field work was done by the three Directors, and the Coordinator who visited Lakshadweep a number of times and the Research Investigators spent several months in collecting data from the field. This is mainly because of non-availability of data regarding the terrain and its people from secondary sources.

Coverage

The following aspects have been covered:

(1) Physical Landscape

(a) Contouring at the horizontal Interval of 100 metres.
(b) Slope analysis (100 m) intervals
(c) Soil Survey: Samples were collected from every 10,000 sq. kms. grid of agricultural land and 1,000,000 sq. m of non-agricultural lands. Thus for agricultural land grids were of 100m and for non-agricultural, the grids were 1000 metres. But it was discovered that since all the soil are the products of decomposed corals by rain, wind and wave actions do not show any significant variation island-wise. Soil erosion both in inland and coastal zones were studied.
(d) Water Resources: (i) Drainage, (ii) Tanks, and (iii) Other water bodies.

(2) Cultural Landscape Survey (100%)

(a) Landuse

(1) General Landuse
(2) Crop Pattern
(3) Crop-combination and Diversification
(4) Land Classification
(5) Agricultural Region

(b) Housing and Settlement Surveys:

(1) Housing Survey at 20 per cent sample study
(2) Settlement Surveys at 20 per cent sample study.

Data Collection

The students from each discipline were responsible for the collection of primary data by field work covering the total period of 60 days, which was done in two phases. These primary data were analysed by regular staff members who were appointed under the scheme.

Mode of Field Work

While the physical landscape surveys consisting of contour survey, slope analysis, soil study and water resources were handled by geography students, the geological surveys were carried out by the geologists. The terrain evaluation were done by Geography, Geology students jointly. The cultural and economic surveys were jointly conducted by the researchers in geography and economics. The students were divided into groups consisting of one geography and one economics. Since the economics students came from Kerala and could speak the local language (Malayalam), they acted as interpreters of the group and field work was conducted as per specified programme.

Data Processing

Most of the questionnaires were pre-coded. The computerising the data were not necessary since the data were not vast. The findings covering geographical, geological and economic aspects are represented in maps and diagrams which have been used as tools to reach conclusions.

The Geological study of the Lakshadweep Islands aimed at the preparation of a Geological map of the Lakshadweep Island. But non-availability of detailed topographical maps acted as a stumbling block. Geological samples were collected from the islands for petrological and palaeontological studies at Bangalore University. A few samples were also analysed chemically.

NOTES

1. Which means islands.
2. A. Galletti, *The Dutch in Malabar*, p. 67, 2-1 Admn/lak/ 76.
3. In Arabic 'Amin' meaning faithful.

2

LOCATION, AREA AND EXTENSION

The Lakshadweep islands consisting of ten islands are irregularly scattered in the Arabian Sea Off the West Cost of India between 8°0′ and 12°30′ North latitude and between 70°0′ and 71°0′ East longitude.

According to the Survey of India, the Geographical area of the Lakshadweep islands is 32 sq. km. Its area according to the revenue records is 28.5 sq. km. which represents only landuse area. Table 2.1 shows the location, area and extension of the individual islands.

TABLE 2.1: Locational details of the Lakshadweep Islands

Islands	Area (sq.km)	Latitude	Longitude	Length (km.)	Breadth (km.)
Androth	4.8	N 10°48′33"	E 73°40′00"	4.8	2.0
Minicoy	4.4	N 8°16′00"	E 73°3′0"	9.8	0.88
Kavaratti	3.6	N 10°33′30"	E 72°36′30"	5.6	1.2
Kadamat	3.1	N 11°13′0"	E 72°47′0"	8.14	0.55
Agatti	2.7	N 10°51′30"	E 72°11′0"	5.6	0.57
Amini	2.6	N 11°5′0"	E 72°44′0"	3.2	1.60
Kalpeni	2.3	N 10°4′0"	E 73°38′0"	4.8	1.2
Kiltan	1.6	N 11°28′0"	E 73°0′0"	3.26	1.2
Chetlat	1.0	N 11°41′0"	E 72°4′0"	2.65	0.59
Bitra	0.1	N 11°35′30"	E 72°09′30"	1.05	0.18

* Data for inhabited islands are given and data for uninhabited islands are not available. The length is calculated by taking the longest point of the island into account. The bradeth is calculated by taking the widest point into account. Data are complied from different sources by the author.

Androth

It is the eastern most island and is the nearest in the group to the mainland. The latitudinal and longitudinal extent is N 10°48′33" by E 73°40′. Its length is 4.8 km and its broadest part is 2.0 km. This island is 158 km from Cochin and is elongated in East-West manner unlike other islands which have maximum north-south elongation. The other peculiarity of this island is, it is devoid of lagoon, as the island occupies the whole of the atoll. The land area is 4.8 sq.km.

Minicoy

The island is situated on the southern extremity of the archipelago. It is the farthest from the mainland being located 388.8 km from the Lakshadweep and Amindivi group of islands. The island is crescent shaped and is 9.8 km in length and 0.8 km in width. It is located on 8°16′0" N latitude and 73°03′0" E longitude. The total area is 4.4 sq. km. This island is separated from the main group of island by 10° channel.

Kavaratti

Kavaratti, the headquarters of the territory, lies between Agatti and Androth, but a little to the south. The island is 5.6 km in the length and 1.2 km in width. At the southern end, the land shrinks to a width of only a few metres. It is located on latitude N 10°33′30" and longitude E 72°36′30". The total area of this island is 3.6 sq. km. This island is 299.2 km from Calicut.

Kadamat

This club shaped island is stretching in north-south direction for 8.14 km and nowhere it is broader that 0.55 km. The area of the island is 3.1 sq km and lies on latitude N 11°13′ and longitude E 72°46′. The southern end tapers down to a very narrow strip and about 9.6 km south of this tip lies Amini, which is easily visible by naked eyes.

Agatti

This is the westerly most island of the group. It is club shaped, broad at the north and tapers in the middle and ends in a narrow strip hardly 95 metres wide in the south. It is 5.6 km. long and 0.57 km. broad. It is located on N 10°51′30" latitude and E 72°11′ longitude. The total are is 2.7 sq km.

Amini

Amini is the northern most island in the Amindivi group. It is narrow on the west and wider towards the north. Its length is about 3.2 km and its width is about 1.6 km. The geographical location is 11°5′ N latitude, 72°44′ E longitude. The area of this island is 2.6 sq. km. It is about 180.0 km to the west of Calicut.

Kalpeni

This peculiarly shaped island, with a bulging to the south, a pointed west and extremely narrowing north lies in latitude 10°04′ N and longitude 73°38′ E. Its area is 2.3 sq km, and lies 228.8 km to the south-west of Calicut. This island is 4.8 km long and 1.2 km broad.

Kiltan

This island lies on 11°28′ N latitude and 73°0′ E longitude. The total area is 1.6 sq km. This island lies 51 km. North-East of Amini. Its length is 3.26 km. and its broadest part is 1.1 km. The islands nearest to Kiltan are Chetlat on the North-West and Kadamat on the South-West.

Chetlat

Chetlat is the northern most island of the Lakshadweep Group. This long narrow island is 56.0 km. due north of Amini. It is shaped like an old fashioned feed bottle complete with the milk is 2.65 km. long and 0.59 kms wide. The area of this island is 1.0 sq km. It lies on the 11°41′ N latitude and 72°4′ E longitude. This island is located 276.8 km to the West of Calicut. The islands nearest to it are Bitra on its West, Kadamat, on its south and Kiltan on its South-East.

Bitra

Bitra is known as the Jewel of Lakshadweep. This island is also mentioned as "Three island". It lies in the North-Western most part of the group and lies in latitude 11°35′30" N and longitude 72°09′30" E. This tiny spot in the vast sea is the smallest inhabitated island in this archipelago.

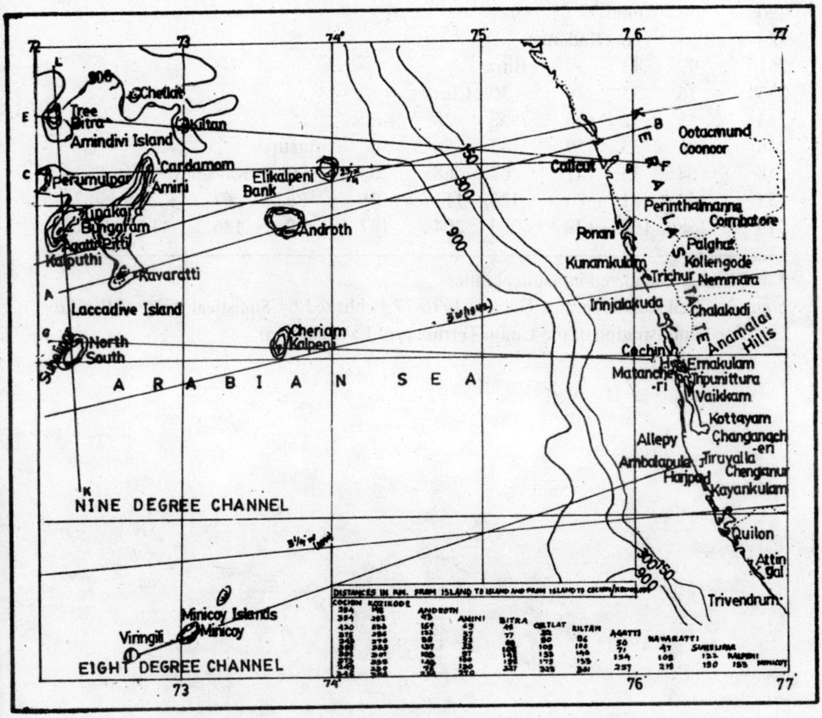

FIG. 2.1: Distance of Lakshadweep from the Mainland

TABLE 2.2: Distance between the Islands

Cochin	And-roth	Ami-ni	Kada-mat	Bitra	Chet-lat	Kiltan	Agatti	Kavar-atti	Kal-peni	Mini-coy
158	Androth									
220	58	Amini								
220	64	6	Kadamat							
261	99	43	39	Bitra						
233	76	35	29	30	Chetlat					
213	55	32	26	48	20	Kiltan				
248	85	33	39	43	56	60	Agatti			
218	64	35	41	67	68	62	31	Kavaratti		
155	47	81	86	123	111	95	36	67	Kalpeni	
215	158	168	178	203	204	187	160	136	114	Minicoy

* Distance calculated in nautical miles.

Source: Lakshadweep at a Glance, 1976-77 Published by Statistical wing of the Administration of the Union Territory of Lakshadweep.

3

HISTORY

Early History

The early history of the Lakshadweep is still obscure. There is no clear information available to tell us when and by whom the islands were first discovered and who were the earliest inhabitants. But the tradition points out that the earliest inhabitants were the Hindus who took shelter in the islands when their ship wrecked nearby. They were the members of an expedition from the Malabar Coast in search of the Perumal who was believed to have gone to Mecca. There are stories and according to which the colonisation took place in the period of Cheraman Perumal who is said to be the last Perumal who ruled Kerala. But the historians have not given the exact period when Cheraman Perumal ruled for which the exact period of colonisation cannot be confirmed. As per the Imperial Gazetteer Cheraman Perumal ruled over Kerala during the 9th century and he went to Arabia in A.D. 827 and died there in A.D. 831.

According to Logan (1887) and Burnell (1878) Cheraman ruled Kerala some time in the 9th century. If this data is correlated with the date of discovery of the islands it can be inferred that the Islands, were first discovered around 9th century.

It is believed that towards the end of his life Cheraman embraced Island and left for Macca without anybody's knowledge. His sudden disappearance created great disturbances throughout the Malabar Coast. So a few members set out for Macca to bring him back. But on the way the vessel in which they were sailing was wrecked near the Island, and the survivors of the wrecked vessel became the first settlers of the Lakshadweep Islands.

Whatever may be the truth of the Cheraman legend, the attempt to link it with the discovery and colonisation of the Lakshadweep would only be an exercise in futility. The Arabs started their trade with the Malabar Coast long before Islam as a religion came to have a foothold in this country and the Arabian Sea had been explored centuries ago by the Indian navigators. It is difficult to believe that these Islands, which lie in the trade route between Malabar Coast and Arab should have escaped the notice of the Indian and Arabian navigators till the 9th century

There are no traces of either any aboriginal race or culture having thrived in this territory or any archaeological relics pointing to an ancient habitation of the Islands. It is well known that the trade of India with the Greeks and the Arabs was very extensive in the centuries preceding the Christian Era.

The discovery of the Monsoon and Trade Winds around the first century A.D. enabled the mariners to avoid the circulatious northerly route touching the coastal ports of Arabia and India. They adopted the direct sailing route from Aden to Muziris in Kerala cutting right across the Arabian Sea. Lying in the direct route, the Lakshadweep served the mariners as a landmark and resting place, which ultimately led to the colonisation of the islands.

Classical References

Among the classical references the most important is the Ptoleny's Geography. He refers to a multitude of Islands in the Indian ocean lying around, *Taprobane* (Ceylone now Sri Lanka) and many other islands numbering about 1378. He gives a long list of islands, out which Mr. Bell identified a few as belonging to Lakshadweep.

The Arab texts do not give any clear picture about the early inhabitants of the islands. Abu Zayd (950 A.D.) writes that " there are in Hind men who are great devotees of their religion". His observation probably indicates the gradual movement of a floating population from the Malabar Coast to these islands during that period. The famous traveller Macro Polo (1254-1324) does not make any direct reference about Lakshadweep. He only gives the idea about Minicoy as "an island of females and Maldives as an island of males". But the available inscription which generally form a valuable source of information for the early history of South India are not much in use in reconstructing the history of the Islands.

So the only possibility is a reasonable conjecture based on a study of the language of the people, their culture, social institutions and also the travel accounts. From Arab accounts it is gathered, that people from the West Coast of India went there to collect coirs and tortoise shells, which were items of commerce. They also probably planted coconuts which they sold to the Arab sailors. A study of the social institutions also rule out the possibility of a migration prior to 11th century. A deeply rooted social institution in the territory is the *Marumakkathayam* system of inheritance which is mainly a Kerala innovation. The political and religious ascendancy of the *Namboothiri Brahmins* during the *Chola Chere War,* their rise to economic ascendancy as the *Janmis* of Kerala, the introduction of compulsory military training and the formation of the Chaver Army to meet the threat of Chola invasion were some of the compelling circumstances which brought about the adoption of *Marumakkathayam* by the people of Kerala in the 11th century A.D. The deep rooted system in the territory leads to the conclusion that the people who migrated from the Kerala coast had already imbibed the institution which they brought with them.

From the language point of view it may be generalised that many of the words which were commonly in use in Kerala during the 14th and 15th centuries are found in use even today in the islands.

It is significant that Ibn Batuta, the African globe trotter, who visited Calicut not less than six times between A.D. 1342 and 1347 left us an interesting account of these islands without making any reference to Lakshadweep. From his view it has been concluded that the permanent colonisation of Lakshadweep (other than Minicoy) had taken place only towards the end of the 14th century or in the beginning of the 15th century.

Early Inhabitants

All the colonisers in the earliest period probably were Hindus, because the typical Hindu temple architecture adopted in the construction of some of the mosques. The pieces of Hindu Icons excavated in some areas and above all the caste distinctions indicate the Hindu Origin of the people. Snake worshipping and adoration of Lord Rama are mentioned in their literature.

The Islands supposed to have been peopled first are Amini, Kalpeni, Androth, Kavaratti and Agathi. The upper class inhabitants of the first four of these islands still claim to trace their descent from *Nayar* or even *Nambudirs* families on the mainland and these islands are known in consequence as *Tarawad* island in distinction to the others which are called *Melacheri* Islands. The lower caste chiefly *Tiyyar* and *Mukkurars* from whom the *Melacheri* class is descended settled on the larger islands as servants of the upper classes and also populated exclusively Agathi and smaller islands like Kiltan and Chetlet. Kadamat appears to have been occupied only recently for *Lieut.*

The influence of Sanskrit is completely absent in the language of the islands. The code of *Manu* describes Brahmins who undertake sea voyage *(Samudrayay)* as not fit to carry out their religious function and hence are not to be invited to religious feasts.

Conversion to Islam

In 1845 Sir Robinson found Kadmat inhabited, but the people were entirely dependent on the people of Amini. They had not even boats of their own and much of the land had been appropriated by the Amini islanders who still hold it. Originally the Hindu the Islanders under the influence of an Arab Saint named Md. Ubaidullah where conversed to Mohammadanism probably in the 14th Century A.D. It is believed that one day when Ubaidullah was sleeping in a mosque in Median, he dreamt that Prophet Mohammad advised him to start for *Deddah.* So he started voyage but in the meanwhile his ship wrecked near some islands and with the help of a wooden peace he reached Amini Island. There he started teaching the principles of Islam but the Islanders revolted against him. A woman being inspired by Islamic faith joined hand with him, and he accepted here as his wife. After Amini, Island they went to Androth where Ubaidullah was successful in his mission. Gradually in this process he converted the Hindu islanders into Muslim in all the islands one by one and lastly died at Androth where his mousoleum stands. But there is difference of opinion regarding the visit of saint Ubaidullah and the date of conversion. The tradition ascribing this to 41 *Hijri* (or 7th Century) is based on a folk song current in some islands. But this date clashes with the *Cheraman* Legend which is ascribed the 9th century.

According to the Robinson's view the conversion took place in the 13th century. He explained that the island remained independent of the chiefs and the rulers on the mainland until after the arrival of the Portuguese on the West Coast. The Portuguese made settlement in Amini and built a fort the site of which is still there. They treated the islanders with cruelty as a result they approached Chirakkal Raja for his assistance. But according to Robinson the period of annexation of the Islands to the Kingdom of the Chirakkal Raja was contemporaneous with the first appearance of the Portuguese on the mainland. The Islanders were successful in poisoning the Portuguese with the help of Chirakkal. After this the entire group of islands remained under the rule of Chirakkal Raja who ruled for a pretty long time. The Islanders suffered from time to time at the hands of the Portuguese. On two occasions the Portuguese killed a great number of people on Chetlat. After a long rule over Islands the Raja of Chirakkal transferred the islands to the Ali Raja, on whom he conferred the title of *Ali Raja* of Arakkal on payment of a tribute of 6,000 *Fanams* (local coin). The principality of the Ali Rajas had always involved of the political manipulation connected with Maldive islands.

The rule of the Ali Rajas continued in the northern islands till the arrival of Tipu Sultan in 1787. The Ali Raja finally become the Lord of the Cannanore Bazar and enjoyed the monopoly of the trade in spices of the North Malabar. He had a good navy under him. The Jagir of Lakshadweep received by him from Kolathiri enhanced the status of the house. During the period of the Mysorean occupation the political power of the Ali Raja increased further as he was given a special status.

In the year 1799 with the fall of Sringapatam, the northern islands were annexed by the East India Company and they formed a part of the South Canara (now Dakshin Kannar) district. Mean while southern Islands (Laccadives and Minicoy groups of Islands) had passed to the East India Company.

Modern History

Modern history of the island began with the gradual extension of the power and influence of the Ali Rajas over islands. By the beginning of the 19th Century, the House of Arakkal had come into prominence. The British control was however nominal and it was the policy to permit Ali Raja to retain her possessions for a return of an annual tribute of Rs. 1,00,000 on these island. The British demanded the islands for arrears of revenue and took over the administration in 1875.

Administration of the Islands under Arakkal Principality

Towards the beginning of 18th Century the islands were kept as colonies by the Arakkal Rajas with an ultimate aim of economic exploitation. There were no public services in the Islands and the main involvement of the government was to maintain law and order in a place where there were very few criminal offences.

The trade was mainly based on barter. The principality appointed known as *Karyakkar* supplied the essential food stuffs to the people who gave him the island produce in return. The boats of Arakkal family shipped the essential articles to the islands and these boats carried back the Island products to the mainland. The exchange rate of rice and other articles was fixed each year by the Arakkal rulers arbitrarily.

All civil and criminal suits were filed before the *Karyakkar.* When these suits were filed directly before the Ali Raja, an enquiry report used to be obtained from the *Karyakkar* before taking a decision in the matter. If the decision of the *Karyakkar* was not acceptable to the concerned parties, they could file an appeal before the Raja. Heavy penalties were imposed for theft.

Tipu's Acquisition of Amindipi Islands

In 1783, the English under Major Macleod stormed Cannanore and compelled the Beebi to enter into a treaty of friendship with them. These develpments had their great impact in the Islands also. The Islanders trade relation had been cut off under Cannanore rule. Revenue raised by the Raja from the islands consisted of duties on export and import, was enjoyed by the prince of the coast. He enjoyed complete monopoly over coir trade as a result, people were economically hard pressed. Consequently, northern islands Amini, Chetlat and Kiltan revolted against Cannanore Rule.

In 1783, four Amini boats sailed to Cannanore with full load of coir, on reaching the coast they found the Cannanore Coast was blocked by the British. Out of these four boats one fell in the hands of the British, one returned to the islands and the remaining two (Belonging to *Taravads* of Kolappu and *Pamadbeli*) sailed on to Mangalore and disposed off their cargo to Tipu at a higher price.

On restoration of peace by the Treaty of Mangalore (11th March, 1784) the Beebi, the head of the Cannanore house, proceeded to punish offenders who had disposed of their coir to Tipu. Before setting in of the monsoon she sent a group of servants to Amini under the leadership of Abdul Kadir Kariyakhar to punish the people. On landing, he confiscated and seized the property and persons and emptied the houses of the principal inhabitants, a form of punishment known in the Island as *Kararcha.* But the whole population rose against him and over powered the tyrant and released the prisoners and jailed Abdul Kadir for the entire monsoon period. As soon as the fair weather started the principal inhabitants sailed to Mangalore taking Abdul Kadir with them and put their allegations before Tipu. By that time Tipu has already developed friendly relations with the Beebi and so Tipu tried his best to calm down the people. But his attempts proved to be unsuccessful and therefore he took over the administration of the Amindivi islands from the *Cannanore House.*

In 1787 he granted a compensation to the Beebi a *Jaghir* from *Chirakkal* territories. Thus the northern group of islands remained under the possession of Tipu Sultan till 1799 (Lo gam, 1887), when Canara fell to the East India Company these islands were transferred to the latter and were attached to the Canara district.

By the end of 1791, the Laccadive Group of islands and Minicoy came under possession of the East India Company and were ceded with all of Tipu dependencies in Malabar by the Treaty of Seringapatam in 1792. But in 1796 they were handed over to the Cannanore Ruler at a *Peiscush* (a kind of annual rent) of Rs. 15,000. Because of accumulated arrears, these islands were taken back by the East India Company a number of times and from 1875 the islands remained permanently under the British control.

From 19th Century onwards the Laccadive and Amindivi group of islands came under the rule of East India company, the former along with Minicoy as a property held in trust on behalf of cannanore Raja and the latter as a part of South Canara district. In 1908 the Raja surrendered even this title to the islands on accounts of heavy arrears of *Peiscush* due from him to the East India Company, and latter to the British Government and so these islands were attached to the Malabar District.

Attempts for Unity of Administration in the Two Groups of Islands

In 1909, the Board of Revenue, Madras, suggested to bring the two groups under one administration, namely. the Malabar district. Mr. R.H. Ellis inspected both the groups but the inhabitants of the Amindivis opposed the idea because of their long connection with Mangalore and for the port facility for their sailing vessels. In 1920 Mr. Ellis again brought the idea of one administration and this time the Malabar islanders agreed with him but due to administrative difficulties it was not materialised. The two groups were put under the jurisdiction of two revenue districts mainly due to their remoteness and isolation the peculiar customs and life of the inhabitants also gave them a separate status. The territory had been declared as a scheduled district. Then it was declared as a "backward tract". Under the Government of India Act, 1935, again the islands were declared as "excluded areas" and were subject to the same immunities until the framing of the Constitution of India in 1950.

Restriction on Entry

The class distinction in the islands give rise to several disputes between the *Koyas* and the *Melacheris* (landlords and tenants) towards the end of 19th Century. There was so many social restrictions for Melacheris which gave rise to disputes. After Independence in 1947, considerable progress could be achieved in removing the discrimination and disabilities which had been imposed on them by social customs and usage.

Shortage of labour was the great problem for *Koya-Malacheri.* There was consequently an inflow of mainland labour to these islands. In 1909, Ellis suggested that some restrictions on the migration must be brought about as this mainland population indulged in petty crimes, but Government did not favour this. In 1912 Government included Collector to enforce reasonable restriction on entry of outsiders. In 1949 "the Amindivi Islands (Restriction on entry and residence) Regulation (Madras Regualtion 4 of 1949) came into force.

Till about 1920, the Inspecting officers were inspired with an empire consciousness, and the establishment of law and order and the settlement of disputes and cases formed their major preoccupation. Due to remote situations in Arabian Sea the Islands did not progress with other parts of India. The freedom movement in India brought Independence which lightened the islanders. But a new chapter of progress and prosperity was opened when these islands constituted into a Union Territory on 1st November, 1956.

March Towards Progress and Prosperity

Buchanan's description of Lakshadweep as 'wretched islands' fitted very well to the condition prevalent during the British period. Some of Inspection officers, indulged in minor developmental schemes, like improvement of coconut cultivation, chiefly by better planting and eradication of disease, or introducing new varieties of flora like bamboo, mango and tamarind. For the rest, they considered that it would be unwise to disturb the placid and amoral isolation of the islanders. Due largely to their inaccessibility to the main land, the islands did not progress with other part of India, in the matter of State help or political awakening. Gradually the freedom movement in India had only a faint impact on the islands. Now the islands are fast catching up with other parts of the country for whatever they might have lost in the past.

4

GENERAL ADMINISTRATION BEFORE CONSTITUTION OF UNION TERRITORY

The earliest form of political authority on Lakshadweep islands was carried by the Chieftains whose number was equal to the number of *Cheris* or localities in each island. It is said by the local people that there existed an 'Amini' a council called *Panchayati* constituted by representatives of the four principal *Taravads* who looked after the internal polity of the island. These chieftains were also known as *Modalals*. These chieftains were assisted by the heads of other important *Taravads* and were called *Mokhyastans* (important people).

The administration of chieftains, assisted by *Mokhyastans* continued even after the annexation of the archipelago to the territory of *Chirakkal Raja*. During the time of Cannanore Raja, the chieftains were replaced by a single Administrative Authority designated as *Kariyakkar*. He was an outsider appointed by the Raja. To help the *Kariyakkar* there was an accountant *(Gumastan)* and four peons. The *Kariyakkar* had powers for the adjudication of petty civil and criminal cases and enforcement of various monopolies. All the servants of the Raja received money by way of salary and they also extracted money from the islanders by abusing their powers. Raja or his higher officials never used to visit the islands to supervise the administration and so the *Kariyakkars* and their subordinates could carry out their tyrannical rule unchecked. The Administrator under the rule of the *Kariyakkar* did not recognise any distinction between civil and criminal cases. For the adjudication of petty civil cases, oaths or arbitration were extensively used. Minor faults, delinquencies and minor breaches of fiscal rules were decided by the *Kariyakkars* and *Mokhyastans* on the spot, and the accused were punished by fine, imprisonment or corporal punishments. Serious cases were referred to Cannanore and were settled by the chief officials of the Raja. Serious crimes like gross breaches of fiscal rules and committing theft on the *Pandaram* lands were punished by looting the house of offender and confiscating his entire property.

With the appointment of the *Kariyakkars* the rule of the Chieftains was terminated, the *Mokhyastans* were continued to help the *Kariyakkar* for the adjudication of civil cases. Some of these *Mokhyastans* were also equally notorious like the *Kariyakkars,* as they used to join with the latter as confederates, and harass the people who refused to grease their palms.

As the two groups of islands came under the rule of the East India Company (1799), the administrative system changed considerably. At that time, the office of the *Kariyakkar* was allowed to continue and was finally abolished in 1842. A *Monegar* was appointed in his place. *Monegar* was a local term used in South Canara District to designate a Revenue Inspector. He was assisted by a clerk called *Karani* and three or four peons (*Kavagars*) stationed permanently on every island.

In 1867, *Monegar's* official position was raised to that of a Village Magistrate and Village *Munsiff* and he enjoyed the powers as defined under Madras Regulation IV, V and XI of 1816 and IV of 1821. In 1948, the post of *Monegar* was upgraded to that of a Deputy Tahsildar, which conferred on him the powers of Second Class Magistrate Appellate powers. With regard to the civil cases, the powers exercised by the Deputy Tahsildar had no monetary limits and the appellate powers were exercised by the Revenue Divisional Officers, Mangalore and the District Collector, South Canara.

In 1957, after the formation of the Union Territory, the status of the Deputy Tahsildar was raised to that of a full-fledged Tahsildar, and the appellate powers in respect of civil and criminal cases were transferred to the Administrator and Secretary to the Administrator respectively.

After Constitution of Union Territory

Prior to the formation of the Union Territory in 1956, the Amindivi Group of Islands were under the jurisdiction of South Canara District and the Laccadive and Minicoy group of islands were under the control of the Malabar District of the erstwhile Madras State. The islands were constituted into an Union Territory on 1st November, 1956. After this the administration is headed by an Administrator, appointed by the President of India under Article 239 of the Constitution of India. His secretariat and the District Administration, are now functioning as compact units under a single file system. Matters pertaining to District Administration, law and order and development in general are under the purview of the Collector-cum-Development Commissioner functioning under the administrative control of the Administrator. The Collector is also the District Magistrate and under him are Additional District Magistrate in the headquarter island and one Executive Magistrate each in three other major islands. There are four Tahsils under each Tahsildar.

There was a Police Department for the maintenance of the law and order which is headed by a Superintendent of Police who is assisted by the Police Staff.

The Secretariat has been divided into six sections: (1) Service Section, (2) Finance and Accounts Section—A, (3) Finance and Accounts Section—B, (4) Planning and Development Section, (5) General Sections and (6) Confidential Branch. The Administrator's Office at Kozhikode is under the Secretary to the Administrator who is also functioning as Central Treasury Officer. Financial powers are vested with the Administrator. Administrator has also powers to sanction schemes other than those related to works, up to Rs. 0.3 million. Few subordinate officers were appointed to work under the supervision of the Administrator for the smooth functioning of the administration.

Long before the formation of Union Territory, these islands formed a part of the Cherayoor Constituency of Malabar District of the erstwhile Madras State. From 1957 onwards one member was nominated by the President of India to represent these islands in Parliament till 1967. When the Laccadive, Minicoy and Amindivi islands Parliamentary Constituency was formed and a representative was elected to the Parliament. Different advisory bodies have also been constituted to ensure the people's close association in local administration and developmental activities.
They are:

(1) Advisory Council
(2) Advisory Committee
(3) Other Government Offices.

In the matters of appointment in various subordinate posts, the posts are reserved for the islanders and if they are not available they are declared unreserved as per the rules of the Union Government of India. The Administrator is generally of the I.A.S. rank and extra island allowances are given from the people appointed from the mainland.

Advisory Council

The Advisory Council was constituted by the Government of India, Ministry of Home Affairs on 29-6-1957 consisting of the Administrator and five other members. Now there are 17 members, nominated by the President of India on the recommendation of Administrator for a period of one year from 1st April every year. The Administrator seeks advice of the Council on the following matters:

(a) Matters of administration involving general policy, schemes for development of agriculture, trade and industry improvement of sanitation, communication, education, health and any other matter intended for the betterment of conditions of population and to make the islands self-supporting, but not on matters relating to the day-to-day administration;
(b) General questions touching the implementation of general policy and schemes of development; and
(c) Any other matter which the Administrator of the Government of India may deem fit to be referred to the Council.

The functions of the Council are purely advisory, but not mandatory. Though their advise is not binding on the Administrator, due weight and consideration are given to such advice while taking decisions or making recommendations to the Government of India. This council meets at least twice in a year.

Advisory Committee

The Advisory Committee associated with the Ministry of Home Affairs was constituted on 12-1-1968. The Administrator, Members of the Parliament and five other non-officials are members of the Committee. Non-official members of the Committee are nominated by the President of India every year. This Committee meets twice a year. Functions of this Committee is defined as under:

(a) General questions of policy relating to the Administration of the Union Territory in the State field;
(b) All legislative proposals concerning the territory with regard to the matters in the State list;
(c) Relating the annual financial statement of the Union and other

financial questions as may be referred to it by the President of India; and

(d) Advisory Committee is consulted on other desirable matters which concerned by the Ministry of Home Affairs.

Suggestions of Advisory Committee are reflected in the planning and administration of the Territory. The judicial organisation in the islands is headed by the Chief Judicial Magistrate and Sub-judge at Kavaratti. There are two judicial First Class Magistrates and Munsiffs at Androth and Amini. There is no separate District and Sessions Court or High Court for the islands.

Other Government Offices

There are nine wireless stations of the Posts and Telegraphs Department for inter island and islands to the mainland wireless communication, one in each island except in Bitra. Telephone Exchanges exist in Kavaratti, Minicoy and Androth. One observatory was established in 1891 in Minicoy for observations of growth and intensity of storms in the South-East Arabian Sea. One Research Unit was established in 1960 at Minicoy under the Central Marine Fisheries Research Institute. There is a Tidal Observatory in Minicoy. It is situated in the lagoon, about 1.2 km S.W. of the Katcheri building. This observatory gives a graphical record of the fluctuations of the water level due to tidal effects. The tidal observatory was dismantled ultimately in 1896, after having functioned satisfactorily for five years.

Revenue Administration

In early times, the private ownership of land was unknown in Lakshadweep. The absolute ownership on land was not in vogue and the property was reckoned in terms of coconut trees and not in terms of land on which they stood. The original colonisers appear to have been accompanied by a number of labourers. There was a patriarchal system of Government and as in all other affairs, the management of land also came under the perview of the *Muthalal* and the Council of Elders consisting of the heads of the families. The heads of the families would have taken up, under arrangements mutually agreed upon among themselves, as much land as they could clear, plant and keep in order. Perhaps the only limiting factor to such acquisitions was the paucity of labour.

The idea of private ownership on land have taken place, when the Cannanore Raja Lunched their policy of economic domination over these islands in middle of the 17th Century. The land tax had never been introduced into the islands at any stage and that the only type of revenue collected from the islands was through the different types of monopolies introduced by the Arakkal Raja.

During the period of Arakkal Raja, a price for coir was fixed, which changed from time to time according to the fluctuation in the price of coir in the mainland market. The payment for coir was fixed to be 1/4th in cash and 3/4ths in rice in the beginning, but later on all cash payments were completely stopped, and rice was given in exchange as rice is not grown in the calcarious soil. The transaction of coir and rice was carried out under the supervision of the post officer who was aided by a Coir Superintendent and one of two assistants. After the formation of the Union Territory, monopoly in coir trade was allowed to continue but it operated on a no-profit no-loss basis. In 1962, the present Administration fixed the exchange rate at 14 kg of coir for 20 kg of rice.

The land tenure system in the Island showed clear resemblance to the traditional land tenure system found on the Malabar Coast. It appears that the people belonging to the highest rung in the society among the early colonisers appropriated for themselves all the land could be brought under immediate cultivation. Thus, they became the *Jenmis* or owners of Jenmam or tax-free land. The low caste people become *Kudiyans* (tenants) of *Serfs* and labourers Tenancy involved perpetual obligations to serve the *Jenmis* in return for occupational rights and for the enjoyment of the use of fruits of the trees grown on the land allowed to be kept under their possession. The tenancy rights were not uniform on all the islands, but the inevitable obligation of the tenants to serve the landlords was common condition appreciable to all types of tenancies.

When the islands came under the rule of the Arakkal Raja, all the areas which had been left unoccupied on the inhabited islands and all the small satellite islets lying around the major islands were appreciated as the property of the States and were called *Pandaram* lands. During the British rule a scheme was drawn up for leasing out the *Pandaram* lands for cultivation of coconut palms to the people of the inhabited islands. The leasees were allowed to keep the lands leased out to them by the government for 40 years or less subjected to the regular payment of the assessment but had no claim for any kind of compensation of the improvement done by them on the land in the event of their relinquishing the land after the lease period. These were, called *Cowle* lands. The intention behind the *Cowle system* was to get the waste lands fully planted with coconut trees and therefore, the conditions of the leases were such as to give sufficient incentive to the people. It was also the intention of the government to allow the leasees who were not in arrears of rent to keep the *Cowle* land leased to them in perpetuity, although, in order to meet exceptional circumstances, the clause limiting the lease period to 40 years had been devised. Many leasees later on gave their *Cowle* lands on tenancy right to others on the same conditions of rent and customary services as obtained in the case of *Jenmam* lands. The right of occupation enjoyed by the other tenants who lived on the private *Jenmams,* the secondary tenants also treated these *Cowle-lands* as inheritable property.

For the *Cowle* lands only Tree-tax was paid to the Government. The Island of Minicoy was free from Tree-tax, and the main source of income from the island was collected in the form of a *Poll-tax.*

5

PRESENT ADMINISTRATIVE UNITS

Prior to 1st November, 1956, administration in the islands was only nominal and as such no distinctive administrative units could be found. At that time each island was treated almost as a separate unit but they were all under a common administration. This was so because it was not a single landmass but separate islands. In its territory for quite a long time the islands were divided into two groups—the Amindivi Group then belonged to the South Kanara district of Mysore State (now Karnataka State) and the rest of the islands were under the administrative control of the Malabar District of Kerala. It was only when the States of the Indian Union were re-organised on linguistic basis and the two groups of islands were separated from the South Kanara and Malabar districts to form an Union Territory.

On the 1st November, 1956 the territory was divided into four Tahsils for administrative purposes. Each Tahsil has a Tahsildar to administer it. The headquarters of Tahsildars and the islands under their jurisdiction are given in Table 5.1.

TABLE 5.1: Jurisdiction of Tahsildars and their Headquarters

Name of the Tahsils and Headquarters	Islands under Jurisdiction
Minicoy	Minicoy
	Viringili
Androth	Androth
	Kalpeni
	Cheriyam
	Kodithala
	Tilakkam(i)
	Tilakkam(ii)
	Tilakkam(iii)
	Pitti(i)
	Pitti(ii)

(Contd.)

Name of the Tahsils and Headquarters	Islands under Jurisdiction
Kavaratti	Kavaratti
	Agatti
	Bangaram
	Tinnakara
	Parali(i)
	Parali(ii)
	Parali (iii)
	Kalpitti
	Suheli Valiyakara
	Suheli Cheriyakara
	Pitti (Biards Island)
Amini	Amini
	Kadamat
	Kiltan
	Chetlat
	Bitra

Source: *Gazetteer of India* (1977) Union Territory of Lakshadweep, p.5.

PHYSICAL BASE

6

EVOLUTION AND PHYSICAL CHARACTERISTICS

The islands extend between 8°N and 12°30′ N latitude and between 71°E and 74°E longitudes. It has an area of 32 sq kms. but the revenue records reveal its area as 28.5 sq. kms. It is a group of 10 habited islands of 26.2 sq. kms and 17 uninhabited islands having an area of 2.3 sq. kms.

The islands do not show any marked topography as they are flat-topped which rise only a few metres above the M.S.L. Occasionally on the storm ward side near the lagoons the old sand dunes rise for a few metres above the M.S.L. The lagoonal shores consists of sandy beaches but at places beach rocks are exposed during the low tide level.

The eastern shore in almost all the islands, except Kadamat, Agatti, Bangaram and Cheriyakara is marked by storm beaches consisting of coral pebbles and boulders piled up well above the high tide mark. They have been piled up by the storms from the east. The islands in the centre of the lagoon i.e. Bangaram, Cheriyakara and others do not have storm beaches and the shores are sandy because the storm waves are protected by the ring atolls

Sub-Marine Topography

These islands lie on the northern edge of the sub-marine Lakshadweep Chagos Ridge which extends for 2500 kms. in N-S direction. The Lakshadweep Chagos Ridge is separated from the Malabar continental shelf by the Lakshadweep Sea and merges with the shelf at some places between 11°N to 14°N latitudes. The Lakshadweep Chagos Ridge rises from a depth of 2000-2700 meters in the Lakshadweep sea and about 4000 metres from the Arabian Sea bed (Indian Ocean bed). The eastern slopes of the submarine ridge is steeper that the western slopes, though the former rises from a shallower depth.

The prominent gaps in the submarine L.C. Ridge are the Nine Degree Channel which separates the atoll of Minicoy from the northern group of islands. In this ridge a large number of atolls and some large banks are situated. The Bangaram, Agatti, Kadamat and Amini atolls are situated on two large submarine coral banks. These atolls and coral banks rise steeply from depths ranging from 1500 to 3000 metres (Fig. 6.1).

Surface Topography

The coral reefs of all the atolls are widest on the S-W side because the growth of the reef has been greatly facilitated by the supply of planktons which are nutrients for the growth of corals. Echosounding on the reefs of the atolls reveals that the first break in the profile of the reefs occur at a depth of about 4-8 metres which extends to about 12 metres on the windward reef of the S-W where a wave-cut platform of recent origin occurs. Then there is a almost vertical steep fall for about 50 metres. In many islands, before this depth is reached there are traces of submerged terraces at 7-12, 15, 21-36 and 43-97 metres, more particularly in Bangaram and Kadamat islands. These wave cut terraces were formed during Pleistocene Glaciation period when there was lowering of the sea level all over the world due to ensiatric change in the sea level as a lot of water was locked up in the form of continental glaciers and continental ice shlets. Traces of numerous groves and furrows called surge channels occur in the sea-ward reef of the atolls in the wind-ward side. These are best developed on the south-western wind-ward reef and are generally aligned in SW-NE direction. They are 1-2 metres deep which have been cut by continuous wave action.

The atolls which form the islands and the lagoons are in various stages of development and are of various sizes, which vary from 1 to 150 sq. kms. The Bottom topography and geomorphology of the lagoons vary considerably. The smaller lagoons in Chetlat, Kiltan, Amini and Kadamat are filled with sediments, where the depth of the lagoons range from 1 to 2.5 meters and are devoid of any significant topographic features. The larger ones in Bitra, Bangaram, and Suheli and Minicoy have deeper lagoons whose depth varies from 10-16 metres. The central part of these lagoons are usually deep and encumbered with numerous coral knolls. All round the deeper central part a Shallow sand bank exists, along the reef margin which is dependent on the continuity of the reef. The banks are not well developed in the vicinity of the opening of the reef. This is clearly evident on the Western Reef of Bangaram, northern reef of Minicoy, N.W. reef of Bitra and Western reef of Suheli.

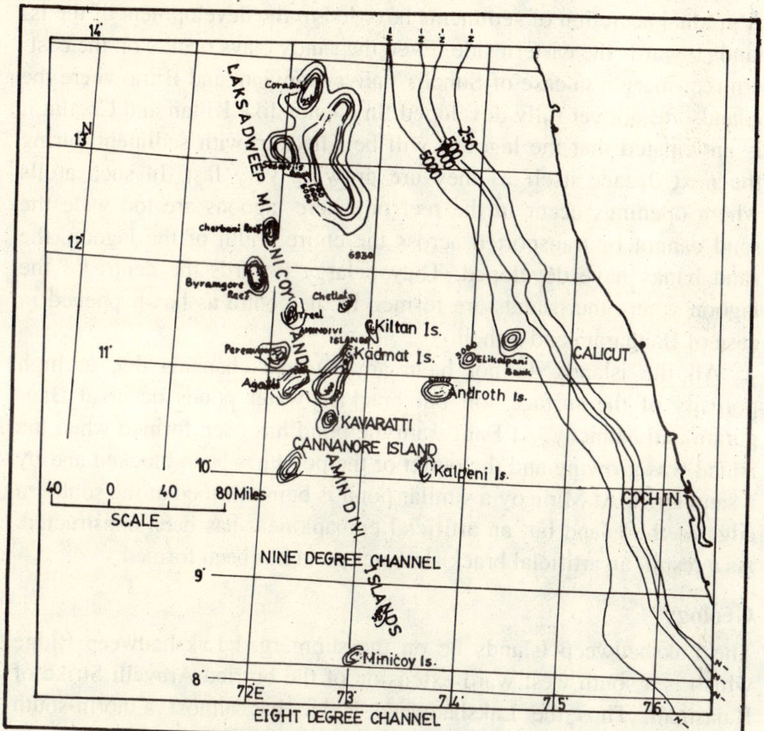

FIG. 6.1: Bathymetric depths of Lakshadweep, Minicoy and Amindivi

Formation and Growth of the Islands

The islands on these atolls are usually found on the eastern reef margin except Bangaram and Cheriyakara which lie in the centre of the lagoon. On Bitra, the island is on the northern edge of the lagoon. The reefs at Cheriyapanniyam, Perumalpar and Suheli reveals the earliest stage of development while Kalpeni, Kavaratti, Agatti and Kadamat are in intermediate stage and Chetlat Kiltan are in an advanced or mature stage of development.

The growth of the islands are generally controlled by the cyclonic wave action on the eastern reef margin which pile up coral debris on the eastern reef while very high waves during S-W Monsoons have broken the reefs and have reduced them to coarse and subsequently fine sediments on the S-W cost of the islands. These sediments in course of time are transported by littoral drift and are deposited on the eastern shore behind the coral boulders and pebbles as the eastern reef. A gradual accretion of sediments have led to the development of the islands towards the eastern side. Even the sandy clays occurs on the eastern reef margin in case of Suheli, Valiyapanniyam and Bitra where the islands are not yet fully developed. In islands like Kiltan and Chetlat it is anticipated that the lagoons will be filled up with sediment during the next decade itself as they are growing very fast. In such atolls where openings occur in the reef or where lagoons are too wide the sand cannot be transported across the entire width of the lagoon, the sand banks have developed. They enlarge towards the centre of the lagoon where the islands are formed in the centre as has happened in case of Bangaram and Suheli.

All the islands do not have any surface channels due to high porosity of the surface soil but brackish water ponds occur at Bangaram and Minicoy. At Bangaram the pond has been formed when the island was growing and the outlet of the pond has been blocked and by a sand Drift. At Minicoy a similar pond is being formed at the southern edge of the island but an artificial embankment has been constructed. As a result, an artificial brackish water pond has been formed.

Geology

The Lakshadweep Islands lie on the submerged Lakshadweep Ridge which is a south west ward extension of the burried Aravalli Strike of Rajasthan. Thus the Lakshadweep Ridge has almost a north-south alignment and the Deccan Traps have been faulted in a north-south direction and down throwed which has given rise to the western scarp of the Western Ghats. To the west of the fault line the Deccan Traps has subsided. Consequently a great thickness of the trapian beds and associated sediments have been deposited in the Arabian Sea between the Lakshadweep Ridge and the west coast of India (Fig. 6.2).

Sesmic studies by the O.N.G.C. in 1965 have revealed that between Malabar Coast and Lakshadweep the thickness of the Sediments in the Vicinity of Kalpeni is about 1.5-2.0 kms. and Elikalpeni about 2.0 to 2.5 kms. of sediments are located.[1] Thus the average thickness of sedimentary deposits is of 2.0 kms. Between Malabar Coast and

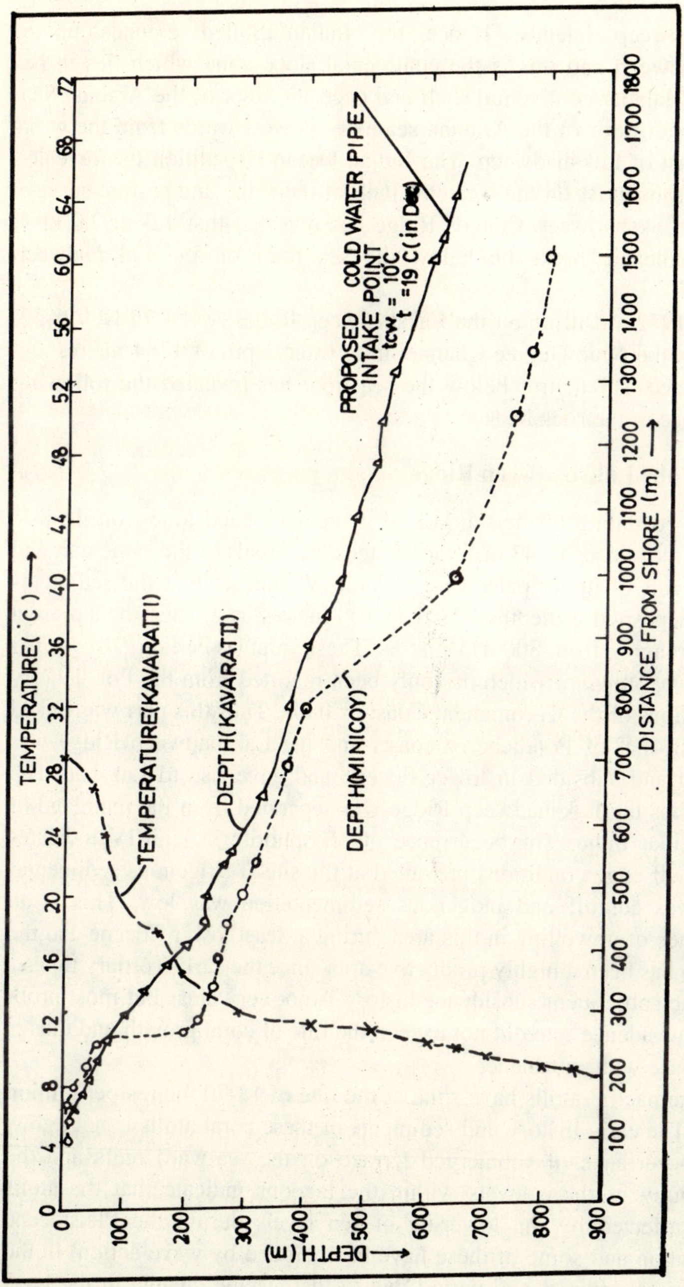

FIG. 6.2: Depth and Temperature Profiles of Lakshadweep

Lakshadweep Islands. Hence the Indian Shiled extends up to Lakshadweep and this is the continental slope zone which lies in between Malabar continental shelf and occeanic floor of the Arabian Sea. The ocean floor of the Arabian sea extends west-wards from the western coast of Lakshadweep. The Indian Ocean Expedition has revealed that basalts exist on the western flank of the ridge and sesmic surveys on the Lakshadweep Chagos Ridge has revealed that 1.5 to 2.0 kms. thick volcanic rocks lie below the sea floor on the Lakshadweep Ridge.[2]

In 1972 a drilling on the Lakshadweep Ridge (9°-01.75 N, 72° 52. 67E) in the Nine Degree Channel in a water depth of 1764 metres and penetrated 411 metres below the sea floor has revealed the following sequence of the rock beds.

Age of the Lakshadweep Ridge

The K-Ar dating of the samples of glauconitic sandstone from Unit-V reveal the age as 41-43 m. years. Paleocene fossils of the same unit and lower part of upper paleocene of Unit-IV indicate that the sediments were deposited at depths less than 100 metres as against their present depth ranging from 300-411 metres. These samples certain *Discocylina remaraoi Samanta* which has only been reported from the Pondicherry formations of the Coromandal Coast of India. Thus this part was linked up with that of Pondicherry coasts and the Lakshadweep Ridge was faulted and subsided in lower Eocene and gave rise to Lakshadweep sea. Thus the Lakshadweep Ridge was separated from the mainland of Peninsular India. The occurrence of phosphorite in Unit-IV indicates that shelf-edge conditions prevailed at the site. Terrigenous sedimentation was cut off and biogenous sedimentation was low. This is an evidence of upwelling in this area during at least lower Eocene and the region has been a highly productive area since the early Tertiary times.

The subsequent subsidence history is not very clear but most probably subsidence rate did not exceed the rate of coral growth and thus is kept pace with subsidence.

The pacific atolls have sunk at the rate of 18-70 metres per million year. The early history and sediments of these coral atolls is not know. The occurrence of submerged terrace on the sea-ward reefs and the continuity of these levels within the lagoons indicate that the atolls were affected by the lowering of sea levels during the Pleistocene Glaciation and some of these have been eroded by wave action. In the subsequent inter-glacial period due to the eustatic change in the level of the sea it started rising with the release of the snow from the continental ice-shelts and continental glaciers. The corals of the Lakshadweep Ridge started growing and kept paces with the rising of the sea level and sedimentation continued uninterrupted in the lagoon till recently.

TABLE 6.1: Stratigraphy in the Nine Degree Channel (9°-01.75 ′ N, 72°-52.67 ′ E)

Stratigraphic age	Absolute age* (million years)	Unit	Depth (in Metres below ocean floor)	Thickness (metres)
Pliestocene to Miocene	1.5 to 26	I Light grey to greenish grey detrital silty clay nanno ooze	0-120	120
Miocene to Oligocene	26 to 37-38	II White foram ooze and chalk	120-146	Ca.26
Late Oligocene Middle Eocene	37-38 53-54	III White Oozes and chalk containing nannos, forams Micarb and rads	146-219	77
Middle Eocene to Upper Paleocene	53-54	IV Grayish yellow to yellow brown micarb chalk and ooze and limestone chert and clay locally tuff bearing	219-300	81
Upper Paleocene	64-65	V Green, yellowish green and greenish black limestone and volcanic tuffs	300-411	111

* Age for beginning of the Epoch Instial Report of the Deep Sea Drilling Project, 23, 1-1180. National Science Foundation, U.S.A., 1972.

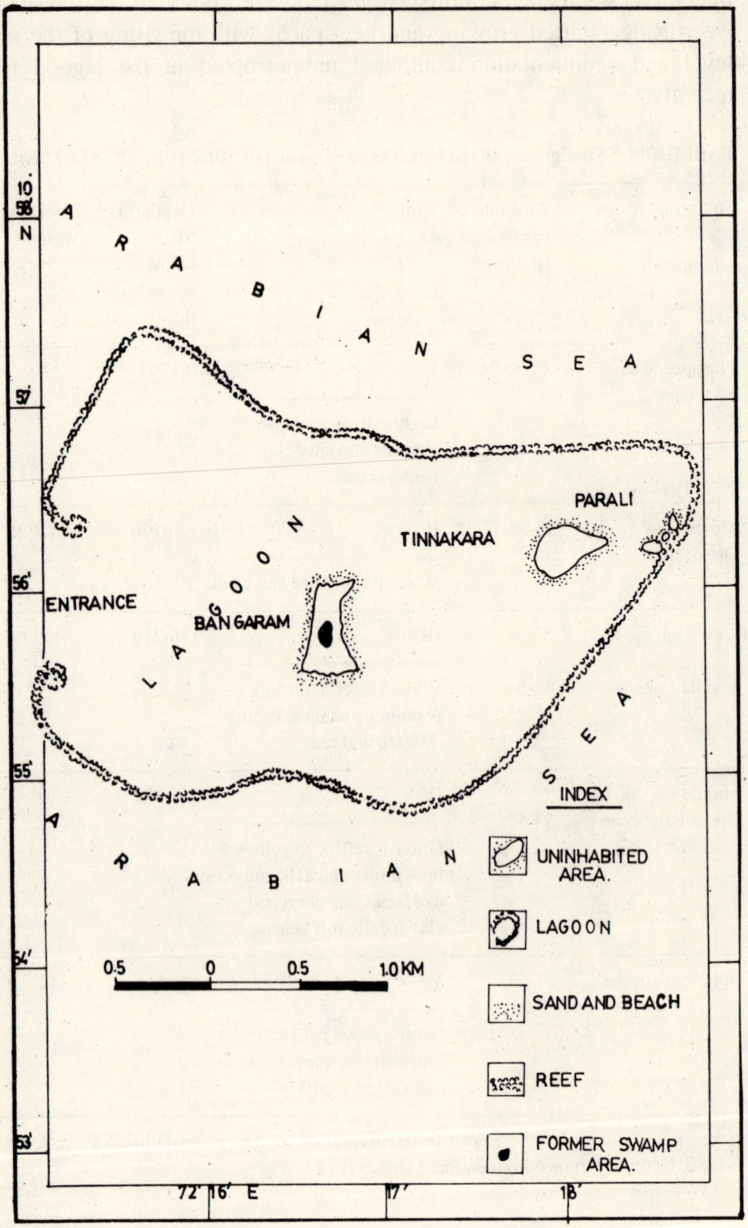

FIG. 6.3: Bangaram etc. Island

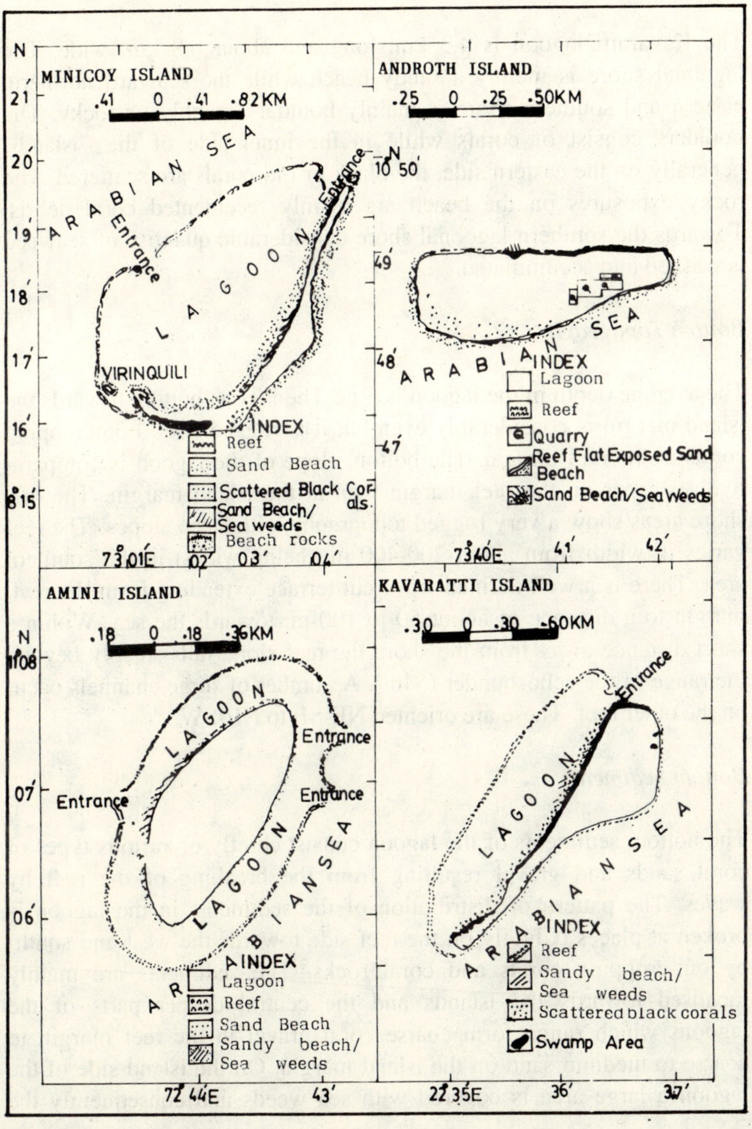

FIG. 6.4: Geomorphology-I

Lagoons and Offshore areas[3]

Kavaratti

Lagoons and Offshore Areas

The Kavaratti lagoon is 4.3 km. long and about 0.8 km. wide. The lagoonal shore is mainly a sandy beach while the seaward northern, eastern and southern shore is mainly bouldary, pebbly or rocky. The boulders consist of corals while in the inner side of the islands, generally on the eastern side, the black or old corals are scattered. The rocky exposures on the beach are mainly recemented coral debris. Towards the southern lagoonal shore considerable quantity of seaweed is washed and accumulated.

Bottom Topography

The average depth in the lagoon is 3 m. The lagoon bottom towards the island margin is considerably even but it is rugged due to outcropping corals at the reef margin. The bottom slope of the lagoon is comparatively steeper on the reef margin than at the island margin. The offshore areas show a very rugged topography with steep slopes. The reef varies in width from about 200-400 m., being widest in the southern area. There is a well defined wave cut terrace extending from the reef, margin to a distance of about 50 to 100 m. towards the sea. Within a short distance away from the shore the reef slope falls steeply beyond the range of the echosounder (54m). A number of surge channels occur on the outer reef. These are oriented NE-SE to NE-SW.

Bottom Sediments

The bottom sediments of the lagoon consist chiefly of various types of coral sands and gravel resulting from the breaking of the reef by waves. The pattern of distribution of the sediments in the lagoon is broken at places (Chiefly on the reef side towards the west and south) by out-cropping corals and coral rocks. The sediments are mainly localised towards the islands and the central deeper parts of the lagoons which range form coarse coral gravel in the reef margin to coarse to medium sand on the island margin. On the island side of the lagoon a large area is covered with sea weeds and consequently the sediments here are rich in humus. The borings near the jetty and the harbour approach channel indicate that the sands are more than 7 m. thick. The sediment in the reef is sparsely distributed; it mainly occurs inpockets and channels and they are mainly coarse coral sand and coarse coral gravel.

Kalpeni

Lagoon and Offshore Area

The Kalpeni island is 5 km. long and 1.3 km in the widest part. The Cheriyam island is situated north of Kalpeni which is 2.8 km. long and the maximum width is 0.3 km. The Kalpeni Cheriyam lagoon is 10.5 km. long and 4.3 wide in the central part. As in Kavaratti the lagoonal shore of the Kalpeni and Cheriyam Islands are sandy with sea weeds at places along the low water line particularly in the southern part. One the eastern, northern and north eastern seaward shore, the beach is bouldary with black coral boulders towards the inner island side. The beach stack is prominent at the low water line of the eastern shore.

Bottom Topography

The depth of the lagoon varies from less than a meter to about 5 m. Geomorphologically the lagoon floor can be divided into three zones starting from the island to the reef margin. These are (a) zone of even topography bordering the island covered with sands; (b) central rugged part with protruding corals and coral knolls indicated by sharp reflections; (c) sand banks in the inward reef margin marked by steep slopes towards the central part which has been formed by the breaking of the reef. Echosounding indicate the terrace extending from the reef margin to a distance of almost about 200m – 300m. towards sea. It is considerably wider north of Cheriyam island but very narrow towards the east. The outer margin of the terrace lies at a depth of about 10m. and the depth falls more than 50 m. rapidly. A number of surge channels occur in the outer part of the reef with orientations varying from NNW-SSE to approximately E.W.

Bottom Sediments

Sediments consist mainly of coral sands, coral gravel and corals. In the southern part of the Kalpeni lagoon the sediments vary from coral gravel near the reef margin and central coralline area to medium to fine sand near the island. The portion near the lagoon side beach of the islands is covered with white coral sands. The central deeper part of the lagoon is covered with sands amongst which outcrop coral knolls are met with. The offshore area contains very little sediments except in channels and pockets. The sediments in the channels consist of coarse sand and gravel. The northern part of Kalpeni is connected with the southern part of the Cheriyam island by a reef of 3.5 km which is exposed during the low water.

Agatti

Lagoon and Offshore Area

The eastern shore of the island is devoid of the usual storm beach common on other islands. The smaller Kalpeni island which is separated from the main Island by a narrow channel has bouldery or pebbly shore (Storm beach) on its seaward side and a sandy shore on its lagoon side. The lagoon shore is characterised by a low sandy beach, outcrops of coral limestone are rare on the lagoon beach but are comparatively common at the low waterline on the seashore.

The northern part of the Island shows a shallow submerged bank (16 m depth) which extends north and connected to the bank at Bangaram.

The depth in the lagoon varies from less than 1 m. near the lagoon shore and reef margin, to about 4 m in the central part of the lagoon. The lagoon floor is devoid of any marked topographic features and the topography of the floor is generally smooth except in the vicinity of coral knolls and reefs where it is rugged. As in other islands the offshore areas show a well marked break in profile at 3-5 m due to wave cutting. Submerged terraces are not well developed though some are seen at a depth of about 12m in the south eastern part. A probable submerged reef also occurs at this depth.

The lagoon floor near the island margin is covered by medium to coarse sand while near the reef margin the floor the covered by coarse to very coarse sand and gravel. The central deeper portion of the lagoon is covered by fine to very find sands. The •offshore area is generally devoid of sediments and only minor quantities of sediments are seen in surge channels, pockets and terraces.

Chetlat

Lagoon and Offshore Areas

The western lagoonal shore is marked by a sandy beach with outcrop of beach rock at or beyond low water line. The eastern seaward shore of the island is marked by storm beach of coral boulders and pebbles and sand is rare but beach rock is fairly common beyond the low water line.

The lagoon is largely shallow with a depth of about 2 m in the central part of the lagoon. In the offshore area the first breach in profile occurs at a depth of about 4 m, this increases to about 8 m in the southern area. The seaward reef is generally devoid of sediments. Mostly samples of corals were collected from this reef.

Kiltan

Lagoon and Offshore Area

Excepting in the north and south the lagoon shores are marked by a sandy beach where beach rock, pebbles and boulders occur. The north eastern and southeastern shore of the islands marked by the "bouldary storm beaches" which is absent in the central eastern shore of the island. Soundings in the lagoons indicated that the lagoon is largely shallow with depths of about 1 m and a maximum depth of about 1.7 m. The lagoon floor is largely covered by coarse sand and gravel, medium or fine sands are rare. Seaweeds are almost absent in the nearshore area in the lagoon as distinct from other lagoons.

On both the northern and southern shores the reef has wide submerged extensions to the north and south respectively. Preliminary observations indicate that the first break in profile is deeper to the north than to the south. The western reef is devoid of sediments and only small quantities occur in the surge channels. Extensive pockets of sediments occur on the outer eastern reef particularly the central part.

Bitra

Lagoon and Offshore Area

The southern (lagoon) shores of the island consists of a sandy beach while the northern shore on the eastern side consists of bouldary storm beach and on the western side a sandy beach with exposures of beach rock dipping westwards is marked.

The western lagoonal margin of the reef is shallow and the topography is considerably evened out by the sand banks. The eastern reef is also shallow but the bottom shows a complicated topography due to coral knolls. Towards the north the western sand bank depends and merges with the coral depression which has a depth of about 10-14m. The central depression shows a complicated topography of coral knolls but the intervening arrears are filled with sediments. The south eastern portion of the lagoon is encumbered with a number of coral knolls. Echo-sounding carried out in the eastern offshore on the reef. Submerged terraces and reefs are also seen in the echograms of offshore areas at certain depths.

The western reef margin is largely covered by the medium to very coarse sand at shallow depth. The eastern reef margin with its complicated bottom topography is covered by fine to medium sand with coral debris. The central deeper portion of the lagoon contains silty fine sand.

Sediment on the reef is rare but it occurs in pockets (eastern outer reef) and surge channels (western reef). The sediment in the pockets is mostly fine to medium sand while those in the surge channels is mostly coarse to very coarse sand.

Kadmat

Lagoon and Offshore Area

The lagoon shore is largely sandy and is distinct from other islands. the eastern seaward shore is devoid of storm beach. Beach rock is exposed just beyond the low water line throughout the entire length of the island.

The lagoon is largely shallow and the maximum depth is about 2.5 km. The lagoon floor is devoid of any marked variations in topography except on the reef margin where some coral knolls occur. The first break in profile occur at a depth of about 6-8 m after which the slope falls of rapidly but submerged terraces are also seen at various depths between 20 and 40 m.

The lagoon floor on the reef margin is covered by gravel and coarse sand while towards the island margin the sand is comparatively fine grained. The seaward reef is generally devoid of sediments and only small quantities of sediments occur in the surge channels on the windward side i.e. western side.

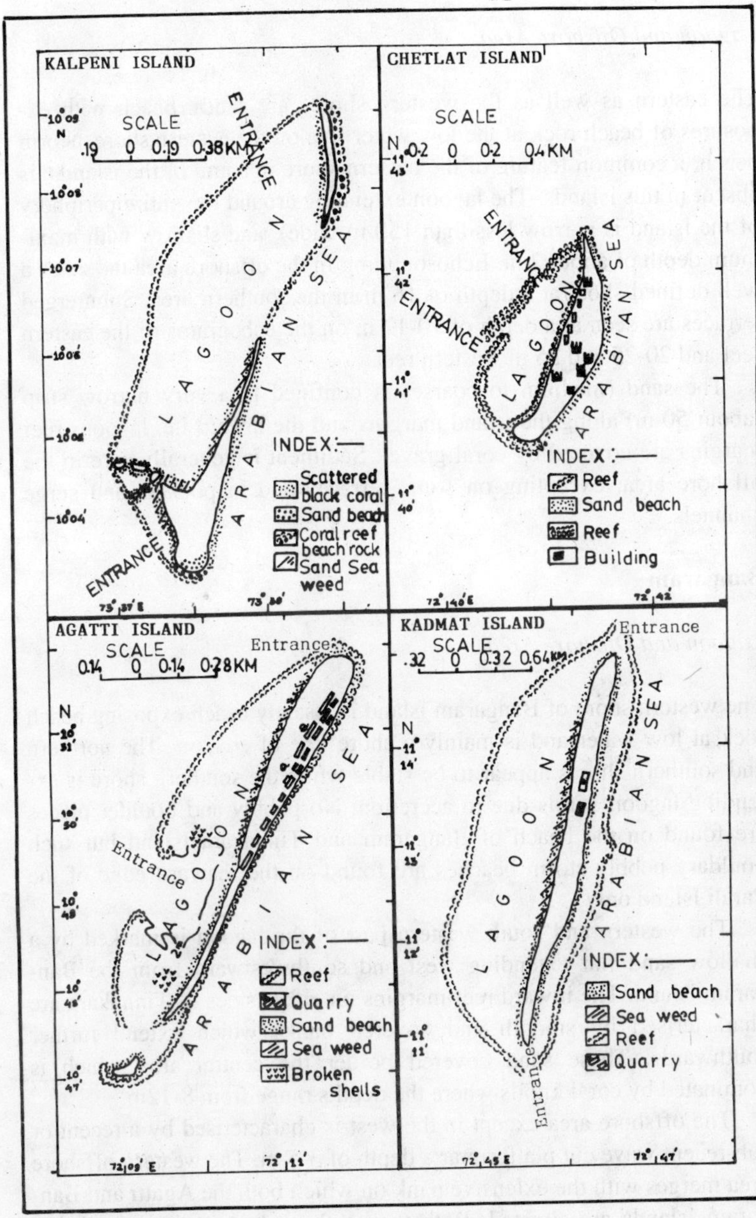

FIG. 6.5: Geomorphology-II

Amini

Lagoon and Offshore Area

The eastern as well as the western shores are sandy beach with exposures of beach rock at the low water line on the eastern shore. Storm beach, a common feature of the eastern shore in some of the islands, is absent in this islands. The lagoon extending around the entire periphery of the island is narrow less than 150 m wide) and shallow with maximum depth of about 2 m. Echosounding in the offshore area indicates a well defined shoal at a depth of 16 m in the southern area. Submerged terraces are seen at a depth of 10-12 m on the echograms of the eastern reef and 20-25 and 35 m western reef.

The sand (medium to coarse) is confined to a very narrow strip (about 50 m) along the island margins and the inward i.e. lagoons reef margins are covered by coral gravel. Sediment is generally care in the offshore area, excepting on some terraces and in pockets and surge channels.

Bangaram

Lagoon and Offshore Area

The western shore of Bangaram island is a sandy beach exposing beach rock at low water and is mainly a shore line of erosion. The northern and southern shores appear to be stable while the southern shore is extending lagoon wards due to accretion. No pebbly and boulder pieces are found on the beach of Bangaram and Tinnakara Island but such bouldary pebbly storm beaches are found on the seaward edge of the Parali Island only.

The western and south western part of the lagoon is marked by a shallow sand flat extending west and southwestward from the Bangaram island. The inward reef margins on either sides of Tinnakara are characterised by smooth and covered banks which extend further southwards. These sand covered border the central area which is dominated by coral knolls where the depths range from 8-12m.

The offshore area except in the west is characterised by a recent or sub-recent wave cut platform ar a depth of 3-5 m. The western offshore area merges with the extensive bank on which both the Agatti and Bangaram Islands are situated. Both the northern and southern reefs besides the wave cut platform show terrace at 12-18 m and some at about 30-40m.

The bottom sediments in the lagoon chiefly consist of coarse sand and gravel on the inward reef flats and reef margins, medium to coarse sand on the shallow sand banks and fine to vary fine sand or silt in the deeper coral region. The offshore area i.e. outward reef flats are devoid of sediment cover and only rarely the sediments occur in pockets or channels. Most of the terraces are covered with sediments but it is doubtful if the sediment is of recent or subrecent origin.

Suheli

Lagoon and Offshore Area

The western shore of the Cheriyakara island consists of a sandy beach while beach rock is exposed intermittently on the eastern shore of the island. The western and southern shore of Valiyakara consists of a sandy beach with intermittent outcrops of beach rock at the low water line. The eastern as well as the northern shores of the island are characterised by storm beach of coral pebbles and boulders.

The central portion of the lagoon is deep (maximum depth about 16 m) and is marked by a complicated topography of coral knolls with intervening areas covered by sediments. The inward reef margins chiefly on the eastern side are characterised by shallow sand banks with depths of the order of 1-2 m. Similar sand banks also occur on the western reef margin but their development is greatly restricted due to the number of openings on the margins which drain out the sediments. The northern portion of the lagoon west of Valikara is largely shallow without any significant topographic features. Echosounding on the offshore area indicates that the eastern reef is extremely narrow and has almost vertical slope towards the sea. Compared to other islands the western reef is also narrow, surge channels are not very prominent on the western windward side of the reef and are almost absent on the leeward side.

Bottom sediments revel that the inward reef margins are characterised by medium to coarse to very coarse sand. The central deeper part of the lagoon is covered by fine sand which in cases approaches silt or clay size. The offshore area is almost devoid of sediments and only rarely sediment occurs on the eastern side in pockets and on the western side in channels.

Minicoy

Lagoon and Offshore Area

The eastern and northern shores of Minicoy Islands are characterised by a well developed storm beach of boulders and pebbles and the lagoon shores are marked by a sandy beach. At the southern end of the Island near the Light House a number of storm beaches probably each representing a particular cyclone are identifiable. Similar set of storm beaches are also identifiable in the central are also identifiable in the central part of the island. The northern part of the island beyond the Leper colony has been built entirely by cyclonic storm as evidenced by the occurrence of coral boulders and pebbles.

Continuous echosounding carried out in the lagoon indicates that the southern and south-western part of the lagoon is largely shallow (1-2 m depth) due to a sand bank. Towards the centre the lagoon is deeper (5-11 m) but this has a large number of coral knolls. Some of them rose to within a metre of the surface. The reefward margin of the lagoon in the north shoals but due to a large number of openings in the reef, sand banks have not developed. Echosounding on the reef indicates that the reef is widest on the south western margin but is considerably narrower elsewhere. Surge channels aligned approximately SW-NE are very prominent on the western-southern and south-western reef but are otherwise absent on the north sides of the reefs. The first break in profile occurs at a depth of 4-8 m no other submerged reefs are prominent on the echograms.

The reef sediments largely comprise of gravel or very coarse sand. The sand banks in the southern and south western portion of the lagoon largely consist of medium to coarse and very coarse sands. In the central and deeper portion of the lagoon the material is usually fine to very fine sand or even silt. Towards the island margin considerable areas are covered by sea weeds as indicated by the occurrence of sea weeds in a samples. As elsewhere, sediments are not very common on the outward reefs most of the sediments being confined to surge channels and sediment pockets. The sediment in the pockets is mostly medium to coarse sand and the one in the channels is mostly coarse to very coarse sand.

Submerged Banks and Reefs

Bassas de Pedro, Cora Dirh and Sesotris

The depths on Bassas de Pedro range from 46 to 50 m, the bank largely appears to be smooth with minor undulations in topography. The Sesotris and Cora Dirh banks with depths of the order of 25 to 50 m largely appear to be flat topped without any significant variations in topography. Bottom samples from Bassas de Pedro consisted of living corals and sands while those from Sesotris and Cora Dirh consisted of sand only.

Beliapani Submerged Reef

The reef has a small island on the northern extremely where guano deposits are being formed at present. A number of sandy days exist on the eastern side of the lagoon. Compared to lagoons of other submerged reef, the lagoon is shallow with maximum depths of the order of 6m and without any significant variations in topography. The lagoon floor is covered with medium to coarse and very coarse sand. Extensive sand covered terrace at a depth of 6-10 m occurs in the eastern offshore area.

Cheriapani Submerged Reef

The reef is largely submerged except at the southern margin where it is seen even at a higher water. The southern part of the lagoon is largely shallow and a number of sand banks occur at the western and eastern reef margins. The central part of the lagoon is deeper with depths extending to 16 m. The sediment in the central part of the lagoon is fine to very fine sand and silt. Echosounding in the offshore area indicates a terrace at a depth of about 10 m.

Perumalpar Submerged Reef

The north-western and south-western portions of the lagoon are shallow, marked by well developed sand banks. The central area is marked by numerous coral knolls but the density of occurrence of coral knolls is not very high and many of the knolls do not rise to the surface. The central coral region has a depth of about 14 m and some of the regions with depths of 10 m and 8 m may be correlated with the terraces on the seaward side of the reef. Echosounding traverses indicated a number of terraces between 8 and 22 m.

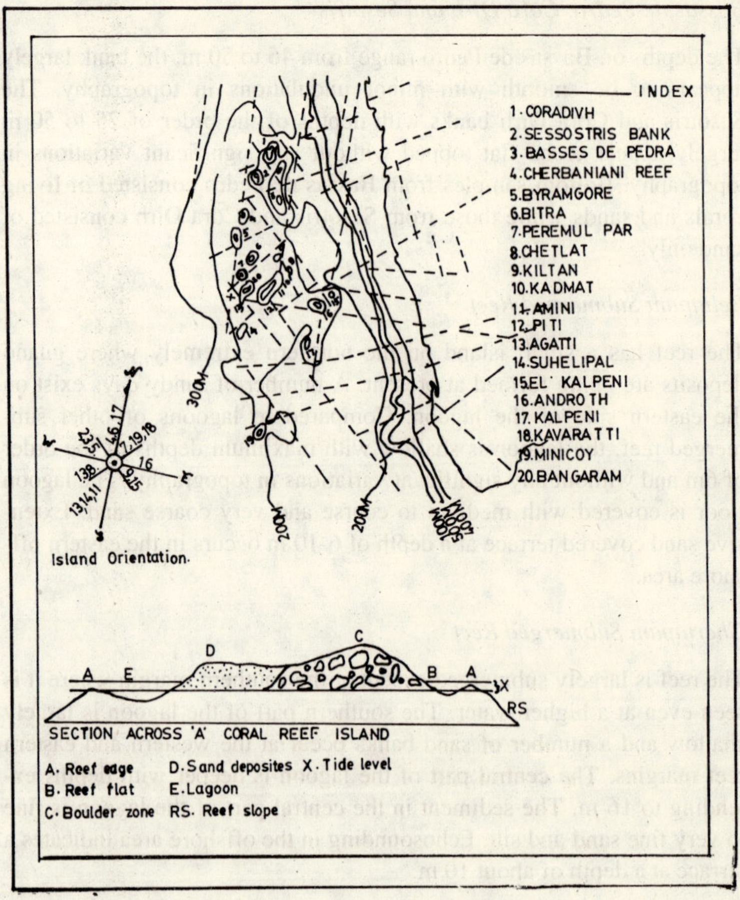

FIG. 6.6: Tectonic Map : Lakshadweep Islands

Androth Island and Submerged Reef

The shores of the Island consist of mostly sandy beach with intermittent exposures of beach rock. On the eastern edge a well developed storm beach consisting of boulders and pebbles is prominent. The offshore bank on the north of the island indicates that down to the depth of 18-20 m the bottom is largely covered with coral growth or strewn with coral boulders and pebbles. Beyond this depth medium to coarse sand occupies the central depression on this submerged bank. In this depression the sediment is fine sand and silt. Sediment appears to be fairly extensively distributed on the south western side of the bank. The southern offshore area shows terraces at about 18 and 28 m.

Amini-Bittin Bank

The depths on this bank range from 15 to 38 m and echograms indicate an irregular topography typical of coral banks. The 10 bottom samples collected from this bank mainly consists of coral pieces towards the north and sand and coral pieces to the south.

TABLE 6.2: The Lakshadweep Islands*

Island	Area(km)	Lagoons		
		Length (kms)	Breadth (kms)	Area (kms)
Agatti		8.1	3.2	17.11
Kavaratti	1.50	4.3	0.8	3.61
Kalpeni	2.87	10.5	4.3	19.97
Chetlat	1.06	2.2	0.75	1.54
Kiltan	1.63	2.6	0.35	1.08
Bitra	0.12	11.5	4.7	45.61
Kadmat	3.15	10.2	1.2	13.40
Amini	2.62	3.5	0.2(W)0.1(E)	1.00
Bangaram	1.00	7.8	3.8	28.06
Suheli	0.67	10.0	6.4	73.96
Minicoy	4.70	9.0	4.2	26.50
SUBMERGED REEF				(Approximate)
Beliapani	—	—	—	50.0
Cheriapani	—	—	—	156.0
Perumal Par	—	—	—	63.0
Androth	—	—	—	70.0
SUBMERGED BANK				
Bssas de Pedro	—	—	—	2400.0
Sesostris	—	—	—	375.0
Coradirh	—	—	—	320.0
Amini-Pitti	—	—	—	430.0
Elikalpeni	—	—	—	88.0

* Siddiquie, H.N. and Mallik, T.K.: Report of the Investigation of the Calcerous sand deposits in the Lagoons of the Laccadives, Offshore Mineral Exploration and Marine Geology Unit G.S.I. 1973, Table. 1.

Elikalpeni Submerged Bank

The submerged bank is situated at a distance of 62 km. north east of Androth. The bank has depth of about 14 m and most of this is a flat topped bank with coral growth. Sand occurs in patches and thin layer on this bank.

Lagunar Sediments

By and large, the gravel and coarse sand form the reef margins while shallow sand banks bordering the reef are covered by coarser sediments. The central part of the deeper lagoons of Cheriyapanniyam, Perumalpur, Bitra, Bangaram, Suheli and Minicoy are covered by fine sands and silt. In bottoms of shallow lagoons of Chetlat, Kiltan, and Kavaratti recovered with medium to coarse sands. These sands are of calcium carbonate with very little silica, alumina or iron. The only impurity is MgO which is particularly high near the reef margins. These are contributed by the calcareous algae.

Minerals

Like all other coral islands phosphate deposits (Guano) on the islands and calcium carbonate in the lagoons are met with.

Phosphate Deposits

The origin of phosphate deposits is due to birds excretions long before these islands were colonised by man. These deposits occur as cappings in all the islands and contain phosphate in varying concentrations. In Lakshadweep phosphate deposits are of low grade where P_2O_3 percentage is only 13.4 and the reserves have been estimated to be 0.12 m tonnes by Indian Bureau of Mines. In Pitti Islands Guan deposits are actively formed where P_2O_5 contents is 11.0 to 15.0 per cent. The Guano deposits could not be mined as these islands are very thickly populated and it would have posed serious problems for settlement.

Calcareous Sands

The G.S.I. discovered large quantities of almost pure calcium carbonate sands during 1967-71. These sands contain low amount of Fe,

Silica and alumina. Only near the reef MgO exceeds 3.3 per cent which is the permissible limit for cement grade limestone. The proved reserves is estimated to be 288.70 m tonnes of Calcium carbonate while the inferred reserves in the lagoons is estimated to be 423 m tonnes up to a depth of 1.0 metres while inferred reserves is estimated at 712 m tonnes between 1-2 metres below the lagoon floor. Thus the total inferred reserves is put at 1135 m tonnes up to a depth of 2 metres in the lagoon floors of the islands. The impurity contain (MgO) varies in per cent of occurrences in the proved reserves of calcium carbonate up to a depth of 1 metre.

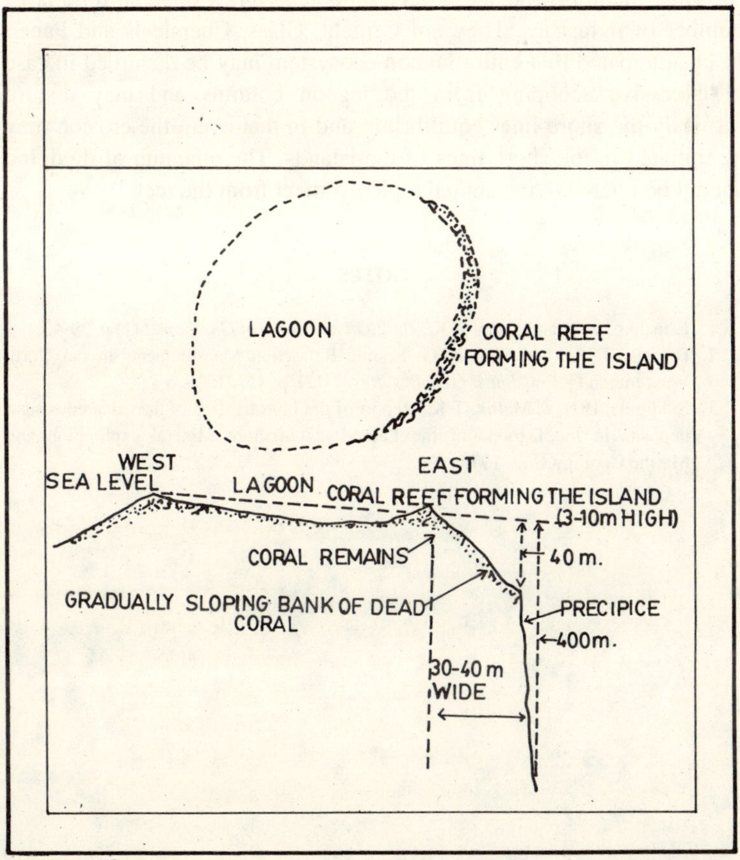

FIG. 6.7: Typical Plan and Cross Section in the Lakshadweep Archipelago

TABLE 6.3: Proved Reserves of Calcium Carbonate

MgO in %	Reserves (in M. Tonnes)
<1	30.65
1-2	173.38
2-3	80.31
>73	4.36
Total	288.70

* Siddiquie, H.N. and Mallik, T.K. Report on the Investigation of Calcareous sand deposits in the Lagoons of the Laccadives. Rep. Geol. Surv. India 1-35.

This calcium carbonate is very suitable as a raw material for a large number of industries. They are Cement, Glass, Chemicals and Paper. In is anticipated that entire lagoon ecosystem may be disturbed in case of excessive scooping from the lagoon bottoms and may disturb seriously the shore lines equilibrium and in that event the erosion may be initiated in the shore lines of the islands. The quantum of dredging should be related to the annual replenishment from the reef.

NOTES

1. Ermenko, N.A. and Datta, A.K., *Bull, Oil and Natural Gas Com.* 5(1) p. 29-40.
2. Francis, T.J.G. and Shor, G.G. Sesmic Refraction Measurements in the North West Indian Ocean. *Jourl, Geophys. Res.* 71(2), p. 427, 1966.
3. Siddiquie, H.N. & Mallik, T.K., Report of the Investigation of the calcareous sand deposits in the lagoons of the Laccadives offshore Mineral exploration and Marine Geology Unit, 1973.

7

CLIMATE

Lying well within the tropics and extending to the Equatorial Belt, the Lakshadweep Islands have a tropical humid, warm and generally pleasant climate, becoming more equatorial in the southern islands of the territory. From the point of view of temperature, there is little variation throughout the year and no distinct and well marked seasons are experienced. South-West monsoon period is the chief rainy season and South-West monsoon is the principal rain bearing wind. The normal data for the onset of the monsoon is from 1st June to 5th June and during this period the entire Lakshadweep comes under the full furry of the South-West monsoons. This monsoon retreats by end of November. But quite often it starts from mid-May. But there are variations between the northern and southern islands.

While the Climatological data shows that the climatology of the three islands is basically similar, there are significant differences among the islands in temperature, humidity, rainfall, cloud amount and winds velocity. It is therefore, extremely important that these outposts of he subcontinent in the Arabian sea and the first fore-warners of the monsoon and any change in weather that takes place in the ocean around then are equipped with the best available instruments as early as possible.

Rainfall

There are four rainfall recording stations in the territory viz. at Minicoy, Amini, Androth and Agati. But records of rainfall for sufficiently long periods are available only for Amini and Minicoy islands. Rainfall at these two stations may be taken as being generally representative of the rainfall over this group of islands. The rainfall data of the islands are shown is Table 7.1. The factors that influence the climate of the islands are its location. The islands spread over from 8° to 12°N latitude, the furthest Southern point is Minicoy island. Because of small extent of these islands the maximum influence of the sea is paramount. Prevalence of land and sea breeze is very imperceptable. These islands are separated from the Mainland by Lakshadweep Sea. In minicoy the monsoon breaks in April, when the rainfall suddenly increases to 53.5 mm from only 17.0 mm in March. It retreats by the end of December when the average rainfall is 75.7 mm but by January it suddenly drops to 35.0 mm. Thus the Monsoon lasts from April to December i.e. for nine months but the rest 3 months of the winter also do not go dry as all these three months i.e. January-March no moth is dry and receives less than 17.00 mm of rainfall.

But in case of Amini, a more northernly located island, the rainfall increases from 2.2 mm in March to 23.6 mm in April, and drops to 23.2 mm in December from 93.9 mm in November. Thus in Amini the monsoon lasts from April to November, a length of eight months, a month less than that of Minicoy.

Further, Minicoy has a higher average rainfall (1588.0 mm) than that of Amini (1490.4mm). This happens mainly because of it is more southerly location. This will evident from (Table 7.1)

In 1966 the average rainfall at Minicoy was 1640.4 mm, while that at Amini was 1504.5 mm. The annual rainfall of Agatti and Androth was 1598.3 mm and 2032.3 mm in the year 1966 respectively. The annual rainfall generally decreases from south to north, but South-West Monsoon rainfall (during June to September) increases from south to north. The rainfall recording stations at the Malabar Coast of Mainland are Mangalore, Kozikode, Fort Cochin, Cochin (Naval Air Station), Alleppey and Trivandrum, where the average rainfall is 2961.8 mm, 2410.2 mm, 3415.6 mm, 3131.05 mm, 2846.7 mm and 1931.7 mm respectively. The average rainfall decreases from Kozikode towards north and south, i.e. Mangalore and Fort Cochin and further decreases towards south i.e. Trivandrum. The rainfall in the southern islands in more evenly distributed due to nearness to the Equatarial Belt than those of the north. During June to September 67.7 per cent of the annual rainfall is received in the north while it is only 53.8 per cent in the South. During the post-monsoon month of October to November, south gets 20.6 per cent of the annual rainfall while north receives only 16.3 per cent.

June is the rainiest month everywhere contributing 23.6 per cent of annual rain in the north and 18.5 per cent in the south. While in the north, rainfall progressively decreases after June, in the south it shows a secondary maximum in October as a result of the influence of North East monsoon.

TABLE 7.1: Normal rainfall (Average between 1931 -1960)

(*Figures are in mm*)

Rainfall Station	January	February	March	April	May	June	July	August	September	October	November	December	Total
Amini (mm)	14.8	2.2	2.2	23.6	172.7	351.1	316.3	203.4	138.1	148.9	93.9	23.2	1490.4
In % of total	1.0	0.1	0.1	1.6	11.6	23.6	21.2	13.6	9.3	10.0	6.3	1.6	100.0
Minicoy (mm)	35.0	25.4	17.0	53.5	199.8	293.6	217.7	199.8	144.1	185.1	141.4	75.7	1588.0
In % of total	2.1	1.6	1.1	3.4	2.6	18.5	13.6	12.6	9.1	11.7	8.9	4.8	100.0

Extremes in Rainfall

The highest monthly average is 351.1 mm at Amindivi and 293.6 m at Minicoy both experienced in June. Agathi has much less monthly maximum rain of the order of 265 mm. The heaviest rainfall ever recorded was 836 mm at Amindivi in June 1924 and 626 mm at Minicoy in May, 1933.

The variation in the rainfall from year to year increases from south to north. During the fifty year period 1901 to 1950, the highest recorded rainfall was 169 per cent of annual normal precipitation at Amini in 1933 while it was 127 per cent at Minicoy in 1902. Similarly lowest recorded rainfall varied from 60 per cent of the normal at Amini in 1934 to 64 per cent of Minicoy in 1939. Again rainfall was less than 80 per cent of the normal in seven years a Amini, while such low rainfall occurred in 5 years at Minicoy during the same period.

Frequency of Rainfall

The frequency of annual rainfall reveals that Maximum frequency occurs (26.2%) in case of 1601-1700 cm rainfall, followed by 1401-1500 and 1501-1600 cms each having 14.3 per cent of years in case of Minicoy. Minicoy has never received rainfall more than 2100 cms during 1901-50.

In case of Amini the maximum frequency (16.4%) of annual rainfall occurs in case of 1301-1400 cms. and 1501-1600 cms. It is followed by 10.2 per cent in case of 1201-1300 cms. Amini has also recorded rainfall twice in excess of 2101 cms. once over 2201-2300 cms. and another year of 2501-2600 cms. This will be clear from the Table 7.2.

Storms and Depressions

The cyclonic depression originate in the Southern Arabian sea and move in North-East direction and hit the islands during the months of April-May which are regarded as South-West Monsoonic cyclones. During October to December a few depressions also occur hear Andaman & Nicobar islands in the Bay of Bengal. They move Westwards and enter the Arabian sea after crossing the Peninsular tip of Tamil Nadu and Kerala to emerge in the South Arabian Sea. They occasionally bring rain to these islands. Table 7.3 gives the average picture during the past 80 years ending in 1970.

TABLE 7.2: Frequency of Annual Rainfall*

Range in M.M.	Minicoy (1901-50)		Amini	
	Nos	In % of total	Nos.	In % of total
901-1000	—	—	2	4.0
1001-1100	1	2.4	1	2.0
1101-1200	1	2.4	4	8.2
1201-1300	3	7.1	5	10.2
1301-1400	2	4.8	8	16.4
1401-1500	6	14.3	4	8.2
1501-1600	6	14.3	8	16.4
1601-1700	11	26.2	4	8.2
1701-1800	1	2.4	4	8.2
1801-1900	5	11.9	1	2.0
1901-2000	3	7.1	5	10.2
2001-2100	3	7.1	1	2.0
2101-2200	—	—	—	—
2201-2300	—	—	1	2.0
2301-2400	—		—	—
2401-2500	—	—	—	—
2501-2600	—	—	—	2.0
Total	42	100.0	49	100.0

* *Gazetteer of India*: Union Territory of Lakshadweep by N.S. Mannadiar, 1977, p. 29.

TABLE 7.3: Cyclones/Depressions (1890-1970)*

Months	Arabian Sea Storms/Depressions	Bay of Bengal Storms/Depressions
April	4	—
May	1	—
October	8	—
November	9	7
December	3	3
Total	25	10

* *Gazetteer of India:* Union Territory of Lakshadweep by N.S. Mannadiar, 1977, p. 26.

From the available records during the past one and half a century it is revealed that Kalpeni has been hit by worst Cyclones thrice (1847,

1922 and 1965), Androth four times (1897, 1922, 1963 and 1964), Kavaratti twice (1891 and 1941). Agatti once (1891), Amindivi once (1891). Suheli once (1922). Amongst all these islands Kalpeni has suffered most in 1847 cyclones when 358 persons died, all houses were damaged, and the island lost 104,232 coconut trees. This will be clear from the Table 7.4.

TABLE 7.4: Effects of the Storms in the Past

Year & date of Commencement		Islands affected	Damaged		
			Death (human)	Damaged (houses)	Coconut Plants uprooted
April, 15th	1847	Kalpeni	246 112 famine and disease	All Houses	Plantations were completely destroyed 104,232 trees uprooted
		Androth	Many died	—do-	—
	1891	Kavaratti	—	—	A large number
		Agatti			were uprooted
		Amindivi		—	—do-
December, 1922		Kalpeni	—	—	Damaged coconut
		Suheli			trees
	1941	Kavaratti	—	—	—do-
	1963	Androth	—	—	540 coconut trees were uprooted
December, 1965		Androth	—	—	11,500
		Kalpeni	—	—	9,500 uprooted

Rainy Days

On an average the number of rainy days* in a year at Amini and Minicoy are 81.7 and 94.4 days respectively. The number of rainy days in a year at Agatti and Androth are 75 and 88 respectively. As in the case of rainfall, the number of rainy days during the South-West monsoon season is also greater in the south than in the north in the Laccadive group of islands. But at the mainland on an average the number of rainy days in a year at Mangalore, Kozikode, Fort Cochin, Cochin (Naval Air Station), Alleppey and Trivandrum are 114, 91, 132, 127 137 and 99 days respectively.

* Days with rain of 2.5 mm or more.

TABLE 7.5: Rainy Days (Numbers) Average Between 1931-1960

Stations	January	February	March	April	May	June	July	August	September	October	November	December	Total
Amini	1.0	0.2	0.2	1.4	6.8	17.1	17.2	12.0	10.0	8.6	5.4	1.8	81.7
In % of total	1.2	0.3	0.3	1.7	8.3	20.9	21.1	14.7	12.2	10.5	6.6	2.2	100.0
Minicoy	2.3	1.6	1.2	3.0	9.5	17.2	14.2	12.3	10.3	10.5	8.1	4.2	94.4
In % of total	2.4	1.7	1.3	3.2	10.1	18.2	15.0	13.1	10.9	11.1	8.6	4.4	100.0

The highest rainfall records in 24 hours in 1965 was 172.4 mm at Mangalore, 228.6 mm at Fort Cochin 209.1 mm at Cochin (Naval Air Station) 177.8 mm at Alleppey (in 1966) and 401.5 mm (in 1964) at Trivandrum, where as it was 224.9 mm at Minicoy and 232.4 mm at Amini in 1965. In 1966 it was 94.5 mm at Agatti and 82.9 mm at Androth. This in a single rainy day in 1966, the rainfall figures are higher in the mainland than those of the islands. In 1965 the single day rainfall figures do not show the same trend. But these rainfall figures reveal that the quantum of rainfall in a single day decreases from the South to the north both in the Main land as well as in the Islands.

Temperature

The highest temperature ever recorded in the island is 37.7°C at Amindivi in 1960 and the lowest temperature ever recorded was 17.2°C at Minicoy in 1942. The average monthly temperature in Minicoy and Amindivi island is fairly uniform. The daily mean maximum is higher in Amini (31.1°C) than that of Minicoy (29.9°C). The daily mean minimum is 25.4°C in Amini and 24.6°C in Minicoy. This is because Minicoy has a southerly location than that of Amini. This higher rainfall brings down the temperature in Minicoy than that of Amini. This trend is also reflected in temperature for highest in the month and lowest in the month. The highest in the month is 35.7°C in Amini compared to 33.2°C in Minicoy whereas it is lowest in the month 20.8°C in Amini and 19.4°C in Minicoy. Thus in the Lakshadweep Island the range is highest in the month in Amini and lowest in the month in Minicoy. In Amini it is 16.3°C (35.7°C-19.4°C) which is quite high. This difference is primarily due to the North-South extension of the island. The Southern Islands are less hot and cold than the northern islands of Lakshadweep.

TABLE 7.6: Temperature (Mean Annual)

Stations	Mean in°C				Extreme in°C	
	Daily		Highest in the month	Lowest in the month	Highest	Lowest
	Maximum	Minimum				
Amini	31.1	25.4	35.7	20.8	37.7	17.8
Minicoy	29.9	24.6	33.2	19.4	36.7	17.2

Agathi is the hotest island in Lakshadweep group of island with a mean temperature of 30.4°C. The warmest months in all the islands are April and May with a mean temperature about 30.1°C in Amindivi and 29.5°C in Minicoy. The corresponding temperature for Agathi is 32°C. The coldest months are from November to February when the temperature drops to 27.8°C at Amindivi* and 27.3°C at Minicoy. Agathi is uniformly warm with the lowest temperature in the rainy season. So far as The recording stations of West Coast of the mainland are concerned, the highest temperature ever recorded is 31.3°C at Mangalore in 1965 which is located at the most northerly point in this part and the lowest temperature ever recorded 29.9°C in 1960 at Fort Cochin. The average monthly temperature in Mangalore, Kozhikode, Fort Cochin, Cochin, (Naval Air Station) Alleppey and Trivandrum is fairly uniform with values of the order of 27.2°C. The warmest months along the West Coast of India are April and May. The cool months are from November to February when 23.7°C temperature is recorded at Mangalore, 23.7°C at Kozhikode, 24.0°C at Fort Cochin, 23.8°C at Cochin (Naval Air Station) 23.7°C at Alleppey and 23.5°C at Trivandrum.

Relative Humidity

The Lakshadweep Islands, being located in close proximity of the Equatorial Zone are very hot and humid. The islands are almost uniformly humid throughout the year only with marginal variations. The humidity values range from 75 per cent to 85 per cent. In Minicoy, the southern most island, it varies from a minimum of 72 per cent in January-March to maximum of 80 per cent during June-August which coincides with the South-West monsoon peak season. In December it is also 74 per cent. The mean humidity of Minicoy is 76 per cent. The same trend is marked in case of Amini Island.

Cloud Amount

The cloud amount is an indicator of rainfall. Data is available for two types of cloud i.e. 'all cloud' and 'low clouds'. The cloud amount varies from 3.7 OKTAS in the month of March to maximum of 7.1 OKTAS in June which are driest month and rainiest month respec-

* Amini is the short form of Amindivi.

tively for Minicoy Islands. In case of Amini in March lowest cloud amount is recorded which is 2.9 OKTAS and the maximum is 7.1 in the month of June when the entire island group is in full furry of the South-West monsoons.

TABLE 7.7: Relative Humidity and Cloud Amount

Humidity in %				Cloud Amount all clouds (in OKTAS)			
Minicoy		Amini		Minicoy		Amini	
Maximum	Minimum	Maximum	Minimum	Maximum	Minimum	Maximum	Minimum
80 (June-July)	72 (Jan.-March)	— —	73 (Feb.-March)	7.1 (June)	3.7 (March)	— —	2.9 (Jan.-February)

Wind Speed

Wind speed varies from 0 to 62 kmph in the Lakshadweep islands. Long range detailed figures are available only for Amini and Minicoy islands which have been analysed in the following paragraphs:

It is quite unusual to find that although Minicoy is nearer the Equator the number of calm days is only 14 as against 26 days at Amini which is further to north of the Equator than Minicoy. However, Minicoy has 301 days with average wind speed of 1 to 19 kmph as against only 242 days at Amini. Further number of days having wind speed between 20-61 kmph is only 50 at Minicoy while it is 97 days at Amini. Thus Amini is more turbulent that Minicoy. It is quite significant to note that in none of these islands the wind speed exceeds 62 kmph which is the gale speed. This is mainly because in the Arabian Sea the cyclones originate in the Lakshadweep and moves in N, N.E. and E directions and hence wind Velocity never exceeds 62 kmph in the islands.

It may be summed up that the average wind speed of Minicoy and Amini is 1-19 kmph. A month-wise analysis of the wind velocity reveals that maximum number of days (24 days) having wind speed of 20-61 kmph is experienced during July and August and gradually diminishes to November when it is only one day and it restarts in April when only one day experiences such wind speed. Thus if the wind speed be any indication of the onsetting of the South-West Monsoon it starts in the month of April and ends in November in Amini islands. In Minicoy it starts from the month of March when one day has a wind speed of 20-61 kmph and lasts up to December. Thus at Minicoy high wind velocity is experienced in March-December while at Amini it is from April to November. This period coincides with the period of South-West monsoons.

Wind Direction

The maximum percentage of days (30-31%) the wind blow from North-West followed by west (25-28%) and from North (17-19%). There is not much of a variation so far as the wind direction is concerned in both Amini and Minicoy islands. Thus it can be summed up that in the Lakshadweep the wind direction is north-westerly, Westerly and Northerly in order of arrangement. The percentage of wind from South S.E. & E are very low. These characteristics of wind direction is mainly because of location of the islands near the Equatorial Belt. This will be clear from the Table 7.8.

Visibility

The visibility position is better at Minicoy that at Amini. This is mainly because in 97.5 per cent of days of the year it is more than 4 kms as against 87.0 per cent of days at Amini. The visibility position is controlled by the cloud amount. Thus at Minicoy visibility is better that that of Amini (Table 7.9).

Conclusion

Thus from the point of view of cloud amount, wind velocity and visibility these islands offer best facilities for a naval base which will be the country's first line of defence in the Arabian Sea. This will also provide protection to India's merchant vessels which passes through Nine Degree Channel Naval and Misile base may be established at uninhabited islands which are good enough for such establishments.

TABLE 7.8: Annual Normal Wind Speed and Wind Direction

Island	Number of day with wind speed kmph				Percentage No. of days of wind form								
	0	1-19	20-61	62 or more	N	NE	E	SE	S	SW	W	NW	Calm
Amini	26	242	97	0	19	8	2	1	1	8	25	30	6
Minicoy	14	301	50	0	17	9	5	2	1	3	28	31	4

TABLE 7.9: Annual Visibility

Stations	Number of days with visibility in kms.					
	Up to 1	1 - 4	4 - 10	10 - 20	Over 20	Total
Amini (day)	2	60	103	176	24	365
In % of total	0.5	16.5	28.2	48.2	6.6	100.0
Minicoy	1	8	152	173	31	365
In % of total	0.3	2.2	41.6	47.4	8.5	100.0

8

EDAPHIC CONDITIONS

In all the island of the group, the soil can be said to be identical. They are poor, porous and calcareous. Everywhere, the fragmentation of coral limestones and sedimentary rocks from the Lakshadweep soil. It is formed by sediments which are consolidated into rocks by the weight of the overlying deposits. Later, by fragmentation of the lime stones and sedimentary rocks, fine soil is accumulated. For centuries, due to the constant accumulation of dead marine organisms, dead birds and bird droppings, the phosphate content of these seeping drop with the rains is gradually replaced the calcium carbonate in the original calcite and led to the formation of phosphorite.

In almost all the islands phosphorite out crops are seen. Fine disintegrated particles of phosphorite are found mixed with calcium carbonate in the soil. Hence, the soils contain appreciable percentages of calcium phosphate and calcium carbonate.

All along the sea shore, the soil tract is white in colour. In the interior of the islands it is generally ash colour due to accumulation of remnants of the plants and animals. Inorganic and organic acids are having profound influence on rapid erosion which changes the white colour of the soil.

The humus content in the soil is very low and hence there is very little retention of moisture. Hence, soon after the monsoon, the surface flora wither away and are dried up. The soil being extremely porous, the water percolates into the fine calcareous sand layer, causing the luxuriant growth of tress having deep roots.

Along the margin of land and sea i.e. on the beach of some islands, sedimentary sandy storms are found. The sudden fall in temperature of water in rock crevices exerts enormous pressure and bring about their disintegration. Further erosion is done by the wind drift and rain which transport the disintegrated materials from the surface of the rocks.

Due to the removal of sand from other parts by strong aeoline action during the South-West Monsoon, Sand dunes are found all along the Western Coast of the islands. So compared to other tracts, the elevation, on the Western Coasts of the island is higher than the eastern coasts and the land slopes from west to east. Generally, in the eastern and central tracts of the islands high concentration of weathered soil is met with.

A number of minerals such as Thorium, Molybdinum Nickel, Silver, Cobalt, Cadmium and Copper are found by the weathering of various felspars present in the soil. Nitrogen and Potasium content of these soils is very low. But with high values of calcium carbonate and available phosphoric acid the soils become excellent as direct fertilisers for correcting acidity and supplying phosphoric acid in soils. These soils are good sources of phosphate and calcium carbonate ores and phosphate Chalk. Bacteria and Fungi though not abundant, are also responsible for the biological weathering of the soil and the formation of minerals as they produce carbonic and other acids by their metabolic activities.

A typical section of the soil will reveal the four horizons of the soil profile.*

(i) *Horizon–A:* This is the uppermost layer of the soil which contains a considerable amount of ash-coloured organic matter about 20 cm in thickness. This provides a congenial surface for root foraging of the crops.

(ii) *Horizon–B:* In this, the leached products of Horizon-A are deposited. The colour of the soil becomes more and more white according to the depth and this horizon represents the sub-soil.

(iii) *Horizon–C:* This forms the immediate weathered parent material having texture of unbound soil particles purely white in colour.

(iv) *Horizon–D:* This is beneath the Horizon-C, where the solid parent rock material known as PARA is seen.

Mechanical composition of the soils in Lakshadweep is such that coarse sand is found in maximum quantum, followed by fine sand and silt. Except for interior shallow belts, clay content is comparatively low. In the coastal tracts the soil is predominantly sandy whereas sandy

---

* *Gazetter of India*, Lakshadweep, p.122, 1977.

loamy soils are found in the interior areas.

A large population of earth worms are found in the soils. These by opening up the soil, allow more air to get into the soil. Azotobacter choroococum and similar type of nitrogen fixing bacteria multiply very largely in earth warm castings. Because of the presence of A. Choroococum and other earth worms, these soils which are never manured, much less with any nitorgeneous one, do not exhibit nitrogen deficiency.

The pH of the soil is neutral, the index ranges roughly from 6 to 8. Generally, Lakshadweep soils are rich in phosphorous and calcium, though deficient in Potash and nitrogen. In Chetlat, Kiltan and Kalpeni Phospatic soil is found with 11 per cent to 24 per cent P_2O_5. The thick layer of bird guano, accumulated over years together is almost black in colour, has a high phosphate value which can be used as a rich fertiliser. A considerable portion of the surface soil in the above islands is a good reserve of phosphates. Though richest in calcium carbonate, the soil in Amini, is generally considered as very poor. Organic matters and calcium phosphate are found in very good quantity in the soils of Pitti Islands. Kiltan soil is good and Chetlat soil is probably the driest.

9

FLORA AND FAUNA

Lakshadweep group of islands though are situated near the Equator and receive considerable amount of rainfall, there are no marked Zones of vegetation. This is because these islands are small in extent and have almost even topography, sandy and very porous calcareous soil and hence without any surface run-off in the form of rivers, streams or lakes. Thus, the herbs, shrubs and climbers the come up during the rains dry up with the ceasation to the rains.

Plant specimens from all the islands have been collected and identified which reveal that there are 290 species of plants. Most of them i.e. 230 belong to *Angiosperm* category (those that produce seeds). The rest are the fresh and sea-water *algae* ferns and moss etc.

Like all other islands of the Pacific, coconut is the commonest plant of these islands which is most extensively cultivated and forms the great bulk of the vegetation. There are a few bread fruit trees, *banyans* and *tamarinds* on all the islands. Other tress that are fairly common, are the *puvarasu* (Thespesio Populnea), the *Punna (Calophyllum inophyllum)* the wild almond (*Terminalia catappa*) and the Horse Radish tree, (*Moringa pterygosperma*) along with *Custard apple, tree, portia, Drumstick catrifolia, Indian coral Tree,* and wild cotton.

Except for the island of Suheli, *Screwpine* (Kaitha) Pandanus Odoratissinuss is found in all the islands and most extensively in Minicoy. The island of Kalpeni has the largest number of bread fruit trees. The *Morinda citrifolia* the root of which was once much used for dying, is found in Kalpeni and Androth. The *Koyam,* a small tree from the wood of which the *tholepin* of the oar is made, is found on Kavarathi and south Kanara islands.

During Monsoon the ferns and Mosses grow almost in every islands. Bordering the shores in every island are thickets of *Pemphis acidula, Scaveola Koneigii* and *Tournea Argentifolia.* The root-parasite-striga *denisflora*—thrives in all islands but is most extensive on Kavarathi island. Thus, barring small differences the distribution of herbs, shrubs and trees are more or less similar in all the islands of the group.

Below is given the list of plants with their common name and Botanical names, that are found in these islands.

TABLE 9.1: List of Plants

Botanical Name	Common Name	Botanical Name	Common Name
Herbs, shrubs and trees:		*Citrus medica*	Lime
Artocarpus incisa	Bread-fruit tree	*Cassia occidentalis*	
Azadirachta indica	Neem	*Clerodendrum SP*	
Argemone mexicana	Mexican Poppy	*Cayratia Carnosa*	
Alstonia scholaris		*Cissus quandrangularis*	
Anona squamosa	Custard Apple	*Cardiospermum Halicacabum*	The ballon vine
Anona muricata		*Carotalaria medicaginea*	
Areca catechu (Kavungu)	Areca Palm	*Corchorus aestuans*	
Abutilon indicum		*Cyanotis cristata*	
Anisomeles indica		*Commelina bengalensis*	
Aerva lanata (Kattucheera)		*Colocassia antiquorum*	
Aeschynomene indica		*Caladium*	
Ammania Baccifera		*Crepis acaulis*	
Ageratum conyzoides		*Cyperus arenarius*	
Acalypha indica		*Dendrocalmus Strictus*	Bomboo
Achyranthes aspera		*Datura stramonium*	The deadly night Shade
Apluda Sp.		*Delonix regia*	(Gold Mohur) Flame of the forest
Alysicarpus SP. monilifer (Pooranpullu)		*Dodenia viscosa*	
Bombax Malabaricum	*Silk cotton tree*	*Disoscorea oppositifilia*	
Boerhavia diffusa		*Desmodium triflorum*	
Cocos nucifera (Thenga)	*Coconut Palm*	*Dactyloctenium agyptium*	
Casuarina equinsetifolia (Chavok)	*Casurina*	*Ery thirna indica*	Coral Tree
Calophyllum inophyllum (Premna integufolia)	*Pinna(Mal) Punna*	*Eclipta prostrata*	
Calatropis gigantea	*Milk Weed*	*Eragrostis tenella*	
Colocassia antiquorum	*Yam*	*Fieus religiosa*	Peepul
Cariya papaya	*Papaya*	*Ficus bengalensis*	Banyan
		Fieus indica	
		Fimbristylis spathacea	
		Gossypium arboreum	Wild cotton Tree

Botanical Name	Common Name
Clyricidia maculata	
Gloriosa superba	
Hibiscus tiliaceus	
Indigofera corditolia	
Indigofera purpurea	
Indigo fera tinctoria	Wild indigo
Ipomaeabiloba (patala)	Goat-foot creeper
Ipomea sp	
Ischaemum indicum	
Ixora coccinea	
Juncellus SP	
Lantana camara (arippoo)	Honey sucker
Leucas aspera	
Mangifera indica	The Mango
Morinda citrifolia	
Macaranga roxburghii	
Moringa pterygosperma	Drumstick
Moringa ollifera (Morigakkai)	Drumstick
Musa sapientum	Banana
Oscimum sanctum	Sweet basil
Pemphis acidula (Cheruthalam)	
Pandanus ordoratt-isimus	Screw Pine
Psidium guavjava	Guava
Plenrostylia wightia	
Plumbage zeylanica	
Piper betel (vettila)	Betel Vine
Polycarpae spicata	
Polygala Erioptera	
Pancratium-Zeylanicum	
Phyllanthus Madaras patensis	
Phyla nodiflora	
Ploygonum barbatum	
Pavetta Indicum	
Physalis minima	Capa Cherry
Physalis peruviana	Cape berry
Quisqualis Indica	Rangoon Creeper
Ricinus communis	Castor
Rungia Parsiflora	
Scaevola koenigii	Kanni
Spinifex littorens	Percupine or spinygrass
Tamarindus indicus	Tamarind
Tournefortia argentea	Tamara
Terminalia catappa	Badam
Typlophora Indica	
Tridax procumbens	
Thespesia populnea (cheerani)	Portia or St. Mary's Tree
Vinca rorea	Periwintle
Vettiverrea Zizanoides	Vettiver
Vitex negundo	
Zizyphus jujuba (elanthapa-zham)	Ber

Besides these there are many other types of hedges, grasses and climbers that go into from Lakshadweep vegetation.

Coconut is the ubiquitous plant and except the island of Pitti all the islands are covered with dense plantations of coconut. Every available area is cultivated in all the islands leaving very little cultivable waste. But Androth runs in irregularly shaped depression of 37 acres through the heart of the island and is easily flooded by sea water during high tides being at a very low level.

Pitti is the only island which has no vestige of vegetation, otherwise there are no barren or desert areas in this group of islands.

Moreover, the lagoons of most of the islands have extensive coverage of sea grass adjacent to the beaches. *Thalassia hemprichil* and *Cymodocea isoetifolia* are the two major plants constituting the Sea Grass. Their presence prevents erosion and movement of beach sediments and wherever these plants are not grown erosion of the beach has been observed to a certain extent.

Apart from all these, *algae* of great economic importance are found in the lagoons and adjacent areas of Lakshadweep. These algae are of following types such as *Ulva, Enteromorpha, Codium, Laminaria, Turbinaria, Sargassum, Padina, Gelidium, Gracilaria, Hypena* and *Ceramium.* These have very wide ranging uses and are used as foodstuff, medicine, fertiliser and cattle and poultry feed etc. But their distribution is rather sporadic in the lagoons, though there may be extensive areas in the shallow regions of the lagoon having *algae* of economic importance.

Fauna

It is almost impossible to give a detailed account of the wide variety of forms observes in these islands. But, the fauna of any oceanic island is generally restricted because of its separation from the mainland by an extensive barrier of sea. Here, the description is limited to the most common terrestrial forms and some commonly observed marine forms.

Flora	Local Name	Botanical Name
Banana	Vazha	*Musa paradisiaca)*
Chilli	Pachamulaku	*Capsicum Aunum*
—	Kattu Patavalam	*Trichosanthes cucmerina*
Cucumber	Vellarikka	*Cucumis sativus*
Drumstick	Moringakkai	*Moringa Obifera*
—	Mulli-	*Spinifex squarrosus*
—	—	*Lanalvulus alsinoides*
—	—	*Kyllinga monocephala*
—	—	*Setaria italica*
—	Pacha	*Blumea membrancea*
—	Chakkarapullu	*Stachytarpheta indica*
—	Katakaspoovu	*Bougainvillaea sepetabills*
—	—	*Codiaeum variegatum*

(Contd.)

(Contd.)

Flora	Local Name	Botanical Name
—	—	*Quamoclit pinnata*
—	Chembaruthi	*Hindisus rosasinensis*
—	—	*Cosmos sulphureus*
—	Arali	*Nerium odorum*
—	—	*Pedilanthus tithymaloids*
Paddy	nellu	*Oryza Sativa*
The common pepper	Kurumulagu	*Piper nigrum*
Tapioca	Marakkilangu	*Manihot utilissima*
—	—	**Crotalaria fysonii*
—	—	**Codiaeum variegatum*
—	—	**Cephalandra indica*
—	—	**Cosmos sulphureus*
—	—	**Spilanthes acmella*
—	—	*Thalassia hemprichii*
—	—	*Cymodocea isoetifolia*

* New plants introduced

Source: Mukundan T.K.,Lakshadweep : *A Hundred Thousand Islands*, pp. 100-103.

Among vertibrates the Cattle and poultry birds are common in the inhabited islands. The only representative of the family carnivora is the common domesticated cat. No indigenous mamalia are found in these islands. Perhaps, the only wild mammal observed belongs to the genus *Mus*, which are again the introduced ones. Atleast, two species are identified and they are common house mice. *Mus. rattus*—the large reddish rat and *Mus.* refescens—the smaller dark brown rat. Each species have colonised different islands and in on island are both seen while, Androth, Agathi, Kavarathy and Kalpeni are colonised by *reddish* ones, the *dark brown* ones are found in Amini, Chethelat, Kiltan, Kadamath and Bitra. Both these varieties though once led a terrestrial life are now almost exclusively arborcal-living and breeding in the crowns of coconut palms. These rats are now the serious pests of coconut causing about 25 per cent to 30 per cent loss.

Among reptiles the most common are the wall-Lizards, Palli (*Gecko* Sp.) garden lizards, *Onthu (Calotes Versicolar* and *Calotes liocephalus)* and *Skinds*, Arana *(Mabuya Carinata). Lycodon Travancoricus (Beddomes Wolf Snakechera)* has been reported at Androth. Though *Colar Snakes* are occasionally seen in the reef area during low tide, snakes are generally not found. The only amphibian reptile is the tortoise which are plentiful in the Lakshadweep waters. Two species of these tortoise are seen here. They are: (1) the *Green Turtle,* mirugom (Chelinia mydas), (2) the *Hawksbill turtle.* The green turtle is killed for its fat and yields a very valuable oil which is used for painting the bottom and sides of the boats to make them water proof. The *Hawksbill turtle* which is not so common, does not attain a size as that of green turtle. This yields the tortoise shell for commercial purposes. The presence of the common frog *Thavala (Rana tigrina)* has been reported at Minicoy island.

Insects of common occurrence are the roaches i.e. *Koorva (Periplanata americana*) and *Periplanata orientalis).* The *Rhino-ceros Beetle, Chellu (Oryctus rhinocerus)* is a pest of the coconut palm and causes lot of damages. In almost all the islands mosquitos are found and the mosquito oriented diseases are also not uncommon. The list of commonly found mosquito and their occurrence have been provided below:

Birds

Among birds, the ubiquitous crow is not seen in certain islands, while they are commonly found in Amini, Androth, Kalpeni and Minicoy, they are absent in Kavaratti. Numerous efforts have been made to introduce crows from Amini in order to check the rats. But Amini being only 5.0 km away from Kavaratti every time the crows flow back to Amini. Some of the birds are commonly seen in these islands and they are permanent residents. But some of the birds are migratory and are seem during a particular period of the year.

TABLE 9.2: Adult Mosquitoes collected from various Islands

Species	Kiltan	Chetlat	Amini	Kadmat	Agatti	Kavar-atti	And-roth	Kal-peni	Minicoy
C.frignas	+	+	—	+	+	—	+	+	—
C.vishnui	—	—	+	+	+	+	—	—	—
C.sitiens	—	—	—	—	—	—	—	—	+
C.tritaeni	—	—	—	—	—	+	—	+	—
Orhyncus									
Armegers	—	—	—	—	—	+	—	+	—
Obturbans									
lutzia	—	—	+	—	—	—	—	—	—
A.varuna	—	—	+	—	—	+	—	—	—
A.subpictus	+	+	+	+	—	+	+	+	—

Note: + = present. — = Absent.

TABLE: 9.3 List of Birds

PERMANENT RESIDENTS:	
Aredea Cinera	The common heron or grey heron
Buttorides Javanica	The little green heron
Corvas Splendens	The crow
Dromas Ardeola	The crab plver
Endynamis Soncrata	The Koel
Gallinula Phoenicula	The white breasted water hen
Netium Creca	The common teal
Sterna Mela Nanchen	The black naped Tern
Sterna Fuliginosa	The sooty tern
REGULAR VISITORS:	
Charadrius Falous	The Golden Plover
Cricus Macrurus	The Pole Harrier
Cricus Cineraceous	Monteagu's harrier
Falco Tinniculus	The Kestrel
Hirundo Urbica	The Martin
Num enius Phaeopus	The Whimbrel
Totanus Hypolencus	The Common Sand-Piper

The small island of Pitti has the largest number of birds. A team of orinthologists from Bombay Natural History Society during 1963 have observed the following birds as stated island-wise.

TABLE:9.4 List of Birds of Different Islands

(A) *AGATHY ISLAND:*	
Anous Stopidus Pileatus	Philippine
Sterna Bergeii	Large erested tern
Streptopelia Orientalis	Turtle dove
Zosterops Palpebrosa Palpebrosa	The white-eye
Caladris Minutus	Little stints (on coral reefs)
Erudy Nami's Scolpacea	The Koel
(B) *CHETHELAT ISLAND:*	
Pluvialis Sonatarola	Grey Plover
Pluvialis Apricaria (domnica)	Golden Plover
Delichon Urbica-House Martin	(a flock of 10)
Zosterops Palpebrosa Palebrosa	The White-eye
Streptepelia Orientalis	The Turtle Dove

(Contd.)

BELIAPANI REEF:	
Catharacta Skua	Antartic Skua
Sterna Anaethotas Antarcitca	Brown winged tern
Sterna Fuscata Nubilosa	Sooty Tern
(C) *PITTY ISLAND:*	
Stoma Bergeii	Large crested Tern (in hundred)
Anous Stolidus Pileatus	Noddy Tern (Breeding)
(D) *KAVARATHY ISLAND:*	
Oceauites Occauicus Occanicus	Wilson's Stormy Petrel
Egretta Sacra	Reef-Hern
Alcedo Athis	Common King Fisher
Hirrudo Rusticas	Swallow—A mile off Kavarathy
Zosterops Palebrosa Palpebrosa	White-eye

(E) BITRA;

The largest number of land birds are seen in the island of Bitra. They Are:

Anthus Similus	The brown Rock Pippit
Ardeola Grayii	The pond Hern—is miles off Bitra
Arenaria Interpres	The Turnstone
Pliuvialis-Apricaria-Dominca	The Golden Plover
Numerius Arquata	The curlew
Tringa Hypolensus	The sand-piper
Dromas Ardeola	Crad plover
Moracilla Have thunbergii	Gray headed yellow wage tail
Caladris Minunus	Little Stint

Of the birds the *Curlew* and the *Golden Plover* are migrants during cold weather. The *Grey heron* is ubiquitous and *Terns* are found in greater number in the island of Pitty. This island has been declared as a bird sanctuary by Lakshadweep administration and therefore they live without the fear of human interference.

Marine Fauna

The Laccadive Marine fauna is much varied and is remarkable for its similarity with the marine fauna of the Atlantic around West Indies. Most remarkable are the Laccadive *Crustaceans* the large *Isopod (Bathynorus giganteus),* the Blind sping lobster (*Phoberus cascus*) and the Spiny hermit crab (*Lithodes Agassizii)* which are again found in the Caribbean Sea. Further Many Types Of fishes and Corals are common to the both regions.

The sea has a wealth of living organisms. Below the 300 fathom line, are 30 different natural orders comprising 80 families,160 genera and 250 species. There are 34 species of star fishes of which 18 are of the *brittle* type. Out of 80 species of crustaceans 40 unable to swim, live on the sea bed. Of *molluscas* there are 40 species and of fishes fifty, of which 20 are peculiar to this area. Some of the molluscas are most attractive like are found in all beaches. Corals of rare types are seen in all the waters round the islands e.g."Stag-horn (*Acropora),* Moose-horn and others". [1]

The varied molluscan forms of Lakshadweep are not only magnificent in their appearance but also important from the economic points of consideration of the islands. The *money cowrie* (Cypraea monita) are abundant in the Lakshadweep shallow waters. The *Cypraeds* have great commercial value. *Cypraea tigris* and *Cypraea caputserpentis* are picked up from the reef at low tide time and are large sold in the mainland for decorational purposes. Other colourful varieties belonging to *Cypraeds* and *Cypraea talpa* and *Cypraea maculifera.* A great variety of shells are found in almost all the islands. These are mostly found on the eastern coast which is open to the sea. The greatest variety of shells are found in Kiltan and Chetelat, Kavarathy has less varieties but they are bigger sized ones. Those usually found are:

Honda Cone, Tulip Shells, Giant Tun Lace Murex, Capritic, Murex (Sping Wood-Cock), *Pacific Pink Scallop, Measeld (Mottled) Cowry, Dwarf Olive, Bubble Shells, Flame Hepnet Queen Scallop, Tower Shell Pelican foot shell, Elephant Tusk Shell and Murex Malabaricus.*

The sea-fauna *Gorgonian* and soft corals are seen in small Umbers Blue coloured coral is common while the pure red ones are very very rare. Both *Hermatypic* and *Ahermatypic* corals occur in the waters of these islands. The reef building corals found here are the *rites* and *Moendrina* species.

Fish are abundant in the waters of the Lakshadweep. Many kinds of the small fishes which are found in the lagoon are wonder-fully coloured. The *Surgeon fish, Gar Fish, Sun fish, Sharks* and *Sword fish* are among the common kinds. A variety of edible fishes that are available include the *Skate,* the *Seer Fish,* the *Tuna* or *Skip-jack* and the shark. The *Devil Fish, Baara-cuda, Marlin, Sword-fish* and *Cybium* are sporadic-in appearance. Commercially, The *Tuna* is the most important. It is almost impossible to give full particulars of all the fishes seen in these waters but a list of very common fishes with their English names and local equivalents is given below:

TABLE: 9.5 List of Marine Fishes

	Scientific Name	English Name	Vernacular Name
1.	Katsumonus Pelamis	Skip Jack	Mas Choora
2.	Neothunnus Rnacropterus	Yellowfin	Poovanchoora
3.	Auxis Thazard	Frigate Mackerai	Ragundi
4.	Euthynnus Alleteratus	Little Tunny	Letti
5.	Sphyraena Sp.	Barracuda	Thriruthakkadian
6.	Acanthocybium Solandri	Seerfish	Ayakura
7.	Corypheanea Hippurus	Dolphin Fish	Avunose
8.	Istiophorus Galdius	Sail Fish	Olameen
9.	Exocoetus Volitans	Flying Fish	Parava
10.	Hermiramphus Far	Half Beak	Kudukka
11.	Belone Annulata	Garfish	Karuthonamkuntic
12.	Elegatis Bipinihulatus	Rainbow Runner	Chameen
13.	Dyphosous Vaigiensia	Chub	Phunji
14.	Lutianus Kashmira	Snapper	Manhan
15.	Lutianus Bohar	Red Snapper	Pulariam
16.	Lutjanus Gibbus	—do-	Chemmali
17.	Lutjanus Argentimaculatus	Grey Snapper	Metti
18.	Thalssoma Sp.	Rainbow Fish	Choolam
19.	Gomphosus Coeruleus	—do-	Irachi Choolam
20.	Echeneis Naucrates	Shark Sucker	Keesakam
21.	Ostracion Lentiginosum	Box Fish	Thomabu
22.	Diodom Hystrix	Procupine Fish	Mullaka
23.	Myrichthys Colubriuns	—	Malanji
24.	Caranx Stellatus	King Fish	Kuluval
25.	Pelatas Quadri Lineatus	Crooker	Manhan
26.	Holuntrus Rubrum	Soldier Fish	Lattam
27.	Cephalipholis Argus	Rock Cod	Chemmum
28.	Cheile Depterus Quinquilineatus	Cardinal Fish	Phootham
29.	Caranx Cruminopthalmus	King Fish	Bangada
30.	Chaetodon Falcula	Butterrfly Fish	Fakkikadia
31.	Chanetodon Auriga	—do-	—do-
32.	Chaetodom Citrinellus	—do-	—do-
33.	Acanthurus Triostefus	Lancet Fish	Kurichi
34.	Acanthurus Lineatus	Surgeon Fish	Varipad
35.	Acanthurus Lineolatus	Surgeon Fish	Neythala
36.	Acanthurs Leucosternon	—do-	Chettipetti
37.	Naso Brevirostris	Unicorn Fish	Karukkan
38.	Naso Unicornis	—do-	Mudiyan
39	Gerrus Punctatus	—	Prachi
40.	Aprion Vivescens	Streaker	Chavadukallan
41.	Chromis Caeruleus	Coralfish	Pachachala

(Contd.)

TABLE 9.5 *(Contd.)*

	Scientific Name	English Name	Vernacular Name
42.	Halichoeres Centriquadrus	Rainbow Fish	Payathalayan
43.	Callyodon Sordidus	Parrot Fish	Pacha Pheesam
44.	Leptoscasrus Coeruleopun-ctatus	Parrot Fish	Pheesam
45.	Siganus Stellatus	Rabbit Fish	Oran
46.	Siganus Rivulatus	Rabbit Fish	Kalloran
47.	Odonus Nigger	Trigger Fish	Kappuvalan Karathi
48.	Balistapus Undulatus	Trigger Fish	Baluppallam Karathi
49.	Rhine Canthus Aculaeatus	Trigger Fish	Vella Karatti
50.	Chaetodon Xanthocephalus	Butterfly Fish	Fakkikadia

* *Gazetteer of India*, Lakshadweep-1977, p. 20-22.

1. *Journal of Bombay*, Nat. History Society for 1892 by Dr. D.Pram.

ECONOMIC BASE

10

AGRICULTURE

The Union Territory of Lakshadweep has a total geographical area of around 32 sq. kms. All the constituent islands were once fringed by a thick growth of *Tamara, Kanni, Chonam* and *Cheruthalam* while large trees like *Punna* (Calophyllum Inophylum), *Cheerani* (Thespesia Populnea), wild Almond and Banyan trees etc. are found inside the islands. The ground flora was thick and knee deep in certain places. Coconut tree was introduced by the earliest settlers who came from Malabar coast of India. Now the entire cultivable area of the Union Territory of Lakshadweep is thickly planted by coconut trees. Nearness to the sea, the high water table, abundant sunshine and porous calcarious soil contribute to the growth of coconut trees and even after centuries, it is still the main play of the island economy.

There were only four persons in the Union Territory engaged in cultivation according to 1971 Census. There was complete absence of agricultural labourers in contrast with other areas of the mainland and Union Territories. Of the total working population, 30.09 per cent were engaged in household industry and 26.68 per cent were engaged in fishing, plantation etc.

At present except Bitra island, in every other inhabited island vegetable gardens are found. Brinjal, *Bhindi* (Ladies figure), Radish, Chillies, Beans, Greens, Tomato and other types of vegetables are being supplied at fairly low prices to encourage the islanders to grow and consume the vegetables. Apart from all these, the plantation of pine apples, soyabean, Tapioca varieties of the Malabar Coast have been introduced in Post-Independence period.

Practically, the only form of plantation found on the islands is coconut. The entire cultivable area of 2855 hectares of the islands of Androth and Kalpeni has been planted with coconuts. The low lying areas which are known as *Thottam* were earlier used for paddy cultivation but with increasing commercial importance of coconut, these areas have been planted up with the latter.

Below is given a detailed account of certain crops which are being cultivated in these islands.

Coconut

Coconut is ubiquitous and is the only crop grown on a massive scale in all the islands. But the method adopted for the cultivation of coconut are crude and primitive. The trees are very closely planted leaving only 2.5 to 3.0 metres distance between them. In many places serious over planting has been practised, resulting in a decrease in the annual crop. Planting is generally done during the South-West Monsoon period. Trees are planted very close and new seedlings are planted only in pits with regard to surface planting which was practised earlier.

Out of the total area of 32 sq. kms. an area of 2855 hectares is under coconut. With about 0.4 million fruit bearing trees, the total number of palm trees in the island exceeds 0.56 million. During 1975-76 the total production of coconut was 214 lakhs. Production of nuts varies with the types of plant. The ordinary type of plant gives about 40-45 nuts whereas a better variety of plant yields 200-300 nuts in a year. The nuts are smaller in size compared to that of the Mainland.

All the palms are tall or medium in height. Dwarf variety is almost absent in these islands. Altogether seven types or coconut palms have been recognised. They have been named as *Chenga, Karunga, Chentengu, Moyiliyar Kooyeydu, Kayyathali* etc. *Chenga* nuts are brown of reddish brown in colour and *Karunga* are green coloured. The nuts are either roundish or oblong in both the *Chenga* and *Karunga* varieties. There are two varieties of nuts one green and the other yellowish-red which is locally known as *Chentengu*. These varieties produce beautiful spherical nuts. *Kayyathali* is a rare variety of coconut. This variety has no commercial importance. About 80 per cent or more of palms are of *Chenga* and *Karunga* varieties. Other varieties such as *Chentengu, Moyiliyar kooyeydu* and the rare *Kayyathali* etc. from about 3 to 5 per cent each.

Cultivation of Coconut

Earlier, coconut trees alone constituted the property, but not the land on which they were planted. But of late, with the survey of land and settlement of the landlord tenant issue, land is being looked upon as a property. So earlier coconut trees bore distinguishing mark of the owner and remained scattered all over.

Nurseries were raised in abandoned sites of wells and pits made by soil excavations and thus they were beyond the reach of cattle and goats. Seedlings were transplanted after 2 or 3 years in nursery. Once planted, they grow by themselves. No attention is paid thereafter, such as hoeing, manuring and irrigation. Irrigation was unknown and manuring was never done. Nuts were taken randomly for seedling.

But now, the agriculture department has effected many changes. Nuts are being raised into seedlings from marked coconut trees. Coconut nurseries have been attached to agricultural gardens from where islanders are getting the seedling at concessional rates. Slowly, the manuring of coconut trees is being appreciated. Fish manure has been supplied at concessional rates for coconut plantation.

Varying uses of Coconut

Copra

Copra making is the most important income earning industry in the island. Copra making is done by splitting open the nut and after draining out the water, the tow halves are dried in the Sun. After the Kernel has shrunk, the copra is scooped out of the shell and packed for export to the mainland. One an average nine coconuts yield a kilogram of copra.

Coconut Oil

Oil is extracted from the coconut by scraping the Kernels, squeezing out the milk from the scraped meat and boiling it in a shallow vessel over a slow fire. The golden coloured oil with a rich appetising smell floats on the top. Which is skimmed off and collected in bottles or tins and are sent to Malabar Coastal towns and Mangalore for sale.

Coir

Next to copra, coir is another article of export. As per 1971 Census, about 92.5 per cent of women folk took part in Coir twisting. The retting of the coconut husks are done either in the pits or no the sea or lagoon beach. The retted fibres are dumped under the shade of coconut trees and women beat out the fibre using strong rods of 'Cheruthalam'. The fibre is twisted into rope and is exported after meeting the domestic requirements. The hand spun coir is mainly used for making coir ropes for sailing vessels. The coir is sometimes bartered for rice. The trade in coir is the monopoly of the government and is done on no-profit-no-loss basis. The production of *Angenogo and Vaikkam* Vaikkam varieties of coir yarn is being encouraged by the government through the coir production-cum-demonstration centres in various islands.

Pests and Diseases

Rats are then main enemies of coconuts. They exist in enormous numbers and due to their arboreal habit causes destruction to incalculable number of coconuts. The traditional rat hunts, use of poison baits and mechanical devices such as rat traps and metal bands around coconut tree trunks are the measures adopted for the eradication of rats. Still rats are in appreciable numbers and it is estimated that 20 per cent to 30 per cent of yield is lost per annum due to the rats. The only remedy seems to be a systematic hunting of rats accompanied by careful protection of trees after they have been cleared.

A large black beetle i.e. the *Rhinocerous beetle* is also one of the common pests of the coconut. It bores into the hears of the crown and the bases of the lead stalks. The traditional practices for the control of beetles are booking them 2 or 3 days before and after the full moon and the new moon, lighting the honfires, filling of leaf axles with sand and tying bones of cattle (shanks) on trees. The grub of *Rhinocerous beetle* is found in manure heaps, fallen tree trunks, piles of rotten *cadjans* etc. and the most effective remedy for the pest is to burn all rubbish and rooten tree trunks. The other minor pests on coconut are *Bombay Locusts (Patanga succincta), Scale* Insects, *Mealy Bugs Epilachna Beetles* etc.

Stem bleeding is the common disease of coconut and cases of bud rot and nutritional deficiencies are also seen.

Bread-Fruit

Next to coconut, bread-fruit tree with thick green foliage and beautiful silk green fruits attracts attention. The tree without much care grows abundantly in all the islands. The tree is called *Chakka* in the Lakshadweep meaning jack fruit. The real jack fruit tree is called Malayam *Chakka* meaning jack fruit from Malabar. A full grown bread-fruit tree reaches upto 15 metres in height. The root sprents which are produced in plenty are transplanted and the tree requires a most and warm climate. In the first few years, the tree can well grow under shade but after that it requires more light for growth. The largest number of trees are found in the island of Kalpeni. These trees bear fruit twice a year i.e. in April-May and September-October. The trees bear profusely but the size of the fruit is much smaller here than those found in the Malabar Coast. Very few fruits are wasted. The mature ones are curried and eaten or sliced and sun-dried and stored for the rainy season.

Apart from a limited extent of use in house construction, the timber is mostly used in boat building.

Papaya

Papaya is the common fruit tree found in Lakshadweep. The leaves are in clusters at the top of the stem or branches. The fruit when it is ripe is very sweet and popular among the people. It is also used as vegetable before it is ripe. The tree requires no manure for its growth. It is soft wooded and milky juice is found almost from every part of the tree. This milky juice has several qualities. All sorts of meat washed with this juice become tender. The decay of the muscular fibre exposed to its influence is hastened. The women folk feed their old poultry with the leaves and fruits of this tree before they are killed so as to make the meat perfectly tender.

Drumstick Tree (Moringa Pterigosperma)

These trees are found in all parts of the islands. They grow of their own and the wood is soft, and brittle. The trees are fast growing with elegant feathery foliage which shed towards December-January. The new foliage appears thereafter with handsome white flowers. The drumsticks grow to a length of one foot and both ends of its area tapering. A large number of seeds are found inside the stick. The sticks ripe from April to June. From the seeds *Ben* oil can be extracted which has many useful applications. *Ben* oil is used by watch makers, for external application for pains in the limbs and for the manufacture of perfumes. Besides, the tree's root, leaves and fruits are also used for various ailments.

Banana

Bananas are planted in low lying areas and house compounds as kitchen gardening. They are grown on a small scale in the islands of Kalpeni, Kavaratti, Androth, Kadamat, Amini and Minicoy. The common varieties of Banana found here are *Mysore, Pooran, Poovan, Kadali, Robusta, Nendran* etc.

Vegetables

Vegetables were never grown in these islands. Rice and fish are sill the staple food of the people. But gradually with the initiative of the agricultural department, cultivation of some vegetables have been introduced. The vegetables which are being grown now-a-days are brinjal, pumpkin, cucumber etc. the seeds or seedlings are supplied by the agricultural department and they are planted during the rainy season. *Cowpea (Vigna Catijang)* is cultivated in December in Androth and Kalpeni and during S.W. Monsoon period in Agatti.

Sweet Potato

In Androth and Kalpeni, sweet potato are being cultivated on a considerable scale. The cultivation of potato in Androth is done during April and may and in September-October in Kalpeni. Harvesting takes place after 3 or 4 months per acre yield of sweet potato is considerably high i.e. 3500 kg. per acre.

Grains, Cereals and Millets

Paddy cultivation was done earlier in the islands of Androth and Kalpeni on a very small scale. But now-a-days paddy is not being cultivated. Ragi cultivation is confined to the *Kharif* season of the S.W. Monsoon period and it is usually grown in the low lying areas of Androth, Kalpeni, Agatti and Kavaratti. Ragi seedlings of 20 or 30 days are planted and are harvested after 3 months of planting.

Agricultural Implements

The cultivation in the Lakshadweep islands is not diversified and is limited only to coconut. So there is no necessity of using various types of implements. The ordinary spade *(Mammutty)* and crowbar are the only agricultural implements used in the island. Spade finds variety of uses and is used for digging pits, earthing up plants and digging out tree stumps. The crowbar used here range from 1.2 to 2.1 metres in length. The big ones find their use in jerking out blocks of cut stones where as short ones are used for digging holes. The *Billhook* is also largely used. There are no working cattle and no ploughs. As the coconut trees and very closely planted, the use of power tillers etc. are not possible. But with the efforts of the Agricultural Department they are being introduced and are becoming popular.

Role of the Agricultural Department

In the year 1955, Agricultural Department of the Government started functioning in the Lakshadweep. The headquarters of this department was at Agatti island. Since then this department has taken a pivotal role in the agricultural development of the islands. As coconut cultivation is the single dominant agricultural activity, Agricultural Department has initiated the production of high yielding coconut seedings and has demonstrated the improved cultural, manurial and intercropping aspect of coconut cultivation. The role of Agricultural Department controlling the pests and diseases cannot be over emphasized. Apart from that, maintenance of vegetable gardens and conduct of experiments on various crops suited to the soil have been carried out by the Department. Barring the island of Bitra, every other island has vegetable gardens. To give an agricultural, bias, small gardens are attached to all schools. The islanders get at subsidised rates, the fertilizers, implements and seedlings etc. from the Agriculture Department. Various types of pesticides are distributed free of cost.

Nearly 6000 quality seedings are distributed to the people from the various coconut nurseries run by the government annually. Vegetable seeds are also distributed to the people at subsidized rates. It has been found out that Hybrid maize, Sugarcane and Red gram can be successfully grown in the islands.

11

LANDUSE

Land Utilisation of Kavaratti

The island was once fringed by thick growth of Tamara (*Tournefortia argentea*), Kanni (*Scaevola Koenigii*), Chonam, and Cheruthalam (*Pemphisacidela*), while inside the island large trees of Funna Cheerani (*Thespesia Populanea*), wild Almond, and Banyan were found.

The ground flora was thick and almost knee deep in certain places. The earliest settlers who came from the Malabar Coast of the main land brought with them the coconut trees, their *Kalpavirksha.* The high water table, nearness to the sea, gentle breeze, abundant sunshine and porous calcarious soil contributed to the rich growth of the coconut tree which served numerous needs of the early settlers. Even after centuries, the coconut trees maintain their supremacy in the domestic economy of the islanders. The edible nut and the coconut husk provide raw materials to the copra and coir industries.

The Kavaratti island is divided into six major divisions and each division is sub-divided into different Blocks. In all, there are twenty-six Blocks, all liked by roads with one another for better economy and administration. Blocks are divided into fields and there are 983 fields in the Kavaratti island. The fields are again divided into sub-divisions which are about 7841 in number (Table 11.1). The area of the island is 362.94 hectares according to the Land Survey Operation Report in 1967, while it is 350.25 hectares as per 1971 Census. It has remained unchanged since then.

The island though still recognised of having primarily a rural settlement pattern, yet it has a number of urban functions, peculiar to suit and administrative headquarter. Mainly in the central-west and north-western parts of the island government quarters are concentrated. In between these two parts private settlements have come up. In the central eastern border settlements of the local inhabitants

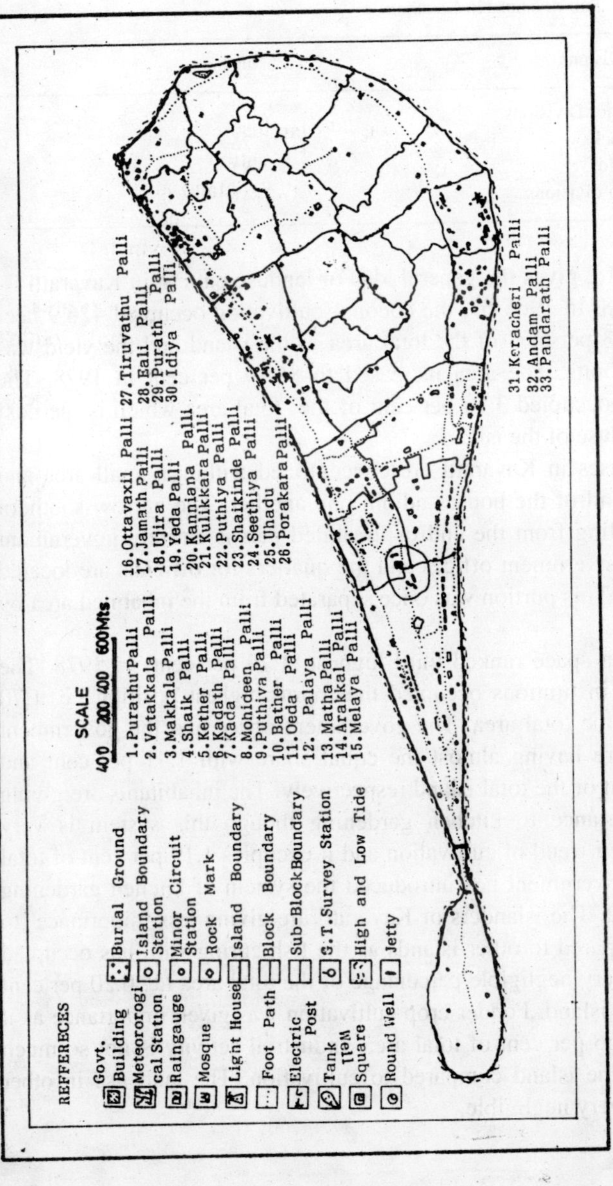

FIG.11.1: Kavaratti Island : Landuse

are met with. The central portion is deprived of Govt. quarters and settlements. The elongated area, penetrating towards the south is lying vacant because the land shrinks to a width of only a few metres.

TABLE 11.1: Sub-divisions in Kavaratti

Divisions	Numbers
Major Divisions	6
Blocks	26
Fields	983
Sub-divisions	7841

Table 11.2 gives the general idea of landuse pattern in Kavaratti island in 1978. In 1966-67, the coconut cultivation occupied 426.9 hectares or 49.3 per cent of the total area of the island and the yield was 18.66 lakh nuts. The area increased to 86.19 per cent in 1978. The settlements occupied 3.10 per cent of the total area which is the next highest landuse of the island.

The houses in Kavaratti are concentrated within a small area and the compound of the houses adjoin one another. The narrow southern portion starting from the end of inhabited part is entirely government land. The Government offices and the quarters for officials are located in this area. This portion was once separated from the inhabited area by a wall.

The open space ranked third highest (1.79 per cent) in 1978. The educational institutions occupied the fourth highest position i.e. 1.70 per cent of the total area. The government office and the government quarters were having almost the equal share with 1.41 per cent and 1.16 per cent of the total island respectively. The inhabitants are giving much importance to kitchen gardening though this system is very recent in their trend of cultivation and it occupies 1.19 per cent of total area. The government has introduced the system of kitchen gardening only in 1972. The islanders of Kavaratti are giving less importance to fishing compared to other islands as the fish curing yard has occupied only only very negligible percentage of the total area i.e. 0.20 per cent of Kavaratti island. Fodder crop cultivation was given importance as it occupied 0.66 per cent of total area. Industrial activity is not so much familiar in the island compared to cultivation. The land use in other aspects are very negligible.

TABLE 11.2: Distribution of Lands into different categories (in acres) in 1978 of Kavaratti Island

Mosques and Madrase	Settlements	Government Quarters	Government Offices	School and Colleges	Recreational	Stores & Godown	Water & Bodies	Power House Light House
(1)	(2)	(3)	(4)	(5)	(6)	(7)	(8)	(9)
5.06 (0.58)	26.80 (3.10)	10.06 (1.16)	12.18 (1.41)	14.70 (1.70)	3.95 (0.46)	2 (0.23)	1.97 (0.23)	1.97 (0.23)

Barren Land	Fishing curring yard	Poultry farm	Industrial Area	Medical and Dispensary	Coconut cultivation Area	Agricultural Demonstration	Area under Fodder crops	Kitchen garden
(10)	(11)	(12)	(13)	(14)	(15)	(16)	(17)	(18)
15.52 (1.79)	1.75 (0.20)	1.03 (0.12)	— —	3.5 (0.40)	745.94 (86.19)	2.52 (0.29)	5.68 (0.660)	10.32 (1.19)

The island does not show any major topographic features as it is largely a low levelled flat topped island and generally rises to a height of a few metres above the mean sea level. It was entirely covered by coconut plantation and settlements. Government buildings are occupying more and more space every year. The number of government buildings is the highest among all the islands of the Lakshadweep Group. The land use map of the Kavaratti island shows that government buildings at the western border of the island are separated from the private buildings. The separation of western border and eastern border is marked by coconut farms and betel orchards.

TABLE 11.3: Landuse Pattern in Kavaratti (1978-79)

Category of landuse	Area in Acres	In % to total area
Settlements	26.80	26.66
Religious Places (Mosques and Madrasa)	5.06	5.03
Educational Institutions (School and Collages)	14.70	14.63
Total	46.56	46.32
Govt. Institutions		
Govt. offices	12.18	12.12
Govt. Quarters	10.06	10.11
Power and Light House	1.97	1.96
Medical and Dispensary	3.50	3.42
Poultry Farms	1.03	1.02
Recreational Facilities	3.95	3.93
Stores and Godown	2.00	1.99
Water Bodies	1.97	1.96
Fish Currying Yard	1.75	1.74
Barren Land	15.52	15.43
Total	53.93	53.68
Grand Total	100.49	100.00

Change in Land use

The spatio temporal change in landuse pattern after 1964 has became very significant and prominent because in 1964 Kavaratti became the headquarters of administration of the Laccadive and Minicoy Islands.

New buildings sprung up in the Kavaratti. A large number of government employees came from the mainland to serve in the island. It has great impact on education, settlement pattern and occupational structure of the original islanders. The island has a literacy rate of 15.95 per cent in 1961. The percentage of male literates was 28.06 in contrast to 3.26 for females. But in 1971, the position changed. The literacy rate increased to 44.37 per cent. The male literacy increased to 60.4 per cent and female literacy became 24.5 per cent. This rise in educational status has influenced the re-arrangement in the lay-out of the dwellings and improvements required any living conditions of the islanders. While almost all the private dwellings in 1961 were of *Kutcha* structure with thatched roofs, in 1971 a remarkable improvement was found in having as more than 80 per cent of the houses were built with *pucca* walls and about 40 per cent of them with improved roofs of either tiles and shingles or C.I. sheets, concrete (R.B.C./R.C.C.) and asbestos sheets etc.

Coming to the non-residential houses including religious shrines and structures, it is observed that back in 1961 there were only 26 such non-residential structures including 7 mosques. The buildings under this category increased to 68 in 1978 which included 34 mosques. The entire island covering only 3.50 sq. km is covered with such structures like mosques, barracks, agricultural store, poultry farm, handicrafts society, radio station, new college campus, textile shop, workshop, workshop yards, furniture unit, clubs and godowns etc. All these mean a considerable addition and transformation in the landuse and cultural landscape of the island. Though the islanders by and large, depend even today on their traditional occupation of coconut farming and fishing, associated with coconut farming and handicrafts. They are also employed in both secondary and tertiary activities but there has been a surprising fall in employment against household industry.

Table 11.3 shows the Land Utilisation statistics available for 858.9 acres or 98.2 per cent of the total geographical area of 865.50 acres. It gives details of land utilization in the island for the year 1978-79. The peculiarity is that there is no forest in the Kavaratti island and only 101 acres are available for cultivation which is about 11.75 per cent of the total area or 11.88 per cent of the total reported area for land utilisation.

TABLE 11.4: Land Utilisation in Kavaratti Island, 1978

Type of use	Reported Area (Acres)	As % to total area
Total geographical area	865.50	
Total reporting area for land utilisation	858.90	98.2
1. *Forest*	—	—
2. *Not available for Cultivation*		
i. Area put to non-agricultural uses	85.5	9.95
ii. Barren and uncultivable lands	15.5	1.80
Sub-total	101.0	11.75
3. *Other uncultivated excluding fallow lands*		
i. Permanent pastures and grazing lands	—	87.65
ii. Land under tree crops and groves	752.9	—
Total	752.9	87.65
4. *Fallow Lands*		
i. Current fallows	5.0	0.58
ii. Others	—	—
Total	5.0	0.58
5. Net Area sown	6.60	0.76
Area sown more than once	3.32	0.38
Total	9.92	1.15
Grand total	858.90	100.0

Out of 101 acres of non-agricultural land about 85.5 acres or 9.95 per cent of the total geographical area of the island or 10.05 per cent of the reported area are under permanent grazing and pastures. The area for "Land under tree crops and groves" has occupied 752.9 acres. The coconut cultivation comes under this category which has occupied the maximum (745.9 acres) area among all categories. In kitchen gardens the inhabitants cultivate papaya, banana and betel vines.

All these categories had occupied 87.65 per cent of the total area. Total cropped area of the island was only 11.52 acres. Out of which 8.2 acres were sown only once in a year and the rest 3.32 acres were cultivated more than once.

Table 11.5 shows only the main crops grown in the island. Coconut cultivation had been the principal crop from time immemorial and it still continues to be so. Some new varieties of crops have been introduced in the island, such as, brinjal, cucumber and pumpkin due to the efforts, of the government. Betel orchard, bread fruit, banana and papaya and sweet potato have been cultivated from very ancient time in limited quantity. The government has opened and agricultural demonstration unit to produce all varieties of food crops but has not yet been successful for various reasons, discussed else-where. The coconut is the only major corp with an annual turnover of Rs. 30 million in 1984 while the area under cultivation was about 2780 hectares.

TABLE 11.5: Crops Cultivated in 1978

Crops	Area (in acres)	Area as % to total reporting area for land utilization
Bread Fruit	2.4	0.27
Papaya	2.1	0.24
Banana	4.5	0.52
Brinjal	4.0	0.46
Pumpkin	2.0	0.23
Cucumber	2.7	0.31
Coconut	745.9	86.84
Betel Orchard	2.0	0.23
Total	765.6	89.13

Land Utilisation of Agatti and Kalpitti Island

The shape of the island is like a club with a broad north. It begins tapering to the south from the middle ending in a narrow strip, barely 95 metres wide in the south. There are no storm beaches to the east which is purely sandy. The very extensive lagoon varying in depth from 2 to 3 metres is the most beautiful in the Lakshadweep Group of Islands. The soil is poor and infertile. The northern part is densely planted with coconuts and bread fruit trees and the southern part has a low scrub jungle, where only a few coconut trees grow. This ends in a spiny grass land at the beach. Separated by a narrow channel on the south lies the rocky 28 acres uninhabited island of Kalpitti i.e. 'Stoney' Island. The whole area is planted with coconuts.

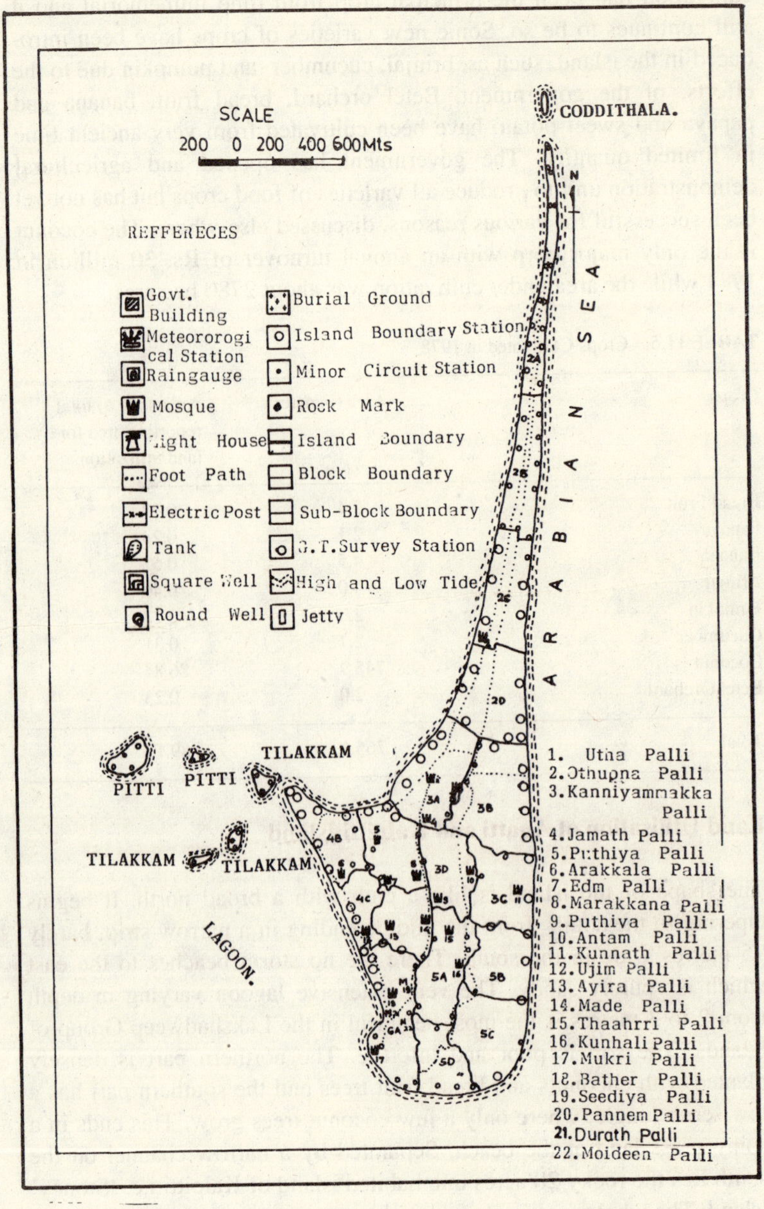

FIG. 11.2: Kalpeni Island: Landuse

The total geographical area of the island is 716 acres (289.75 hectares). It has been divided into 25 Blocks; 1,321 fields and 13,471 sub-divisions, as per land survey operation of 1967. All these are interconnected with roads. The island lies on the eastern side of the coral shore and is about six kilometres long and one kilometre wide at the broadest point. Habitations are mainly confined to the northern portion of the island which is broad and well protected from annual topical cyclones. Coconut plantation is however sparse, compared to the other islands of Lakshadweep group of islands. There is a large and beautiful lagoon on the western side of the island which is ideal for Dishing. It is however deep, compared to other islands and consequently ripples are larger than the average waves which make it impossible for the inhabitants to net coir nets in the lagoon as done in other islands. Attempts were evidently made in the past to construct a *Thottam* (Garden) for cultivation of paddy and cereals, but all those failed. A sort a bean plantation and a few betel vine were however, grown in the gardens.

The earlier settlers had planted coconut trees only on a small scale. There were vast areas of waste land when the British took over the islands. The policy of the British Government was to let out such government lands to granting lands to individuals on *Cowle* (a system of granting lands on improved lease). The *Cowle* system boosted the coconut plantation which soon covered the entire island. At present there is little scope for further expansion of coconut cultivation. The other draw back for cultivation of crop is soil erosion. Most of the soil of the western shore has been blown away by the local strong wind during the off monsoon season and left baren. The soil in Agatti island has become so shallow that even lapping of the small waves is strong enough to uproot some of the coconut trees over the shore. Cassurina has been planted in some areas to protect the soil erosion. Our Survey of 1978 has given in Fig. 11.3 of landuse in Agatti island.

Out of the total area,the coconut cultivation occupied 661.46 acres (267.8 hectares) which was about 92.28 per cent of the island and the output was 20.29 lakh nuts in 1966-67. The 1978 survey has revealed that the land under coconut cultivation has decreased to 573.4 acres i.e. 80.08 per cent of the total area. Thus in about a decade, the percentage of reduction of coconut cultivation is 11.46 per cent of the total area of the island. The coconut cultivated areas has been put to other used like settlements. The number of settlements have increased from only 470 in 1971 to 906 in 1978. All these settlements have occupied 36.5 acres or 5.09 per cent of the total area of the island.

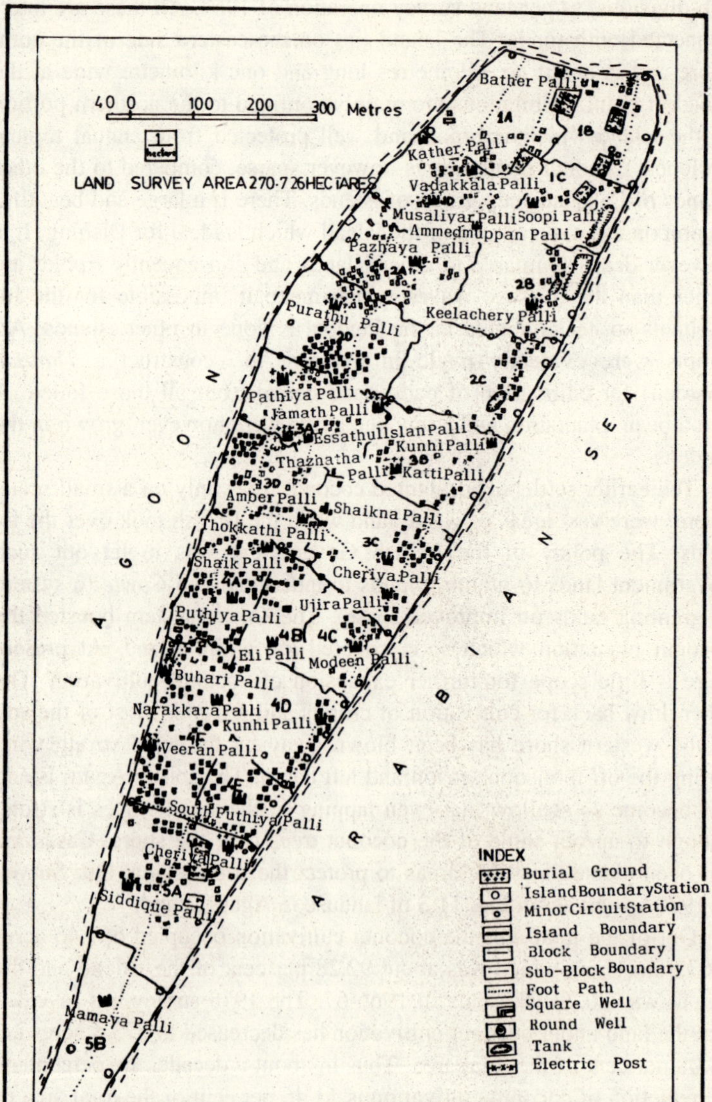

FIG. 11.3: Agatti Island: Landuse

The forests occupy 0.50 acres which is only 0.07 per cent of the island. This is very negligible whereas the land not available for cultivation amounts to 126.50 acres constituting 17.67 per cent of the total area. This includes the non-agricultural uses, barren and uncultivable lands. Most of the baren land is confined to the southern part of the island which is 40.7 acres or 5.68 per cent of the total area of the island. Other uncultivated excluding fallow lands is fully covered by coconut groves which accounts for 573.4 acres (80.08 per cent). Current fallow lands are very minor as it occupies only 3.5 acres which is 0.48 per cent of the total geographical area.

Net area sown and areas sown more than once which is 15.10 acres constituting 2.1 per cent of the total geographical area. It is the fourth largest landuse category of Agatti. This includes the kitchen gardening which was introduced by the British under the *Cowle* System for improving leases.

Table 11.7 reveals that the land is not available for cultivation in detail in 1978-79 when the survey was conducted. Apart from barren lands (40.70) acres and settlements (36.50 acres) which have been discussed in the above paragraphs, the educational institution occupy 10.02 acres or 1.42 per cent of the total area of Island. The government institutions include government office (6.00 acres), government quarters (5.80 acres), power and light house (0.90 acres), medical and dispensary (1.90 acres) and poultry farm (1.50 acres). All these account for 16.10 acres or 2.24 per cent of the total area of the island.

"Quarrying" a secondary activity which is found in Agatti island is most peculiar and prominent. It occupies 3.50 acres or 0.48 per cent of the total area of the island. The industrial activities such as boat repairing and construction is more pronounced in this island compared to the Kavaratti island having 4.50 acres which is 0.63 per cent of total area. The islanders have also shown keen interest in fishing which is the oldest traditional activity among the people. Fishing, quarrying etc. occupies 3.80 acres and 3.50 acres or 0.53 per cent and 0.48 per cent of the total area respectively.

The survey made by us in the year 1978 reveals the general surface configuration of the island. The privately constructed houses are found in the eastern and western part of Agatti. The open space between the eastern and western part is occupied by coconut cultivation where scattered quarters are met with. Most of the government quarters are situated in the western part of the island. There were five government buildings including one court, five schools, a society and one post office.

TABLE 11.6: Land Utilisation in Agatti Island (1978-79)

(*in Acres*)

Total Geographical Area	716.00	% of total geographical area
Total reporting area for land utilisation	713.30	99.62
1. Forest	0.50	0.07
2. Not available for cultivation		
(i) Area put to non-agricultural uses	85.30	11.92
(ii) Barren and uncultivable lands	40.70	5.68
Total N.A.C.	126.50	17.67
3. Other uncultivated excluding fallow		
(i) Permanent Pastures and grazing lands	—	—
(ii) Land under tree crops groves	573.40	80.08
(iii) Cultivable waste	—	—
Total Cultivated	573.40	80.08
4. Fallow Lands		
(i) Current fallows	1.00	0.14
(ii) Others	—	—
Total	1.00	0.14
5. (i) Net Area sown	12.40	1.73
(ii) Area sown more than once	2.70	0.38
Total Cropped Area	15.10	2.11

For the purpose of recreation there is one hall called Nehru Hall and one pendal at the centre of the island. Four Agricultural Farms were at the north-eastern part of island. There were 32 mosques and there *Madrasa* schools in close proximity of the mosques.

The household industry includes one canning factory, a coir factory and three boat shed was found at the eastern border. A fishing industry has been located at the north-western part of the island. To extend medical facilities one Primary Health Centre (PHC) is functioning.

The above analysis reveals that majority of area is covered by coconut cultivation, houses and barren land which put together accounts for 90.89 per cent of the total island. The land which are not suitable for cultivation are heavily eroded. Unfertile soil and sand deposition during off-monsoon season are peculiar features.

Table 11.8 shows the preponderance of food crops over non-food crops. The total area cultivated for this purpose was 577.60 acres or 80.67 per cent of the total geographical area. As stated above, the coconut cultivation is main cash crop in the island. Betel vine and bean were the two other crops grown mainly during the season 1978-79. The area occupies by total betel vine was 4.20 acres, which accounts for 0.59 per cent of total area and bean was occupying 20.5 acres or 2.86 per cent of the total area of the island.

TABLE 11.7: Non-Agricultural Landuse (1978-79)

Category of Landuse	Area in Acrs.	In % of non-agricultural area	In % of total area
Settlements	36.50	28.96	5.09
Religious places (Mosques and Maidans)	4.60	3.65	0.64
Educational institutions (school and colleges)	10.20	8.09	1.42
Govt. Institutions			
(a) Govt. Offices	6.00	4.76	0.83
(b) Govt. quarters	5.80	4.60	0.81
(c) Power and light houses	0.90	0.71	0.12
(d) Medical and Dispensary	1.90	1.50	0.26
(e) Poultry Farms	1.50	1.19	0.22
Total	16.10	12.76	2.24
Recreational facilities	2.40	1.90	0.83
Stores and Godown	3.20	2.53	0.44
Water Bodies	0.57	0.45	0.07
Fish drying yard	3.80	3.02	0.53
Industrial area	4.50	3.57	0.63
Barren land	40.70	32.30	5.72
Quarrying	3.50	2.77	0.48
Grand Total	126.50	100	17.67

TABLE 11.8: Detailed Agricultural Landuse (1978-79)

Crops	Area (in acres)	In % of total Area
Betel Vine	4.20	0.59
Coconut	573.40	80.08
Bean	20.50	2.86
Total	598.10	83.53

12

MARINE RESOURCES AND THEIR DEVELOPMENT

Historical Resume

The history of the fishery of Lakshadweep is as old as the history of human settlement in these tiny tots of islands. The marine biological and fishery research in the Lakshadweep Sea dates back to the end of the 19th century, when the surgeon naturalist A. Alcock set sail on 17th October, 1891 by R.M.S. Investigator. He has given an account of the deep sea fishes collected from the Lakshadweep Sea. The Cambridge University Expedition under the leadership of Prof. J. Stanley Gradiner was the next significant event in the marine resource of Lakshadweep. Later Hornell (1910) and Ayyanger (1922) described briefly the tuna fishing methods in the Lakshadweep. The establishment of the research centre of Central Marine Fisheries Research Institute (CMFRI) and the Department of Fisheries in the Lakshadweep dates back only to 1985 and 1959 respectively which gave a fillip to the fisheries research in this remote area. In the past 28 years scientists of the CMFRI and the National Institute of Oceanography has furthered our knowledge on the environmental characteristics, fishery resources, fishing methods and fishery biology of important tunas and live-bait fishes of the Lakshadweep Sea. Researches on corals and coral reefs have also been strengthened.

Jones and Kumaran[1] have documented information on 603 species of reef fishes including many bathy-pelagic forms. Due consideration has been given to the systematics of commercially important tunas and related fishes as well as the common live-bait fishes. The earlier estimates (Jones, 1968) revealed that only a total of 650 tonnes of Dish were caught from the Lakshadweep waters annually against a potential yield of 3300 tonnes of pelagic and demersal fishes. George *et al.* (1977) estimated a projected exploitation potential of 50,000 tonnes of tunas against the total local annual exploitation of 2740 tonnes.

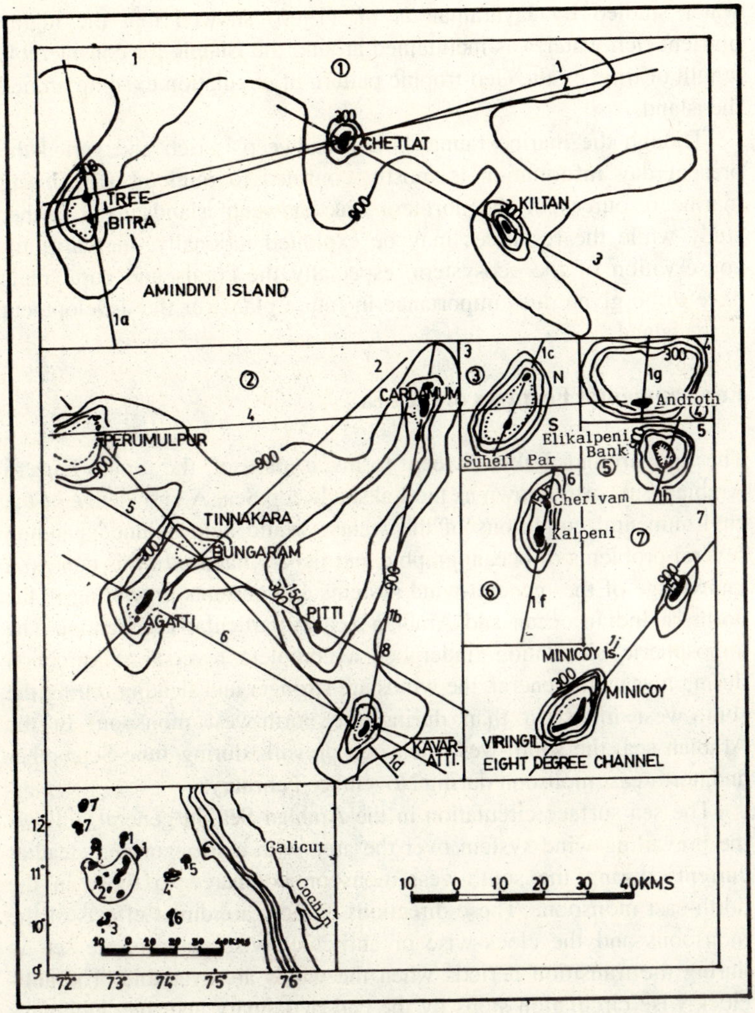

FIG. 12.1: Cross-section along the Lakshadweep, Minicoy and Amindivi Islands

The physical, chemical and biological parameters of the marine environment and also some oceanographic features such as currents, water masses, upwelling etc. have been studied by the CMFRI in the recent past. Prasad (1951) and Jayaraman *et al.* (1960) have brought to light the influence of the nutrient rich Antarctic bottom water in the

Lakshadweep Sea area. The physio-chemical characteristics of the water studied by Jayaraman *et al.* (1960) showed that the highly nutrient rich water was maintained around the islands for considerable length of time by the Geo-trophic pattern of circulation existing around the island.

Though the marine fauna of Lakshadweep is rich and varied the present day information is mostly confined to minicoy. The living marine resources of the northern Lakshadweep islands need further study while the resources may be exploited rationally, measures for conservation of the ecosystem, especially the corals and coral reefs have to be given due importance in future plans for the development of the islands.

Environmental Features of the Sea

The sea around Lakshadweep forms a part of the South-Eastern Arabian Sea, also known as the Lakshadweep Sea. A knowledge of the environmental conditions of the waters would help in understanding several problems of oceanographic and fishery nature. In this context a knowledge of the general wind systems and currents prevailing in the northern Indian ocean and Arabian Sea in particular is essential. The atmospheric circulation undergoes a complete reversal in direction during a year. In general, the winds are stronger and steadier during the south-west monsoon than during the north-west monsoon. In the Arabian sea, the south-west monsoon prevails during June-September and north-east monsoon during November-February.

The sea surface circulation in the Arabian Sea, in general, follows the prevailing wind system over the area with a stronger and steadier currents during the south-west monsoon compared to those in the north-east monsoon.[2] These directions of flow are direct effects of the monsoons and the clock-wise or anti-clock-wise patterns are set up during the transition periods when the winds are available. The anti-clock-wise circulation stops by the end of January and the clock-wise coastal current is gradually established by May. This reversal of the coastal current system along the coasts in the Arabian Sea in not simultaneous all over the area. During Feb-April the predominance flow in the upper layer of sea is towards west or north-west. The existence of circulatory water movements (eddies) or/and the islands at practically all levels down to 500 m has been observed from the nature of the density surfaces and geopotential anomalies. Anti-cyclonic movements (eddies) are present in the upper 100 m and reverse of that below that level. These eddy-like circulatory motion of the waters helps to keep the fish eggs and larvae within the highly productive waters in the vicinity of islands for a considerable length of time.

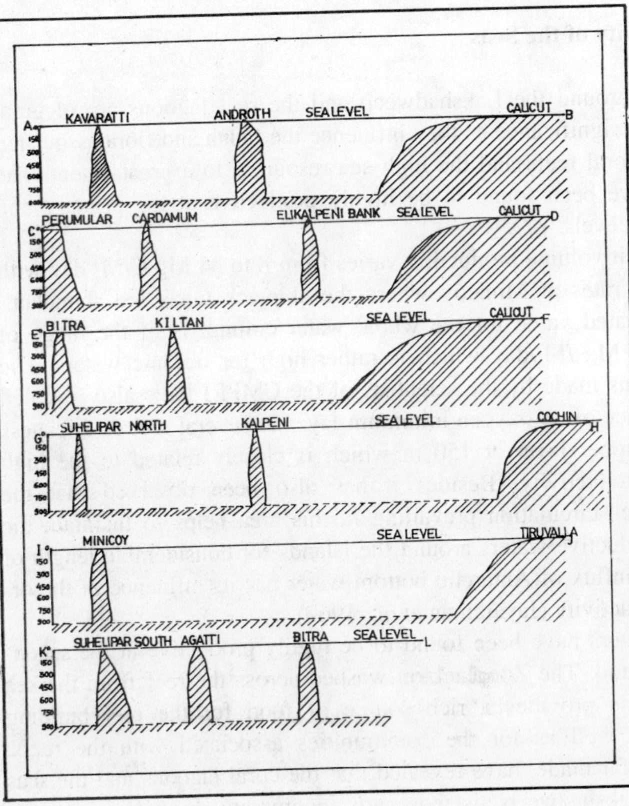

FIG. 12.2: Cross-section along the Lakshadweep Islands

The importance of the sea around Lakshadweep from the point of tuna fishery is well known. It is seen that the sea around these islands are highly productive. The circulatory movements (eddies), the vertical turbulent mixing and wind induced upwelling in the region are contributory to this high productivity. The coral island of Minicoy is a major tuna fishing centre in the Indian Ocean and the importance of this region from the point of tuna fishery has been well recognised.

Productivity of the Seas

The seas around the Lakshadweep and the reef lagoons are of great ecological significance as they influence the fauna and flora associated with the coral reefs and the high sea resources to a great extent. The waters have been found to be highly productive at the primary and secondary levels.

The unit volume production varies from 8 to 34 Mg C/M^3 day with maximum rates at Minicoy where the skipjack tunas are abundant.[3] The integrated value for the whole water column is of the range of about 300 Mg^C/M^2/day which is rather high for oceanic waters. The observations made by the scientists of the CMFRI have also revealed the existence of an oxygen minimum layer of several metres thickness with the upper layer at 150 m which is closely related to the high organic productivity. Besides it has also been observed that the geostrophic circulation prevailing in this area helps to maintain the highly productive waters around the islands for considerable length of time. The influx of Antarctic bottom water has its influence of the organic productivity (Jayaraman *et al.*, 1960).

The waters have been found to be highly productive at the secondary level too. The Zooplankton washed across the reef from the sea into lagoons provides a rich source of food for the reef building animals as well as for the communities associated with the reefs. Studies so far made, have revealed that the coral lagoons and the seas of the Lakshadweep islands are comparatively rich in their Zooplankton assemblages.

Exploited and Potential Resources

Oceanic species of tunas such as *skipjack and yellow fin* tuna constitute the major tuna resources taken from the Lakshadweep water from September-October to May every year. They are being exploited from

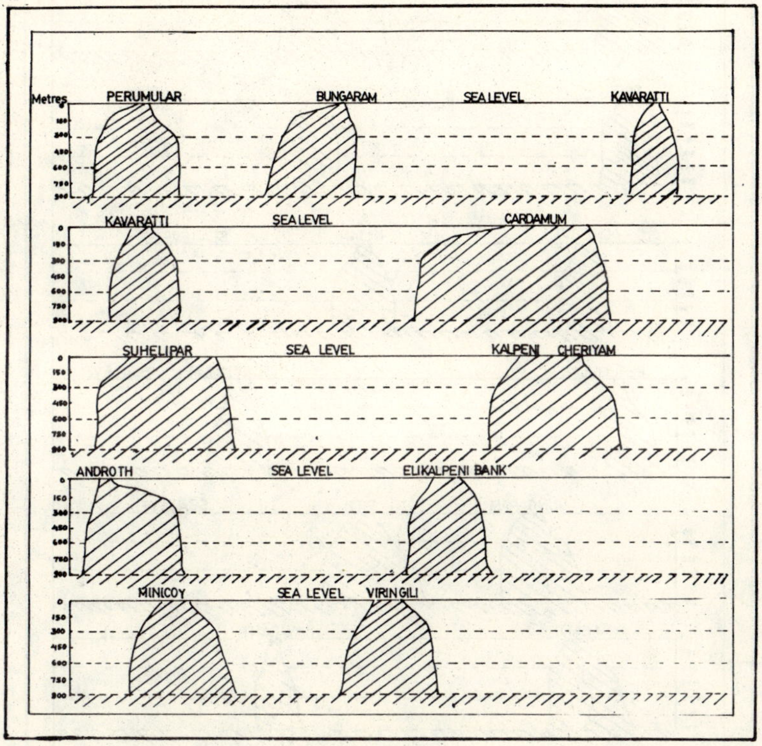

FIG. 12.3: Bathymetric features of Lakshadweep Islands-I

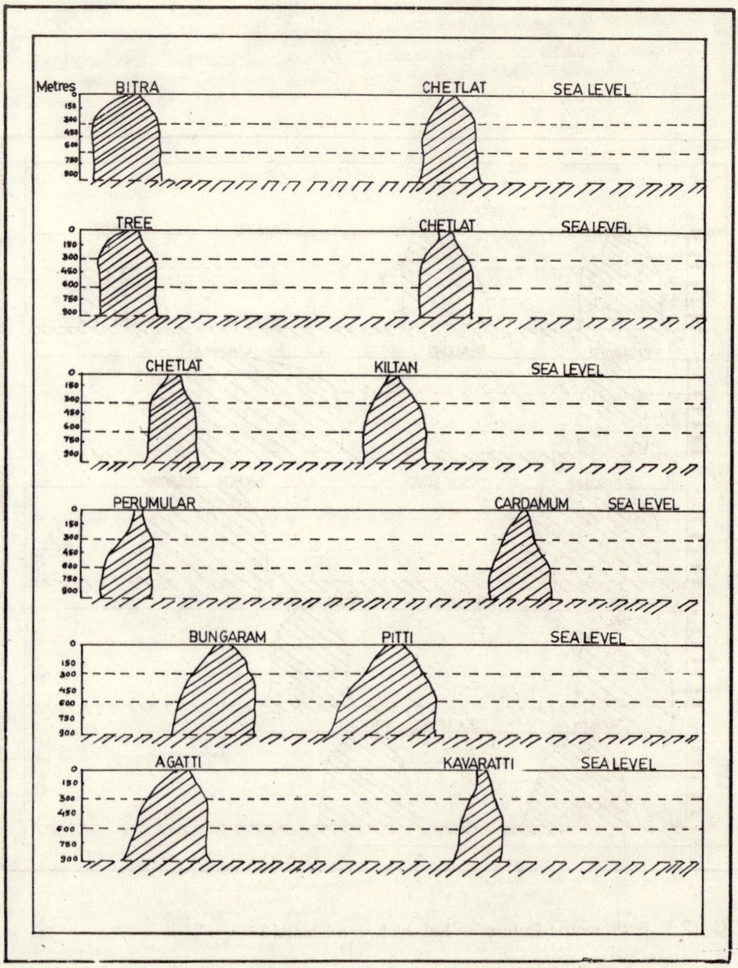

FIG. 12.4: Bathymetric features of Lakshadweep Islands-II

these islands by pole and line fishery with live-baits. The total tuna-fish catch in the Lakshadweep islands has increased considerably from 571 tonnes in 1970 to 4,101 tonnes in 1984. Island-wise tuna catch data and the number of mechanised boats available for the period 1978-83, are presented in Table 12.1.

TABLE 12.1: Island-wise and Year-wise Production (in tonnes) of Tuna in Lakshadweep*

	NAME OF THE ISLAND											
Year	Agatti	Amini	Androth	Bitra	Chetlat	Kadmat	Kalpeni	Kavaratti	Kiltan	Minicoy	Suheli	Annual total tuna landing (mt)
1978	899	64	173	92	36	49	21	211	19	311	—	1875
1979	1314	72	303	118	116	100	62	207	86	415	—	2793
1980	490	46	179	104	33	43	27	150	54	643	—	1759
1981	820	81	196	126	38	37	41	395	24	485	—	2236
1982	550	77	243	345	148	38	63	150	102	427	823	2966
1983	731	53	283	166	96	36	59	164	55	273	1121	3037
Annual Average	801	66	230	159	78	50	45	213	57	426	972	3097
No. of Mechanised fishing boats (25 ′ and 30 ′)												
1978	29	14	16	6	9	12	7	16	9	27	—	145
1979	31	17	21	8	12	14	11	21	12	29	—	177
1980	35	18	24	9	13	14	12	25	13	30	—	194
1981	35	18	24	9	13	14	12	25	13	31	—	223
1982	40	22	29	10	15	14	13	30	16	31	—	223
1983	49	29	33	10	17	16	14	37	22	36	—	263

* Silas, E.G., Rao, K.V.N. and others. *Exploited and Potential Resources of Tunas of Lakshadweep.* Marine Fisheries Information Service. Special Issue on Lakshadweep. No.68, July, 1986. p. 15-25.

George *et al.* (1977) estimated a projected exploitation of potential of 50,000 tonnes of tuna from Lakshadweep. Silas and Pillai (1985); proposed that by A.D. 2000 the total production of skipjack and young yellowfin tuna should achieve a commercial production target of 150,000 tonnes.

The introduction of larger pole and line boats recommended by Silas and Pillai (1982) is particularly significant to the Lakshadweep islands. For undertaking prolonged fishing trips and improvements in operational techniques, navigational aid and catch storage facilities will be great advantage and would increase tuna production.

The scarcity of live-baits is no doubt a limiting factor for the expansion of the fishery. Research inventory on live-bait fishes including the assessment of the availability and abundance of live-bait recourses in space and time, along with large culture of suitable live-bait fishes for supplying to the fishermen deserve special attention.

Live-Bait Fishes

Different fish species associated with corals are used as live-bait at Minicoy. Whichever species is available in good numbers are made use of as live-bait. But only a few of them are considered superior for pole and line operation. A live-bait fish can be more successful on one occasion in a particular area than at others.

Fishermen of Minicoy Island generally complain about the gradual decline in the live-bait fish catches. To ascertain whether really live-bait catches are declining year after year, live-bait catch data were collected during 1981-82, 1983-84 and 1984-85 fishing seasons (Table 12.2).

The fact remains that although the supply has increased in 1984-85 compared to 1981-82, the demand for live-baits now-a-days exceeds the fishable stock in the atoll regions. At least, three major reasons can probably be attributed to this shortage:

(a) Environmental deterioration;
(b) Fluctuation in the seasonal recruitment of migrant bait fishes; and
(c) Demand exceeds available stock.

The cumulative effect of these, is an apparent shortage of live-baits not only of Minicoy but probably also at the other islands of Lakshadweep. The chances of resident species sharing improvement appears to be very bleek, recourse of the deterioration of the environment caused by human interference.

Status of Coral Reefs

The Lakshadweep has twelve atolls three reefs and five submerged banks with a total of 27 islands. The total land area is 32 km² and the total extent of the lagoons is about 420 km² (Mannadiar, 1977). Raised reefs, found in Kiltan atoll, indicate a relative change in the level of land with the sea in the pliestoune glaciation times. According to Alcock (1902) the Lakshadweep Islands are the remains of eroded atolls raised only a few metres above the M.S.L. and formed entirely of coral rock and coral sand. They rise quit abruptly from the sea within 800-1000 metres of the shore often close upon 1000 fathoms deep.

TABLE 12.2: Species Composition of Tuna Live-bait at Minicoy during 1981-82, 1983-84 and 1984-85 1883-85 seasons * (kg.)

Species	1981-82	1983-1984	1984-85
1. *Spratelloides delicatulus*	1,795.65	1,053.5	2,019.0
2. *S. Japonicus*	263.00	395.0	435.0
3. *Archamia lineolatus*	622.00	985.0	—
4. *Chromis caeruleus*	65.50	—	119.1
5. *C. Ternastensis*	—	—	41.5
6. *Caesio caerulaureus*	52.50	219.0	1,031.9
7. *C. Chrysozona*	—	265.55	722.1
8. *C. Pisang*	—	20.5	—
9. *Gymnocaesio argenteus*	—	82.5	683.9
10. *Lepidozygus tapeinosoma*	—	—	26.0
11. *Apogon sangiensis*	—	—	118.7
12. *Rhabdamia gracilis*	—	—	63.0
13. *Archamia fucata*	—	—	98.6
14. *Dussumieria hasselti*	—	—	124.0
15. *Pranesus pinguis*	—	202.0	—
Total of all species	2,798.65	3,222.5	5,482.8

* Pillai, P.P., Kumaran, M., Gopinadha Pillai, C.S. and Others; *Exploited and Potential Resources of Live-Bait Fishes of Lakshadweep. Ibid.* pp 25-32.

Our knowledge of the coral fauna of Lakshadweep is based on Minicoy with a total of 28 genera comprising of 73 species of stony corals which were recorded by Pillai (1971,1972). The Octocorals are represented by *Heliopora Coerulea* which form a very conspicuous element in the inner lagoon reefs throughout Lakshadweep. The *gorgoneds* are not found in shallow waters. The hydrozoans are represented by *Millipora* with three species known. The genous *Acropora* is the richest as they from about 25 per cent of the total species known from Minicoy. A marked feature of the coral fauna of Lakshadweep is the absence of foliaceous forms such as *Montipora foliosa* and *Echinopra lamellosa.*

More or less three distinct coral communities are found in the reefs and lagoons of Lakshadweep. They are *Porites* community, the *Acropora* community and *Holiopora* community.

The siltation interferes with coral growth as it smother the corals and kills them. The rate of siltation in the lagoons of Minicoy and other islands have increased due to sea erosion and disturbances in the lagoons. Details of human interference has been studied by Pillai in 1983. Removal of corals from the shore and reefs is the main cause of Minicoy of Sand Stone in Kiltan for construction work is the problem.

A proper assessment of the deep water Mollusca, Lobsters algae and gorgoneds need to be surveyed and documented.

Ecological Stress in Minicoy Lagoon and its Impact on Tuna Live-Baits

The lagoon possesses two ecologically distinct habitats, viz. coral shoals and sand flats. The former provides habitat for many important live-baits belonging to the families Pomacentridae and Apogonidae and form the traditional site of live bait-fishery.

The lagoon fishes in general can be classified into either resident or migrants. Those that are found on coral heads are resident, while those that sporadically appear in the lagoon waters are migrants.[4]

A few species of small fishes enter the lagoon at sporadic intervals as juveniles and are caught of and when available. None theless they form a major component of the live-baits of Lakshadweep though their appearance is unpredictable and there is a lot of inconsistance in their recruitment to the fishery. Often their massive recruitment is coupled with a bumper catch of tunas. It is likely that tunas follow this group of fishes along with the oceanic current. Though tunas never enter the lagoon, the live-baits make their way into the calm lagoon waters along with the water current.

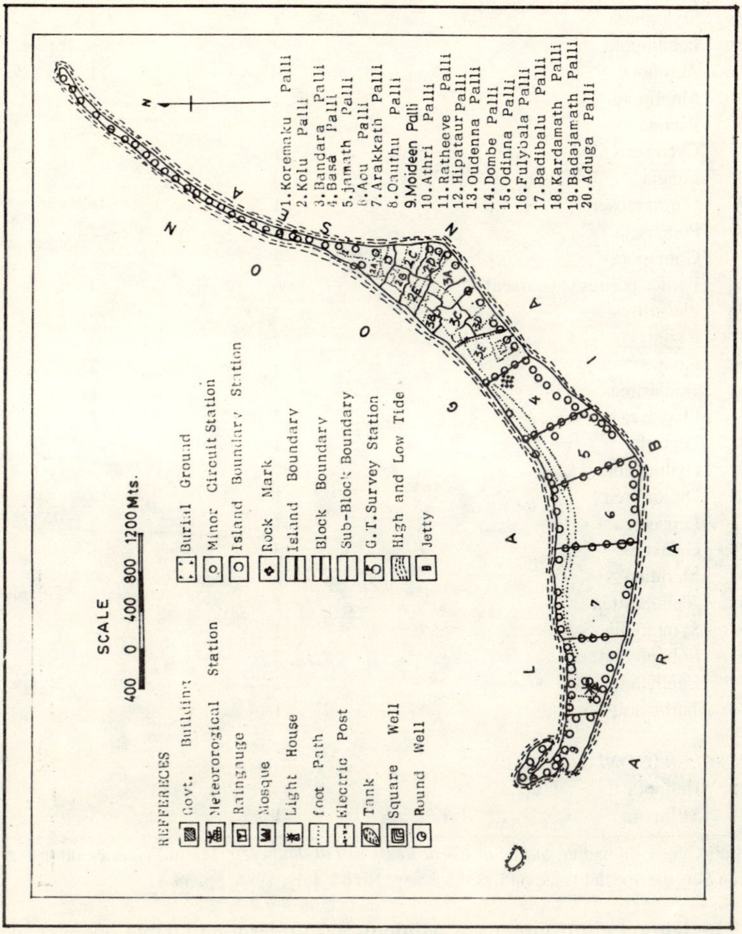

FIG. 12.5: Minicoy Island: Landuse

TABLE 12.3: Coral Species Occurring in Minicoy and Kiltan Atolls*

Genera		*No. of Species Recorded*	
		Minicoy	Kiltan
SCELERATINIAN CORALS			
1.	Psammocora	3	3
2.	Stylophora	1	1
3.	Pocillopora	4	5
4.	Acropora	20	11
5.	Montipora	1	1
6.	Pavona	2	2
7.	Cycloseris	1	1
8.	Fungia	3	1
9.	Gardineroseris	1	1
10.	Podabacia	1	—
11.	Goniopora	2	—
12.	Porites porites (Synaraea)	6	4
13.	Plesiastrea	1	—
14.	Favia	1	—
15.	Favites	3	2
16.	Goniastrea	5	1
17.	Platygyra	2	1
18.	Leptoria	1	—
19.	Hydnophora	1	—
20.	Diploastrea	1	—
21.	Leptastrea	1	2
22.	Galaxea	3	1
23.	Merulina	2	—
24.	Acanthastrea	1	—
25.	Symphyllia	1	—
26.	Lobophyllia	2	—
27.	Euphyllia	1	—
28.	Turbinaria	1	1
NON-SCLERACTINIAN CORALS			
1.	Helipora	—	1
2.	Millipora	1	3

* Pillai, C.S., Gopinadha, *Status of Coral Reefs in Lakshadweep.* Marin Fisheries Information Service Special Issue on Lakshadweep. No.68, July, 1986, pp. 38-41.

The lagoon environment of Minicoy has undergone visible changes in the last decade due to both natural and artificial factors. The current prevailing feeling among the fishermen is that the live-baits are on a declining trend and the available stock is insufficient to meet the local demand.

Environmental Degradation

At present the lagoon of Minicoy is a modified eco-system compared to that of a decade ago. Corals of all genera and species have suffered mass mortality during the Last five or six years (Pillai, 1983). The large number of *Acropora* thickets that formed the habitat of many reef fishes including live-baits are all dead and are getting disintegrated. The lagoon bottom is strewn with dead branches and is slowly getting covered by sand. The major reason for this mass mortality of corals is undoubtedly excessive siltation. The dead *ramose* corals are efficient sediment trappers which aid the filling up of the lagoon. Small polyped corals like *Acropora* are very sensitive to the smothering effect of sediments and are easily killed (Pillai, 1971s). In 1980 *Acanthaster Planci* was also recorded in fair number among the *Acropora* thickets and several patches of freshly killed corals were observed (Muety *et al.*, 1980). The mass mortality of corals has adversely affected the resident ichthy fauna. The dominant species like *Chromis Caeruleus, Pomacentrus pavo and Dascyllus aruanus* have markedly dwindled in the lagoon and the present lagoon looks depopulated when compared to a decade ago.

Sale *et al.* (1984) have shown how some of the *Pomacentrids settle more profusely on wider live coral* coverage than on area with sparse coral coverage. This indicates that intensity of coral growth is a factor that determines the settlement of coral reef fishes including tuna live baits in many cases.

Potential Resources of Fishes other than Tuna

The tuna fishery of the Lakshadweep in the South-Eastern Arabian Sea is over emphasized to the extent to create an impression that there is no other exploitable resources of fishes other than tunas.[5] The highly productive waters around the islands (numbering 27), the submerged banks and the crevacies of coral boulders and reefs offer ideal habitats for a large number of economically important groups of fishes which offers scope for extensive fishing by simple crafts and gears. Most of the other fish resources are now caught either as by-catch of pole and line tuna fishery or as incidental catches in surface trolling. Hence, the diversification of fishing effort for the exploitation of fishery resources other than tuna evolving cheaper preservation methods and effective marketing become essential for the futurological development in the fisheries sector of these islands.

The group-wise annual catch, average catch and the percentage contribution of each group in the landings of other fishes for the years 1971 to 1984 are given in Table 12.4.

The average contribution (average of 1982-84) of the fishery resources other than tunas to the total fish production of the islands is 24.0 per cent. However, it varies from island to island and is inversely related to the development of pole-and-line fishery for tuna of different islands. The average landing in the islands was 3,527 tonnes and other fishes 1,118 tonnes. The landings of other fish resources excluding tuna was the lowest in 1971 (403 tonnes) and the highest in 1976 (1,241 tonnes). It could be seen from Table 12.4 that the commercially important resources other than tunas in the Lakshadweep in the order of abundance are: sharks and rays (25.6%), perches (20.5%), carangids (12.1%) half beaks and belonids (7.5%); seer fishes (6.4%), flying fishes (2%) and goat fishes (2.5%).

Since fishing effort is concentrated mainly for tuna in most of the islands, the catch of other fishes generally vary according to the fluctuations in the availability of tuna shoals around the islands. When the tuna catch became poor in a particular season, the effort expended for other groups of fishes increased and consequently the landings of other resources also increase. This indicated that if the effort is diversified, the catches of other resources could be enhanced.

The month-wise landings of the various other resources for 1984 and 1985 at Minicoy are given in Table 12.5.

The annual average landings of other fishes is about 10.4 tonnes. It is evident that the island have a resource potential for at least four major groups of fishes other than tunas viz. *Acanthocybium* Solandri, *Carangids*, perches and sharks. The other two species i.e., *Elagatis bipinnulatus* and *Coryphanea hippurus* are landed mainly as a by-catch of pole and line fishery.

Hence, diversification of fishing effort, effective improvements in the existing crafts and gears and providing financial support to develop traditional practices by artisanal fishermen employing indigenous crafts and gears are of prime importance for the development of small-scale sector aimed at the exploitation of resources other than tunas. This is labour intensive and can bring about economic uplift and generate employment to the increasing population.

Ancillary Living Marine Resources

Besides corals, tunas and other fish resources, a number of other ancillary resources are also found in the sea around Lakshadweep. These ancillary resources mainly constitute sea weeds, *crustaceans, molluses,* sponges, *echinoderms,* reptiles, such as turtles, birds etc.[6] There are few others like beautiful coral reef fishes which are of potential value as an export item for marine aquaria all over the world. Varieties such as *Abudefduf amphiprion, Apogon, Coris, Balistes, Platax* and several other beautiful coral reef fishes are available in Lakshadweep. Ornamental invertebrate such as sea *anemones, crustaceans, echinoderms* and sedentary tube worms are also reared in marine aquaria and hence have marketing possibilities.

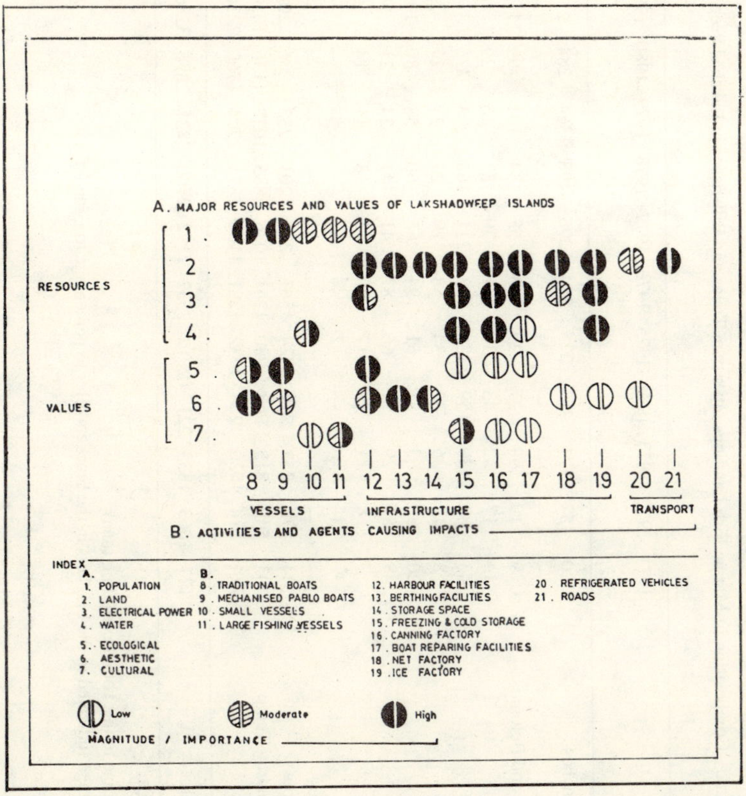

FIG. 12.6: Impact of Fisheries Development Projects on Resources and Environment of Lakshadweep Islands

TABLE 12.4: Composition of Marine Fish Landings other than Tunas and Bill-fishes in Lakshadweep During 1971-84

(figures in tonnes)*

Category	1971	1972	1973	1974	1975	1976	1977	1978	1979	1980	1981	1982	1983	1984	Average (82-84)	percentage**
Elasmobranches	120	157	171	253	325	354	296	198	364	284	211	240	332	287	286	25.6
Catfish	—	—	—	—	1	—	—	—	—	—	—	—	—	—	—	—
Half beaks and Belonids	9	19	99	27	29	33	58	144	101	99	113	87	103	62	84	7.5
Flying fish	14	17	42	43	30	41	30	33	16	29	16	25	25	15	22	2.0
Perches	43	83	130	159	186	193	211	163	203	376	315	230	252	205	229	20.5
Goat fishes	8	12	36	32	34	58	29	27	27	27	25	27	32	24	28	2.5
Carangids	20	30	63	61	61	94	65	60	58	80	105	214	147	45	135	12.1
Seer fish	48	51	29	91	66	87	41	41	24	21	50	99	59	59	72	6.4
Barracuda	7	8	11	18	17	20	15	18	11	14	12	10	14	14	14	1.2
Sciaenids	—	—	—	—	2	—	—	—	—	—	—	—	—	—	—	—
Silver bellies	—	—	—	—	5	—	—	—	—	—	—	—	—	—	—	—
Miscellaneous	134	172	232	279	224	361	281	201	233	206	203	239	237	265	248	22.2
Total (excluding Tuna)	403	549	813	963	980	1241	1026	885	1037	1136	1050	1171	1206	976	1118	(24.0)
Tuna	774	514	1020	1254	1932	1291	1166	1875	2794	1760	2236	2966	3303	4313	3527	(76.0)
Grand Total	1177	1063	1833	2217	2912	2532	2192	2760	3831	2896	3286	4137	4509	5289	4645	—

* *Ibid*. page.42

** Percentage to the Total (excluding tuna)

Percentage indicated in the brackets in the brackets refer to percentage to Grand Total.

TABLE 12.5: Landings of Fishes other than Tunas and Bill-fishes at Minicoy during 1984-85 (in kg.)

Category of fishes	1984	1985
Acanthocybium Solandri	3057.0(22.8)	2826.0(38.7)
Carangids	1448.5(10.8)	629.0(8.6)
Elagatis bipinnulatus	2417.0(18.1)	2042.0(27.9)
Coryphaena hippurus	193.5(1.4)	429.0(25.9)
Sphyraena spp.	792.5(15.9)	45.0(0.6)
Perches	2592.0(19.4)	20.0(0.3)
Sharks	2885.0(21.6)	1318.5(18.0)
Total	13,385.5(100)	7309.5(100)

Limited exploitation of these hitherto untouched resources for capturing a share of the worlds ornamental marine organism trade is worth attempting.

Prospects of Development of Marine Fisheries Resources

Tuna Resources

It is well known that the chief marine resource of Lakshadweep is tuna fishing. To obtain better catches introduction or larger pole and line boats with storage facilities and simple navigational aids would facilitate the fishermen to move beyond the traditional grounds to scout for tuna shoals.

In Lakshadweep, a beginning has already been made in the setting up of 'Payao' type of fish aggregating device off Kavaratti island by the Fisheries Department. The *aggregating* tunas are caught by the traditional gears. The method with modification if needed can be extended to the whole region for increasing tuna catches in the small scale sector.

The Maldive region is a highly productive semi-enclosed and self-contained ecosystem that supports a safe, sure and rich tuna fishery. In fact it is fishermen's paradise and probably one of the best in the world. No wonder more than 30 per cent of the population are engaged in tuna fishery.

Chagos-Lakshadweep ridge, the widely scattered micro-island system of the Lakshadweep separated by deep ocean has none of the features of the Maldive archipelago to consider the development of the tuna fishery by taking the Maldive fishery as the standard.

Total lack of any harbour facility is another major disadvantage of these islands. The development of the Lakshadweep fishery has therefore to be considered on the basis of its own characteristic features and limitations:

(a) Lakshadweep fishery for tuna has the characteristics of an unsheltered open ocean fishery requiring vessels larger than the small pablo boats;
(b) Both natural supply and the avenues available for bait fishery culture are limited and hence only restricted live bait fishing of tuna can be adopted for expanding the fishery;
(c) Maldive fishery has so far been developed without causing serious damage to the ecosystem by introducing only minimum mechanisation. It has always been export-oriented, yet has none of the modern shore based secondary and tertiary level industries. It may worthwhile to acknowledge these facts in developing the Lakshadweep fishery—these islands being ecologically more vulnerable than the Maldives, for economic reasons and due to the serious scarcity of other major inputs;
(d) Pablo boat fishery using the traditional fishing methods can be encouraged in nearby waters in view of their efficiency and other advantages; and
(e) Capital outlay required in developing the Lakshadweep fishery will be more than that required for Maldives and the amplitude of the annual fluctuations in landings should also be expected to be larger. Hence it may be wiser to adopt initially a more modest scale of development.

It thus appears that phased development of the Lakshadweep fishery will require the deployment of larger vessels and without depending on the islands for shore-based facilities. Two possibilities open for consideration are to have the associated industries and facilities in mainland and the introduction of mother ship into the industry. If fishery is to be export oriented, handling and processing technology to suit the consumer preferences in foreign market may have to be adopted along with other innovations to make it competitive.

Live-Bait Resources

In recent times, acute shortage of live-bait fishes for the tuna fishing has been faced. For a proper management of the tuna fishery and steady supply of live-bait fishes for the local tuna fishery, reliable estimated of potential and exploited stocks are necessary. It would then be possible to plan ways and means of augmenting the live-bait resources.

Surveys should be conducted to identify suitable resources of live-bait in the vicinity of the island and develop methods to transport and maintain the stock for later use in the tuna fishery.

Attempts should be made to identify promising species of fishes for artificial propagation and development of stocks to be used as live-baits. Attempts, should be made to identify alternate species which could be used as live-baits. The possibilities of using artificial bait for catching tuna could also be a part of the over-all programme on live bait fishes.

Coral Conservation

It is essential to preserve the coral reef eco-system of the islands as it forms the habitat of live-bait fishes which are essential for the pole-and-line tuna fishery. The preservation programme of coral reefs should involve (i) creation of marine park for the protection and preservation of marine wealth, (ii) transplantation of live and suitable species of corals into regions where they thrived earlier, and (iii) cautious dredging and blasting operations in the lagoons. It assumes paramount importance in any future plans for the development of Lakshadweep.

Resources other than Tuna

The islanders have little attraction for fishes other than tuna. But one-fourth of the landings in Lakshadweep is accounted for by fishes like sharks, perches, cerangids, half-beaks, belonids and seer fishes. It may not be possible to exploit these groups of fishes by following the traditional methods. Hence, diversified fishing efforts like drift/gillnetting coupled with improvements in crafts to fish in farther waters would go a long in tapping these resources. It would help in providing employment and income to the fishermen during the tuna off season.

Several colourful coral reef fishes like butterfly fish, surgeon fish and parrot fish which are found in plenty in Lakshadweep are of great export value. Collection methods, packaging technologies and transportation facilities need to be developed to tap these resources for export trade.

Preservation of marine ecosystem and introduction of aquaculture programmes for resources suitable to the island conditions will go a long way for batter exploitation of marine resources of Lakshadweep.

Turtle Farming

This is another potential resource for development although, unlike other resources, the conservation of the species has also to be an integral part of the turtle farming programme. Currently the turtles are caught indiscriminately by the islanders despite the ban on catching them. The stock is dwindling at an alarming rate. During the breeding season the females always come to the same island for laying eggs. The eggs are poached for human consumption. They are also heavily predated upon by birds and hermit crabs until they hatch and move the sea.

Turtles have great commercial importance. The oil is highly priced for its use in the manufacture of cosmetics. The calipee – the cartilegenous material between the shell bones – the component in making turtle soup, is a delicacy in many countries. Turtle skin is very expensive and is considered high quality leather. The tortoise shell mostly comes from the Hawksbill turtle (*Eretmochelys imbricata*). Turtle fish is edible and considered a delicacy.

Looking at the returns, it is obvious that presently export is not significant and this can be definitely enhanced, if turtles are available in large numbers and the market properly combed.

Two of the most common species of turtles seen in Lakshadweep are Chelonia mydas (Green turtle) and *Eretmochelys imbricata* (Hawksbill turtle).

"Farming" the turtles has been thought over by a few countries and experimental farms have already been started in the Carribean as well as in Torres Strait island of Queensland.

There are reasons to believe that only less than one per cent return to the shallow waters for grazing on the sea grass.

TABLE 12.6: Summary of Scenario for Fishery Development

Method of fishing	No. of Vessels X 10^2	Size of vessel LOA. m.	Employment potential X 10^3	Capital Investment (Rs. in million)	Expected catch in tons X 10^3
Local Fishery					
Pole and Line diversi-	2.0-2.5	9.75-12.2	3.0-4.0	30-35	4.5-5.0
fied Fishing	1.5	9.75-12.2	1.0-2.0	15-20	4.5-5.0
Middle and Distant Water Fishery					
Method of Fishing	No. of vessels	Size of Vessel LOA.m.	Employment potential (Direct)	Capital Investment (Rs. in million)	Expected Catch in tones X 10^3
Pole and Line	12-15	20-25 (50-100 GRT)	250-300	100-120	12-15
Long liner	12-15	30-35 (100-200 GRT)	250-300	150-180	12-15

The points in favour are the following:

(i) Turtle eggs are available in large numbers in many of island;
(ii) The eggs collected from wild rookaries of different islands can be transported to the hatchery. The young ones are reared for a year before releasing them into the sea there by increasing the number of breeders in one island until such time, artificial stock of layers is maintained;
(iii) At the end of one year, when they are free from dangers of predation, they can be liberated to the shallow waters of the lagoon, to feed on the rich *Thalassia* beds. The shallow water of the lagoons can even be properly utilised for cultivating the sea grass, providing sufficient food for young ones kept in captivity; and
(iv) At the end of two or three breeding seasons, when they attain marketable size they are harvested after retaining a stock for breeding to build up successive generations. The size attained in captivity however, has been much lower than those of natural populations.

Ocean Thermal Energy for Lakshadweep

Although the area of Lakshadweep is less than 30 sq. km the Exclusive Economic Zone (EEZ) is about 0.07 million sq.km from where ocean resources are to be exploited by India covering ocean resources, living will require large power resources. Power is required to mine huge reserves of mineral resources, for cold storage to preserve fishes and run fish processing plants. The present power generation of only 2000 kW is grossly insufficient and the cost of diesel power generation is 10 times higher, compared to the mainland.

Ocean thermal energy offers a huge potential for future requirement of Lakshadweep islands which is commercially viable. Ocean Thermal Energy Conversion (OTEC) will utilise the temperature difference existing between the surface sea water of (28°C) and cold deep water of around 8°C-10°C at a depth of 800-1000 metres in the Lakshadweep. This OTEC system is continuous, renewable and pollution free and cold sea water is rich in nutrients and can be utilised for aquaculture. This system also provides fresh water as a by-product of which there is a great dearth in these islands. It can be utilised as an important alternate source of power for remote islands.

It is proposed to have ocean thermal energy plants at Kavaratti and Minicoy of 1.0 MW OTEC plants one each in these two islands. The bathymetry off Kavaratti indicates that the bed profile is steeply falling down to about 600 metres and becomes flater to a depth of 900 metres at a distance of 4 kms from the coast. The cold water will be taken through pipelines of less than 2 km long, reducing the cost of transporting cold water. This plant at Kavaratti will cost only Rs. 95.35 million.[7]

Offshore Wind Energy

If availability of land is not a serious constraint, the structures for tapping wind energy can be based on the island. Offshore wind energy has certain advantages over the other alternate sources of energy. A major point in its favour is that it is pollution free. It requires comparatively simple technology and less maintenance and will also be economically cheaper. It is also feasible to provide this system to each of the major inhabited island. Its disadvantage in the tropics is the variable wind system prevailing here which may restrict the production of energy to a particular season necessitating its storage for offseason.

Introduction of even smaller class vessels of the size range between 9.75 and 12.2 LOA on a modest way to double the production from the present level by pole and line require and addition of nearly 200 to 250 vessels, a manpower of nearly 3 to 4 thousand and other facilities. Even if this could be attained the problem of live bait remains unsolved. The capital investment for the above is estimated to be about Rs.30-35 million.

It may not be desirable to expand the localised fishery beyond this limit. A modest estimate of an additional annual production of 25000-30000 tonnes of tuna, like fishes and bill fishes can be attained by the exploitation of middle.

This will indirectly develop the island and the socio-economic condition of the people without any imbalance or adverse effect on the islands' ecology.

Shore-based Infrastructural Facilities

This will require a self-supporting shore-based infrastructural facilities comprising a fully mechanised berthing and bunkering jetty, a canning factory of capacity nearly 100 tonnes per day, a 200 tonnes capacity freezer storage at −20°C, an ice factory of 50 tonnes per day and by-product factory of 20-25 tonnes of fish meal/silage etc. costing nearly Rs. 350-400 million. A recurring expenditure on the operational cost of vessel including the purchase of bait and live bait comes to nearly Rs.3 million and on infrastructural facilities Rs.100 million.

A package project of this type of capital investment ranging from Rs.650-750 million could be attained during a period of 10 years.

In the same plateau and almost same fishery exist in the area, the natural harbouring facilities available with deeper lagoons and inlets to the different groups of island favourable for fishing and culture of bait fishery doesn't exist in the Lakshadweep area. The second phase of fishing with pole and line and long lining with base in the mainland can be taken up in two stages.

Conclusion

The economy of Lakshadweep depends solely on its marine resources. Hence, all the developmental efforts of the island are to be so lined that they will help development in presentation and exploitation of marine resources. Remote sensing technologies should be developed to estimate the basic productivity in the sea around Lakshadweep so that aggregation of fish shoals could be predicted. It would also help to evaluate the ecological changes, nature of vegetation, extent of pollution and shore-line changes.

Preservation, processing marketing of tuna and other fishes assume great importance for the development of the island. Suitable post-harvest technologies and he needed infrastructure will have to be provided for marketing the fish and fish products both in the main land and in the other countries. It is desirable to follow a systems approach where the various components are treated as essential parts of the system instead of dealing each problem or groups of problems in isolation at their own merits.

NOTES

1. Jones, S. and Kumaran, M., *Fishes of the Laccadive Archipelego*. Nature Conservation and Acquatic Sciences Se[illegible]e, Trivandrum, 760 pp.
2. Nair, P.V.R., Murty, A.V.S., Remamirtham, C.P. & Others: Environmental Features of the Sea Around Lakshadweep. *Marine Fisheries Information Service*. Issue on Lakshadweep, No. 68, July, 1986, p.10-13.
3. Nair, P.V.R., Subbarajee, G., Mathew, K.J.*et al.*, Productivity of the Sea Around Lakshadweep. *Marine Fisheries Information Service*. Special Issue, on Lakshad-

weep. No.68. July. 1986, pp.13-15

4. Gopinath, C.S. and Mohan, M., *Ecological Stress in Minicoy Lagoon and its Impact on Tuna Live-Baits. Ibid.* pp. 33-37.
5. Kumaran. M. and Gopakumar, G., Potential Resources of Fishes other than Tuna in Lakshadweep. *Marine Fisheries Information Service*, Special issue on Lakshadweep. No. 68, July, 1986, pp. 41-45.
6. George. K.C., Thomas, P.A. and others, Ancillary Living Marine Resources of Lakshadweep. *Marine Fisheries Information Service*. Special issue of Lakshadweep. No.68, July, 1986, pp. 46-50.
7. Ravindran, M., *Ocean Thermal Energy for Lakshadweep*, Ocean Engineering Centre, I.I.T., Madras-600036.

13

INDUSTRY

By and large the islands are very backward so far as industries are concerned as most of the people are engaged in the primary sectors of occupation. Non-availability of mineral resources, lack of cheap power and far away from market which are located in the main land are the principal reasons for the industrial backwardness of the islands. Most of the industries are small scale village industries type, centring round local raw material like coconut from the agricultural sector and fish from the marine sector.

Fishery

For the development of the fishery in the island a sum of Rs.52 million has been earmarked during the Seventh Plan. Fishing is the main industry of the island as the sea around the island is very productive. The number of mechanised boats have been increased to 279 from almost nil during the seventies. These boats operate from both the inhabited and the uninhabited islands. The islands occupy the pride of place in the country for having the highest per capita availability of fish among the States and Union territories of India.[1]

Dairy Industry

There are dairies at Kavaratti and Minicoy islands. Poultry farms are found in the Andorth, Kadmat, Kaopeni, Minicoy, Kavaratti, Agatti and Kiltan Islands. During the Seventh Plan for animal husbandry a sum of Rs. 20.0 million has been earmarked for expenditure.

Coir Industry

The coir industry is very labour intensive in nature but has a low productivity and has meagre per capita income. Only the dropouts from schools and the people who fail to find out employment in government and other gainful occupations are mostly engaged in coir industry. There are coir extraction units which are operating to their optimum capacity. Reactivation of the operation units in selected areas will go a long way to solve the problem of this industry.

Raw Material

Coconut as a raw material is being cultivated on 2740 hectares is produced 23.56 million coconuts.

Amongst all the islands Androth produces the maximum coconuts of 4.7 million nuts and this island has also the maximum area under coconut cultivation (464 hectares) followed by Kavaratti (4.05 million nuts). Kalpeni produces the third maximum coconut (3.3 million) in Lakshadweep.

Extraction of coir from coconut husks by the natural ratting processes and hand spinning of coir yarns, since mid-18th century has been introduced. The "Coir Monopoly Scheme" was introduced by the old rulers. The production in those days was of the 1210 quintals in 1984-85. The entire production of coir under the coir monopoly scheme is marketed by Government in the mainland at Mangalore. The processing of coconut fibres into yarns, ropes, and other products are important.

Minerals and Mineral-based Industries

The calcareous sands are the only minerals of the islands which have been located in the islands, lagoons, submerged reefs and submerged banks of Lakshadweep up to a depth of 2 metres below the lagoon floors. They have been categorised as per their MgO contents into four classes. They are less than one per cent MgO, 1-2 per cent Mgo 2-3 per cent MgO and more than 3 per cent MgO content. The indicated reserves of the above categories are 30.65 m. tonnes, 173.37 m. tonnes, 80.31 m. tonnes and 4.36 m. tonnes respectively. Thus indicated calcareous deposits of all grades are of 288.70 m. tonnes. (Table 13.2).

The inferred reserves of calcareous sands are 712.20 m. tonnes up to a depth of two metres below the lagoon floor (Table 13.3). The MgO content in the lagoons is higher towards the reef, generally low in the central deeper parts of the lagoons.

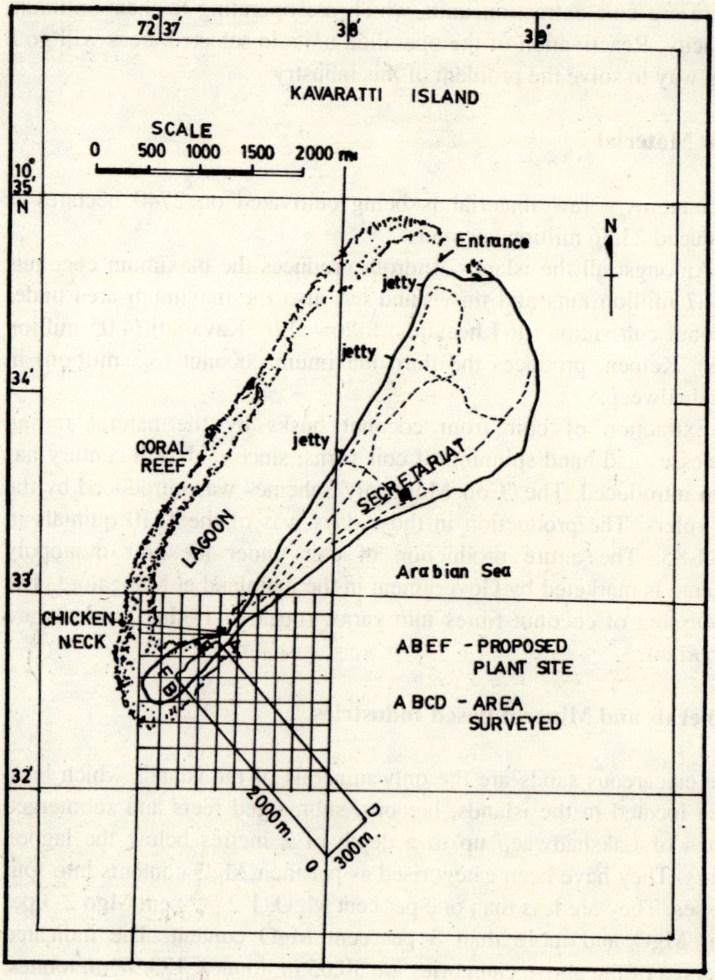

FIG. 13.1: Ocean Thermal Energy Proposal

Mineral-based Industries

The calcareous sands of the Lakshadweep Islands are suitable for cement industries. Since the average FeO_3 content of sands is only 0.12 per cent and the physical characteristics of these sands are eminently suitable for the production of white cement of which there is a great demand in the mainland and fetches a very high price (about Rs.300) per bag in 1988.

TABLE 13.1: Island-wise Population and Annual Production of Coconuts in the Union Territory of Lakshadweep*

Island	Population (1981 Census)	Area under coconut cultivation (hectares)	Annual production of coconuts (000's)	Power generation (installed) kW
Androth	6812	464	4700	349
Amini	5367	255	3040	209
Agatti	4111	369	2620	236
Bitra	181	9	70	24
Chetlat	1484	100	540	75
Kadmat	3114	305	2330	188
Kalpeni	3543	298	3350	231
Kavaratti	6604	360	4050	535
Kiltan	2375	160	1050	156
Minicoy	6658	420	1810	424
Total.	40249	2740	23560	

Note: Data on the annual production of coconuts is provided by the Directorate of Agriculture, Lakshadweep Administration. The other Particulars are drawn from the publications of the U.T. Administration.

These calcareous sands can also be used for iron and steel industries if it can be aggregated. These sands are physically unsuitable for manufacture of calcium carbide because it is not lumpy but suitable for bleaching powder, soda ash, caustic soda production. These sands can also be used in sugar, glass and paper industries. The calcareous sands can also be used for paints, distempers, silica brick manufacturing, mineral treatment process, rubber, soap and allied industries, for water and sewage treatment.

But the moot problem is although the indicated and inferred reserves of the calcareous sands are quite adequate for setting up industries in million scale and export to the mainland for use in the industries, it is very difficult to predict how much can be mined without disturbing or even destroying the fragile ecosystem of these

TABLE:13.2 Indicated Reserves of Calcareous Sands in the Laccadive Lagoons (Area in km, Reserves in million tonnes up to a depth of one m. below lagoon floor)*

Lagoons	Area covered by 1% MgO or less	Reserves	Area covered by 1-2% MgO	Reserves	Area covered by 2-3% MgO	Reserves	Area covered by 3% MgO or more	Reserves	Total reserve of all categories
Agatti	0.03	0.03	9.00	11.20	8.00	9.37	0.08	0.10	20.70
Kavaratti	—	—	1.50	1.87	2.00	2.50	0.02	0.02	4.39
Kalpeni	5.75	7.18	12.50	15.62	1.50	1.87	0.07	0.09	24.76
Chetlat	0.25	0.31	0.56	0.70	0.62	0.77	0.11	0.13	1.91
Kiltan	0.03	0.03	0.70	0.87	0.15	0.18	0.20	0.25	1.33
Bitra	0.05	0.62	30.00	37.50	15.00	18.75	0.11	0.13	57.00
Kadmat	—	—	2.50	3.12	9.00	11.25	1.90	2.37	16.74
Amini	—	—	—	—	1.00	1.25	—	—	1.25
Bangaram	2.10	1.37	9.50	11.87	16.50	20.62	0.96	1.20	35.06
Suheli	2.90	3.62	66.00	75.00	11.50	13.75	0.06	0.07	92.44
Minicoy	14.00	17.50	12.50	15.62	—	—	—	—	33.12
Total Reserves	—	30.65	—	173.37	—	80.31	—	4.36	288.70

* Siddiquie, H.N. and Mallik, T.K., *Report of the Investigation of the Calcareous sand Deposits in the Lagoons of the Laccadives.* Off-shore Mineral Exploration and Marine Geology Unit, G.S.I., 1973, Table -1.

coral islands. This calls for a detailed study without which the bottoms of the coral lagoons should not be scraped for calcareous sands to be used for economic upliftment of the islanders. It may spell disaster for the islanders in the long run and may cause irreparable damage to the island environment. Hence a judicious policy be followed with regard to the exploitation of the calcereous sand is the Lakshadweep and a detailed study is called for before a final decision is taken since the problem hinges between short-term gains in the economy of the islanders versus the long-term irreparable damage to the ecosystem of the islands.[2]

TABLE 13.3: Inferred Reserves of Calcareous Sands in Lakshadweep Lagoons*

Lagoons	Area(km^2)	Reserves (m. tonnes upto a depth of 1.0 metre below lagoon floor	Quality	
			CaO in %	MgO in %
Baliapani	50	62.5	49.0-51.83	1.20-1.80
Cheriapani	156	195.0	49.22-51.06	1.81-2.90
Perumal Par	63	78.6	48.70-51.17	1.58-3.95
Androth	70	87.5	50.30-52.80	1.17-2.92
Total	339	423.6		

	Up to 1-2 m below lagoon floor
Surveyed in detail	
Agatti	20.70
Kavaratti	4.39
Kalpeni	24.67
Chetlat	1.91
Kiltan	1.33
Bitra	57.00
Kadmat	16.74
Amini	1.25
Bangaram	35.06
Suheli	92.44
Minicoy	33.12
Reconnaissance only	
Baliapani	62.50
Cheriapani	195.00
Perumal Par	78.60
Androth	87.50
Total	712.20

* Ibid. Table 13.2

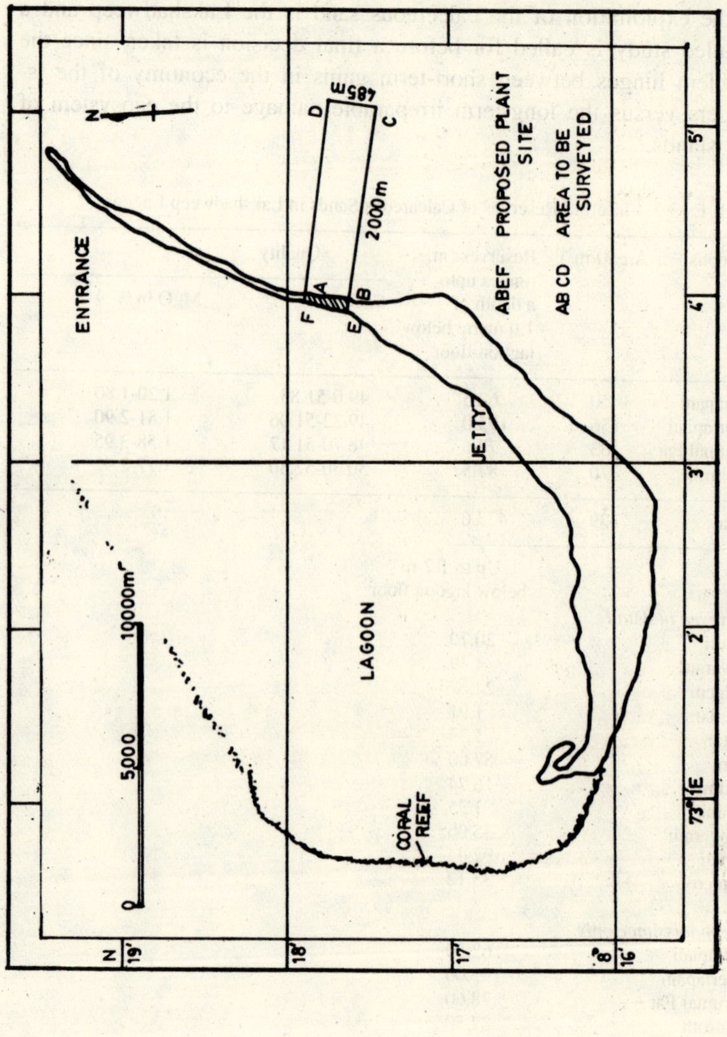

FIG. 13.2: Ocean Thermal Energy Proposal of Minicoy

Power Generation

Supply of electricity as an infrastructure is now available in all the ten habited islands after Bitra was electrified in 1983 which has an area of only 0.1 sq.km and population of only 181 as per 1981 Census. But all the power is generated by diesel generators and hence to costly for industrial purposes.

Tourist Industry

Tourism has been recognised as an industry of the islands. In 1984-85 about 1181 tourists from the mainland and 41 foreigners visited. There are 16 tourist huts, five beach resorts, one tourist bungalow and one honey-moon hut are located in the islands for tourists.

NOTES

1. *India, 1986: A Reference Annual,* Publication Division, Ministry of Information and Broadcasting, Government of India, pp. 666-667.
2. Siddiquie, H.N. and Mallik, T.K., *Report of the Investigation of the Calcereous Sand Deposits in the Lagoons of the Laccadives,* Off-shore Mineral Exploration and Marine Geology Unit, G.S.I. 1973, Table 6.

SOCIAL BASE

14

DEMOGRAPHY
A Comparative Picture

Growth Rates

While analysing the demography of the Lakshadweep, it is very pertinent to consider the growth of population since 1911. The Lakshadweep Islands had only 14.6 thousand population in 1911 which increased 40.2 thousand in 1981 and thereby recorded a growth of 275.3 per cent during the past seven decades (1911-81). During this period the country as a whole recorded a growth of 271.8 per cent in her population which increased from 252.1 million in 1911 to 685.2 million in 1981. Thus the growth rate in the islands was higher than that of the national average. It is quite pertinent to note that decennial growth rate was accelerated during the past two decennial growth rate was accelerated during the past two decades i.e. during 1951-61 when Indian growth rate was 21.63 per cent. This higher growth rate in the past two decades in the islands was primarily due to influx of population from Mainland to the island. (Table 14.1).

Density Variations

With the growth of population the density of population per sq.km has changed. This change has been faster in the country as a whole compared to Lakshadweep. During 1911-81 the density of population has increased from 485 in 1911 to 1342 in 1981 in Lakshadweep as against 76 to 216 in case of India as a whole. Thus India has recorded a growth of 284.2 per cent in 1981 with 1911 as the base year as against 276.7 per cent in case of Lakshadweep. This slower rate of growth in case of Lakshadweep is primarily due to a higher base year figure in case of Lakshadweep than that of India.

But when the density per sq. km is considered it was 485 persons in case of Lakshadweep in 1911 as against only 76 in case of India as a whole. Thus Lakshadweep had a more than six times higher density figure than that of India in 1911 and in 1981 it was 1342 persons per sq. km as against only 216 of the country as a whole. Thus in 1981 the density figure was also more than six times in Lakshadweep than that of Indian (Table 14.2). Thus the island is much more crowded than India as whole in 1981 and it will continue to do so in future decades also.

The Quality of Population

To assess the quality of population it is necessary to analyse the literacy figures in 1981. In 1981 in the Lakshadweep 22,165 persons were literates comprising of 13,293 males and 8,872 females. Thus, literacy figure was 55.07 per cent in case of Lakshadweep compared to only 36.23 per cent in India as a whole. Thus the islanders were more literate than the country as a whole. As usual, the male literacy is higher (65.24 per cent) than the female literacy (44.65 per cent) in the Lakshadweep. The same trend is revealed in India as a whole where male literacy is 46.89 per cent as against only 24.82 per cent in case of females (Table 14.3).

Scheduled Castes and Scheduled Tribes Population

By and large, the Scheduled Caste and Scheduled Tribe population is considered as a drag for economic growth. Higher the percentage of S.C. and S.T. Population lower is the growth rate. In the Lakshadweep there are no Scheduled Caste population but most of them have been classified as S.T. population. In the Lakshadweep 93.82 per cent of the total population are S.T. as against only 23.51 per cent in case of India as a whole. Thus this high ratio of population of Schedule Tribe category is a drag for the economic growth of the islands. (Table 14.4).

Size and Growth of Population in Lakshadweep: 1901-1981

If we consider the growth of population during the 1970s it increased from 31,810 in 1971 to 40,249 in 1981 adding 8,439 persons in ten years. As indicated in Table 14.1 the growth of population was slow from 1901 to 1921 and in fact the population declining during 1911-21 and there was a rise in the trend during the decade 1921-1931. Again there was a decline trend in the growth rate during 1931-41 decade. But the next three decades of 1931-41, 1941-51, 1951-61 recorded more or less an uniform decennial growth rate i.e. 14.43 per cent, 14.60 per cent and 14.61 per cent respectively. However, the decade ending in 1971 recorded and abnormal increase in the growth rate while the decade of 1981 recorded a downward trend of growth rate where the growth rate came down from 31.95 per cent in 1961-71 to 26.53 per cent during 1971-81.

TABLE 14.1: Growth in Population*

Year	Lakshadweep(in thousands)		India (Million)	
	Absolute	Decennial Growth in %	Absolute	Decennial growth in %
1911	14.6	—	252.1	—
1921	13.6	–6.85	251.3	–0.32
1931	16.0	17.65	270.0	7.44
1941	18.4	15.00	318.7	18.04
1951	21.0	14.13	361.1	13.30
1961	24.1	14.76	439.2	21.63
1971	31.8	31.95	548.2	24.82
1981	40.2	26.42	685.2	24.99
Growth during 1911-81	275.3	—	271.8	—

* *India,* 1985 Table 1.1, p.8

TABLE 14.2: Growth in Density of Population (per sq.km.)

Year	India		Lakshadweep	
	Absolute figure	Decennial variation in %	Absolute	Decennial variation in %
1911	76	—	485	—
1921	81	6.6	455	–6.2
1931	90	11.1	535	17.6
1941	103	14.4	612	14.4
1951	117	13.6	701	14.5
1961	142	21.4	804	14.7
1971	173	21.8	1060	31.8
1981	216	24.9	1342	26.6
Growth % during 1911-81	284.2	—	276.7	—

India 1981, Table 1.3, p.11.

TABLE 14.3: Literacy Rate 1981*

Region/Country	Literates			Literates in % total population		
	Persons	Male	Female	Persons	Male	Female
India ('000)	241,032	161,680	79,746	36.32	46.89	24.82
Lakshadweep	22,165	13,293	8,872	55.07	65.24	44.65

* *India 1985*, Table 1.5, p.12.

TABLE: 14.4 Population of Scheduled Castes and Scheduled Tribes 1981*

Region/country	Scheduled Castes	Scheduled Tribes	Total	
			Numbers	In % of total
India ('000)	104,755	51,629	156,384	23.51
Lakshadweep	—	37,760	37,760	93.82

* *India 1985*, Table 1.7, p 15.

No castes were scheduled by the President of India for Lakshadweep.

However, it is observed from Table 14.6 that except during 1951, Androth ranks first on all the census decades as regards the total population is concerned. Bitra is the smallest island which has the lowest population in all the censuses. The four islands, i.e. Kadmat, Kiltan, Chetlat and Bitra have retained the same rank from 1951 to 1981 and there is no variation at all. But Minicoy Island which the largest populated island during 1951 has become second in the rank during the later decades. Agatti Island which was holding 6th rank during 1951 and 1961 has improved her position to 5th position during 1971 and 1981 where as Kalpeni which was holding 5th rank during both the periods i.e. 1951 and 1961 went down to 6th position during 1971 and remained in the same rank in 1981. Kavaratti Island has improved her position and has gone up to 3rd rank in 1981 pushing Amini Island down to the 4th place.

TABLE 14.5: Growth in Population in Last Eighty Years in Lakshadweep Island

Year	Population	Decade variation	% decade variation	Sex Composition		Sex ratio number of female per 1000 male	Density sq.kms.
				Male	Female		
1901	13,882	—	—	6728	7154	1063	498
1911	14,555	+673	+4.85	7325	7230	987	522
1921	13,637	–918	–6.31	6727	6910	1027	489
1931	16,040	+2403	+17.62	8045	7995	994	576
1941	18,355	+2315	+14.43	9096	9259	1018	659
1951	21,035	+2680	+14.60	10295	10740	1043	755
1961	24,108	+3073	+14.61	11935	12173	1020	831
1971	31,810	+7702	+31.95	16078	15732	978	994
1981	40,249	+8439	+26.53	20377	19872	1258	975

TABLE 14.6: Growth of Population (Island-wise)

Island	Population				Percentage decadal variation				Rank			
	1951	1961	1971	1981	1951-61	1961-71	1971-81	1951-81	1951	1961	1971	1981
Minicoy	3804	4139	5342	6658	8.81	29.06	24.63	75.03	1	2	2	2
Androth	3500	4183	5425	6812	19.57	29.69	25.57	94.63	2	1	1	1
Amini	3159	3530	4542	5367	11.74	28.67	18.16	69.90	3	3	3	4
Kavarathi	2390	2828	4420	6604	18.33	56.29	49.41	176.32	4	4	4	3
Kalpeni	2269	2613	3152	3543	15.16	20.63	12.40	56.15	5	5	6	6
Agatti	2029	2411	3155	4111	18.83	30.86	30.30	102.61	6	6	5	5
Kadmat	1641	1851	2416	3114	12.80	30.52	28.89	89.76	7	7	7	7
Kiltan	1249	15020	2046	2375	21.70	34.61	16.08	90.15	8	8	8	8
Chetlat	948	953	1200	1484	0.53	25.92	23.67	56.54	9	9	9	9
Bitra	46	80	112	181	73.91	40.00	61.61	293.48	10	10	10	10

As regards the growth rate of Bitra Island being the smallest island has recorded the highest growth rate during 1951-81 and Kavaratti Island which has recorded highest growth rate during 1961-71 ranks second, next to Bitra during 1971-81. Kalpeni Island has the lowest growth rate during 1951-81. Chetlat Island which has less than one per cent growth rate during 1951-61 has improved to 23.67 per cent during 1971-81. Similar is the case with Minicoy which improved from 8.81 per cent during 1951-61 to 29.86 per cent in 1961-71 and 24.63 per cent during 1971-81.

Density of Population

As regard the density of population it has steadily increased from 1901 till 1981 except the year 1981. The 1981 Census show a sudden increase in the density from 994 per sq.km in 1971 to 1258 per sq.km in 1981. Amini Island has the highest density (Table 14.8) and Island-wise Kadmat has the lowest density (1005 person). However,. density of population has increased in all the islands considerably over the decades during 1961-81. The maximum increase in density during 1961-81 is observed in Bitra Island (126.25%) followed by Kavaratti (125.2%). The least growth has been recorded in Kalpeni (17.29%) whereas the growth rate in density of the Lakshadweep is 51.38 per cent. The Amini island and Androth Island have also lower growth rate than that of the Lakshadweep (Table 14.7 and 14.8).

TABLE 14.7: Density of Population in Lakshadweep

Year	Density
1901	498
1911	522
1921	489
1931	576
1941	659
1951	755
1961	831
1971	994
1981	1258
Growth rate during 1901-81 in % of 1901	152.6

Composition of the Population

For the first time during 1981 Census the three islands namely, Minicoy, Kavaratti and Amini were classified as Census towns. Hence, 46.28 per cent of the total population of this territory constitute urban population.

Among the Scheduled Tribe population about 44.68 per cent represent the urban population. As the Islands are mainly dominated by Scheduled Tribes only about six per cent of the total population are other than Scheduled Tribes. The detail picture about the percentage distribution of Scheduled tribe population to total population is given in Tables 14.9 and 14.10. From these tables it is clearly observed that the Union Territory is dominated by S.T. population but their percentage has declined from 97.03 per cent in 1961 to 93.82 per cent in 1981. So the characteristics of Scheduled Tribe population largely resemble with that of general population which form only six per cent of that total population.

TABLE 14.8: Density of Population in the Island by 1961, 1971 and 1981 with their ranks.

Name of Island	1961 Density	Rank	1971 Density	Rank	1981 Density	Rank	Variation in density 1961-81 in % of 1961
Amini	1406	1	1747	1	2072	1	47.37
Kalpeni	1313	2	1370	2	1540	4	17.29
Androth	966	3	1130	8	1419	9	46.89
Kiltan	944	4	1279	3	1484	7	57.20
Chetlat	916	5	1200	6	1484	8	62.00
Minicoy	914	6	1214	5	1524	5	66.74
Agatti	861	7	1169	7	1523	6	76.88
Kavaratti	808	8	1228	4	1819	2	125.12
Bitra	800	9	1120	9	1810	3	126.25
Kadmat	611	10	779	10	1005	10	64.48
Lakshadweep	831	—	994	—	1258	—	51.38

TABLE 14.9: Distribution of S.T. Population (1961-81) in Lakshadweep

Scheduled Tribes (in % to total population)									Growth rate of S.T. during the decade	
1961			1971			1981			1961-71	1971-81
Persons	Male	Female	Persons	Male	Female	Persons	Male	Female		
97.03	96.07	97.96	92.86	90.89	94.88	93.82	92.58	95.08	26.29	27.83

TABLE 14.10: Percentage Distribution of S.T. Population to Total Population in the Islands, 1981

Island	Proportion of S.T. Population to total Population			Growth rate during 1971-81
	Person	Male	Female	
Minicoy	92.29	90.13	94.17	27.94
Kalpeni	97.15	96.30	98.06	14.43
Androth	96.51	95.23	97.71	26.96
Agatti	96.52	96.11	96.96	29.72
Kavaratti	84.57	83.66	85.68	53.06
Amini	95.83	94.67	97.07	19.13
Kadmat	97.21	96.45	97.98	31.38
Kiltan	95.92	95.54	96.29	16.05
Chetlat	95.55	93.46	97.60	23.63
Bitra	99.45	99.01	100.00	66.71

Sex Ratio

The sex ratio means the number of females per 1000 males. In other words, it is the ratio of distribution of men and women in a population. In 1901 for every thousand males there were 972 females in India. The figure declined to 930 in 1971 and it rose to 935 during the decade 1971-81. But the Lakshadweep shows a very significant fluctuating figure of sex ratio from 1901 to 1981. It shows a surplus female population in the year 1901, 1921, 1941, 1951 and 1961 where as in other census periods (1910, 1931 and 1981) there is surplus female population. During the last three decades the highest sex-ratio is seen in Minicoy. The lowest sex-ratio is seen is Bitra during 1981 and 1961 Census whereas Kavaratti has the lowest during 1971. The detail pictures of the sex ratio is shown in Table 14.11.

Work Force of Lakshadweep

In the Lakshadweep Islands the volume of work force is too small since out of 1000 persons only 244 are workers and 756 are non-workers, which means only 24.4 per cent are workers while the balance 75.6 per cent are non-workers. Thus every working population supports 3.10 persons. This is one of the major primary reasons for the economic backwardness of the islands. An usual amongst the females the percentage of non-workers is very high which is 90.8 per cent while the female work force account for only 9.2 per cent.

TABLE 14.11: Sex ratio in Lakshadweep (Females per 1000 Males)

Names of Island	1961	1971	1981
Minicoy	1307	1196	1154
Kalpeni	974	1019	928
Androth	1045	1033	1057
Agatti	903	907	925
Kavaratti	954	810	823
Amini	870	869	933
Kadmat	1030	1027	973
Kiltan	995	945	997
Chetlat	1122	1034	1022
Bitra	702	1000	792
Lakshadweep	1020	978	975

This dismal picture is further worse when we consider only 'main workers'. Out of every 1000 persons the main workers in the Lakshadweep is only 198 which means they support in the ratio of 1:5.05 persons. Thus one person works to support 5.05 persons.

Non-Workers

Island-wise there is a difference in the problem. The maximum non-workers (827) are met with in Minicoy followed by Androth (819), Kalpeni (768) and Amini (759), all above the islands average. To this extent Minicoy is worst off amongst the ten habited islands. Bitra is the best so far as non-workers are concerned since it has only 669 non-workers of every 100 persons.

Main Workers

Bitra has the maximum number of main workers which is 320. It is followed by Agatti (318) and Kavarathi (277) all of which are above the Island's average figure of 198 persons per 1000 persons. Thus seven out of the islands are below Lakshadweep's average figure so far as main work-force is concerned.

Marginal Workers

So far as marginal workers are concerned the picture is different. The island of Kiltan has the maximum number of marginal workers (123) per 1000 persons. It is followed by Kadmat (910), Chetlat (80), Kalpeni (72) and Amini (68). The least number of marginal workers are found Minicoy (7), preceded by Bitra (11), Kavaratti (13) and Androth (35).

All these points at only one thing i.e. economic backwardness because of lack of labour force. This is primarily due to lack of employment potential in the islands. It can be revealed from the Table 14.12.

Occupational Pattern of the People

The striking difference between the mainland and the Island's employment pattern is the absence of agricultural employment. Practically it is absent since the edaphic conditions are not suitable for cultivation. Whatever little that exist do not attract 'Main workers'. The main workers are engaged in equal proportion i.e. 27 out of every 1000 main workers in manufacturing, processing and servicing in the islands. But in case of "other workers" maximum are engaged in processing (308), followed by manufacturing (171) and servicing (29).

Island-wise the picture changes from an Island to the other. Agatti has the maximum number of main workers engaged in processing (192), manufacturing (175) and servicing (157) out of every 1000 persons. It is followed by Kadmat when in manufacturing 35 persons are engaged, 66 persons in servicing and only four persons in processing. Amini ranks third in this aspect. In this Island 45 are engaged in servicing, 29 in manufacturing and 15 processing out of every 1000 persons.

The Bitra Island tops the list in having 535 other workers in processing, 320 persons in manufacturing and 50 persons in servicing out of every 1000 persons. Amongst the 'other workers' it is Kavaratti Island which stands second. In this Island 455 persons are engaged in processing and 270 persons in manufacturing. It is quite surprising that both Chetlat and Bitra islands do not have main workers. But one of them are 'other workers' which Minicoy and Kiltan have very nominal figure (Table 14.13).

All these lead to an inevitable conclusion i.e. quality of population is very low, compared to other States of the country, which if not informed the future for economic prosperity of the islands is very bleak.

TABLE 14.12: Work force of Lakshadweep in 1981 (per 1000 population)

Island	Total Main Workers			Marginal Workers			Total Workers			Total Non-Workers		
	Persons	Male	Female	Persons	Male	Female	Persons	Male	Female	Persons	Male	Female
Minicoy	166	319	33	7	9	5	173	328	38	829	672	962
Kalpeni	160	281	31	72	127	11	234	408	42	768	592	958
Androth	146	281	19	35	67	3	781	348	22	819	652	978
Agatti	318	445	181	48	29	69	366	473	250	634	527	750
Kavaratti	277	467	46	13	20	4	290	487	50	710	513	950
Amini	173	273	66	68	76	59	241	349	125	759	651	875
Kadmat	190	273	105	91	64	118	281	337	223	719	663	777
Kiltan	123	226	19	123	126	121	246	352	140	754	648	860
Chetlat	181	341	25	80	107	52	261	448	77	739	552	923
Bitra	320	535	50	11	10	13	331	545	63	669	455	937
Lakshadweep	198	335	56	46	57	36	244	392	92	756	608	908

TABLE 14.13: Classification of Workers as Per Their Occupation (per 1000 persons)

Islands	Cultivators Agricultural and labourers	Household Industry Main Workers			Other Workers		
		Manuf-acturing	Processing	Servicing	Manufacturing III	Processing IV	Servicing V VI-IX
Minicoy	—	1	1	2	165	318	31
Kalpeni	—	3	6	—	157	275	31
Androth	—	5	10	—	141	271	19
Agatti	—	175	192	157	143	253	24
Kavaratti	—	7	12	1	270	455	45
Amini	—	29	15	45	144	258	21
Kadmat	—	35	4	66	155	269	39
Kiltan	—	2	3	—	121	223	19
Chetlat	—	—	—	—	181	341	25
Bitra	—	—	—	—	320	535	50
Lakshadweep	—	27	27	27	171	308	29

MARITAL STATUS

A Total Population

(a) *Never Married and Unspecified*

Although marriage is universal for males and females above the age of 15 years in the Lakshadweep Island 12.5 per cent male and female have never married. This is a significant departure from the normal Indian conditions. Further, another 4.2 per cent of both the sexes are either divorced or separated while another 1.9 per cent of males and females have not specified their marital status and hence they have been categorised as "unspecified". Thus the divorced or separated and unspecified people above the age of 14 years account for 6.1 per cent of the total population whereas only 40.1 per cent of the total population are married and a total of 18.6 per cent of both the sexes are not enjoying marital status, which is a significant portion of population above the age group of 14 years who account for 58.6 per cent of the total population.

Age structure and marital status are co-related. Marriage is practically absent for infants and boys and girls of below the age of 14 years as only 0.1 per cent of the total population of this group are married.

(b) *Married*

In all 40 per cent of the total population are married and incidentally all of them belong to the age group above 14 years. Married females are more (20.8%) compared to married males (19.3%) and more males (30.0%) have never married compared to females whose percentage is 23.9.

(c) *Divorced or Separated*

Since the bulk of the population are Muslims, Mohammadan law of separation is prevalent. More females (3.5%) are either divorced or separated than males whose percentage is only 0.7, about one-fifth of those of the females. Age has no relationship in divorce or separation since 1.6 per cent of the females above the age of 60 years fall in this group.

TABLE:14:14 Age, Sex and Marital Status of total population

Age group	Never Married		Marital Status							
			Married		Divorced/Separated		Unspecified		Total*	
	Male	Female	Male	Female	Male	Female	Male	Female	Male	Female
Below 14	8623 (21.5)	7996 (19.9)	4 (-)	16 (0.1)	— —	— —	— —	2 —	8627 (21.5)	8014 (19.9)
15-29	3267 (8.1)	1536 (3.8)	1435 (3.6)	3530 (8.8)	7 (-)	79 (0.2)	35 (0.1)	206 (0.5)	4744 (11.8)	5351 (13.3)
30-44	114 (0.3)	36 (0.1)	3511 (8.7)	3099 (7.7)	37 (0.1)	205 (0.5)	71 (0.2)	204 (0.5)	3733 (9.3)	3544 (8.8)
45-59	19 (0.1)	13 (0.1)	2055 (5.0)	1399 (3.5)	61 (0.2)	487 (1.2)	49 (0.1)	117 (0.3)	2184 (5.4)	2016 (5.1)
60 & above	11 (-)	5 (-)	797 (2.0)	268 (0.7)	175 (0.4)	650 (1.6)	28 (0.1)	30 (0.1)	1011 (2.5)	953 (2.4)
Of all ages	12034 (30.0)	9586 (23.9)	7802 (19.3)	8312 (20.8)	280 (10.7)	1421 (3.5)	183 (0.5)	559 (1.4)	20299 (50.05)	19878 (49.5)

* 40,177 As per details of calculation while as per 1981 Census it is 40,249 persons. Figures in bracket are in percentage of total population.

TABLE 14.15: Rural Age, Sex and Marital Status in Lakshadweep Island.

Age group	Marital Status									
	Never Married		Married		Divorced/Separated		Unspecified		Total	
	Male	Female	Male	Female	Male	Female	Male	Female	Male	Female
Below 14	4813 (22.3)	4473 (20.7)	3 (-)	11 (0.1)	0 (-)	0 (-)	0 (-)	2 (-)	4816 (22.3)	4486 (20.7)
15-29	1545 (7.1)	760 (3.5)	807 (3.7)	1851 (8.6)	5 (-)	50 (0.2)	25 (0.1)	125 (0.6)	2382 (11.0)	2786 (12.9)
30-44	37 (0.2)	17 (0.1)	1876 (8.7)	1681 (7.8)	21 (0.1)	96 (0.5)	52 (0.2)	118 (0.5)	1986 (9.1)	1912 (8.8)
45-59	5 (-)	3 (-)	1129 (5.3)	759 (3.5)	35 (0.2)	257 (1.2)	36 (0.2)	74 (0.3)	1205 (5.6)	1093 (5.1)
60 & above	6 (-)	2 (-)	392 (1.8)	113 (0.4)	82 (0.4)	331 (1.5)	17 (0.1)	15 (0.1)	497 (2.3)	461 (2.2)
All ages	6406 (29.6)	5255 (24.3)	4207 (19.5)	4415 (20.4)	143 (0.7)	734 (3.4)	130 (0.6)	334 (1.5)	10886 (50.3)	10738 (49.7)

(d) *Unspecified*

It is quite interesting to note that 1.9 per cent of the total population, all of whom belong to the age group of above 14 years have not specified their marital status. Out of whom 1.4 per cent are females and only 0.5 per cent are males.

Child Marriage

Child marriage which was quite prevalent in the island, a few decades ago, by 1981 it has almost vanished since only 0.1 per cent in the age group of below 14 years are married, and there are no cases of divorce or separation among them.

Marital Status of Rural Population

(a) *Never Married*

Out of the total population above the age group of 14 years 10.9 per cent of the total rural population have never married whereas such percentage is 12.5 of the total population of the island. This proves that such category of people is more among the urban dwellers who constitute 46.28 per cent of the the total population.

(b) *Married People*

Marriage is more universal among the rural population than urban dwellers in the country as a whole. In Lakshadweep, 39.9 per cent of the total rural population were married in the islands although 57.01 per cent of the rural people were eligible for marriage since they were above 14 years of age. Such figures were higher for the total population of the islands since 40.1 per cent were married as against 39.9 per cent of rural population. Thus, married people were less in the rural areas than in the urban areas. This is because percentage of unspecified category is higher in the rural areas compared to the total population.

(c) *Divorced or Separated*

In the rural Lakshadweep, 4.1 per cent of the rural population were either divorced or separated which is lower compared to the total population of the islands. In the islands 4.2 per cent were categorised in this type of population. This proves that more urban people are divorced or separated than the rural population. The percentage of female divorced or separated is 3.4 as against only 0.7 among the males. Thus, the condition of rural female is worse than that of the rural males.

(d) *Unspecified*

In this category 2.1 per cent of the rural population are classified. This is higher than that of the total population amongst whom they constitute 1.9 per cent.

(e) *Child Marriage*

Although child marriage is banned in the country, it was more prevalent in Lakshadweep, compared to the mainland because of prevailing customs, a few decades ago. In 1981, 0.1 per cent of the rural population below the age of 15 years were married and most of them are girls. The Table 14.15 shows the rural age, sex and marital status of the population is Lakshadweep Island.

Urban Age, Sex and Marital Status

In Lakshadweep 53.8 per cent of the urban dwellers were never married in 1981. Out of this 39.3 per cent were below 14 years of age. Thus 14.5 per cent of the urban dwellers, above 14 years have never married. This percentage is highest compared to total population and rural population. The percentage of married people was also only 40.2 per cent which is also lowest among the total rural and urban population of the island. Divorced or separated people constitute 4.4 per cent of the total urban dwellers. It is also quite strange that marital status of 1.4 per cent of the urban dwellers have been declared as 'unspecified'. Thus amongst the urban dwellers only 40.2 per cent are married while the balance 59.8 per cent do not enjoy marital status. This will be clear from the Table 14.16.

Immigration

Immigration as a factor of population growth is of minor consequence in Lakshadweep since only 2191 are enlisted as immigrants. They constitute only 5.44 per cent of the total population as per 1981 Census. The bulk of these immigrants comes from the different States of the Mainland since 2169 persons out of a total of 2191 persons belong to this category. Hence the immigrants from mainland account for 99 per cent of the total immigrants to the island.

TABLE 14.16: Urban Age, Sex and Marital Status in the Lakshadweep Island

Age group (in years)	Never Married		Marital Status							
			Married		Divorced or Separated		Unspecified		Total	
	Male	Female	Male	Female	Male	Female	Male	Female	Male	Female
Below 14	3,811	3,523	1	5	0	0	0	0	3,812	3,528
	(20.4)	(18.9)	(-)	(-)	—	—	—	—	(20.4)	(18.9)
15-29	1,794	776	628	1,680	2	29	10	81	2,434	2,566
	(9.6)	(4.2)	(3.4)	(9.1)	(-)	(0.1)	(-)	(0.4)	(13.0)	(13.7)
30-44	77	19	1,636	1,417	16	109	19	86	1,748	1,631
	(0.5)	(0.1)	(8.7)	(7.6)	(0.1)	(0.6)	(0.1)	(0.5)	(9.4)	(8.8)
45-59	24	10	926	641	26	230	13	43	989	924
	(0.1)	(-)	(5.0)	(3.4)	(0.1)	(1.2)	(-)	(0.2)	(5.3)	(5.0)
60 & above	5	3	404	155	93	319	11	15	513	492
	(-)	(-)	(2.2)	(0.8)	(0.5)	(1.6)	(-)	(0.1)	(2.8)	(2.6)
Average	5,711	4,331	3,595	3,898	137	687	53	225	9,496	9,141
	(30.6)	(23.2)	(19.3)	(20.9)	(0.7)	(3.7)	(0.2)	(1.2)	(51.0)	(49.0)

The bulk of the mainland immigrant come from Kerala which number 1890 persons or 87.14 per cent of the immigrants of the mainland. Kerala is surprisingly followed by Uttar Pradesh in north India from where 58 immigrants have come. They constitute only 2.68 per cent have come. They constitute only 2.68 per cent of total immigrants from the mainland. Uttar Pradesh is followed by Tamil Nadu 51(2.35 per cent), Madhya Pradesh 44(2.35) and Karnataka 39(2.03 per cent). Thus all the three Southern States (Kerala, Tamil Nadu, and Karnataka) have contributed 91.52 per cent of the total immigrants to Lakshadweep. This is mainly because of physical proximity of these states of the islands and affinity of language particularly of Kerala.

Only 22 immigrants have come from countries other than India, the maximum immigrants (16) have come from Nepal. Table 14.17 shows the immigrants to Lakshadweep.

Growth of Towns in Lakshadweep

The Lakshadweep Islands were purely rural till 1971. During the decade 1971-81 the process of urbanisation started in the Lakshadweep. Towns started developing in three islands i.e. Minicoy, Amini and Kavaratti. By 1981, the largest town was Minicoy having a total population of 1154 persons, followed by Amini (933, persons) and Kavarathi (823 persons). All these towns are no bigger than villages in the mainland and as per urban hierarchy all these are class VI Towns as classified in 1981 Census.

The Lakshadweep has a total urban population of only 2910 which is only 7.23 per cent of the total population. Thus it is much lower than the national average of about 20 per cent Hence the islands are much less urbanised than the country as a whole.

When the degree of urbanisation is taken at the basis of individual islands and Tahsil-wise, it is revealed that Amini Tahsil is maximum urbanised (17.30%) followed by Minicoy' Tahsil (17.33%) and Kavaratti Tahsil (7.68%) but when the islands are considered individually the same order of arrangement is followed. Minicoy Island is most urbanised (39.66%) followed by Amini Island (32.06%) and Kavarathi Island (28.28%) and peculiarly all these percentage figures and higher than that of the national average of (20.0%) urbanisation. Thus the Lakshadweep is lowely urbanised when taken as a whole but highly urbanised when the islands are taken individually. This will be clear from the Table. 14.18.

TABLE 14.17: Immigration into Lakshadweep, 1981

Birth Place	Total Male	Total Female	Rural Male	Rural Female	Urban Male	Urban Female	Total Immigration
Andhra Pradesh	10	5	4	1	6	4	15
Assam	1	—	1	—	—	—	1
Bihar	12	1	3	1	9	—	13
Gujarat	3	—	1	—	2	—	3
Haryana	2	—	1	—	1	—	2
Himachal Pradesh	—	1	—	—	—	1	1
Jammu & Kashmir	1	—	—	—	1	—	1
Karnataka	18	21	11	12	7	9	39
Kerala	1,116	774	335	213	781	561	1,890
Madhya Pradesh	41	3	11	1	30	2	44
Maharashtra	4	2	1	2	3	—	6
Manipur	4	—	—	—	4	—	4
Meghalaya	—	1	—	—	—	1	1
Orissa	3	2	—	—	3	2	5
Punjab	3	—	—	—	3	—	3
Rajasthan	5	—	3	—	2	—	5
Tamil Nadu	33	18	8	4	25	14	51
Uttar Pradesh	56	2	25	—	31	2	58
West Bengal	3	2	2	—	1	2	5
Andaman & Nicobar Island	8	10	1	—	7	10	18
Delhi	1	2	—	—	1	2	3
Pondicherry	—	1	—	—	—	1	1
Total Indian States & Union Territories.	1,324	845	407	234	917	611	2,169
Malaysia	2	1	—	—	2	1	3
Burma	—	1	—	—	—	1	1
Nepal	16	—	8	—	8	—	16
Pakistan	1	—	—	—	1	—	1
SriLanka	—	1	—	—	—	1	1
Total from other countries	19	3	8	—	11	3	22
GRAND TOTAL	1343	848	415	234	928	614	2191

TABLE 14.18: Growth of Towns in Lakshadweep in 1981

Islands	Population			
	Total	Urban	Population	
		Number	In % of Total island	In % of Lakshadweep
Minicoy Tahsil	6,658	1154	17.33	39.66
Minicoy Island	6,658	1154	17.33	39.66
Kavaratti Tahsil	10,715	823	7.68	28.28
Kavaratti Island	6,604	823	12.46	28.28
Amini Tahsil	12,521	933	7.45	32.06
Amini Island	5,367	933	17.38	32.06
Lakshadweep	40,249	2,910	7.23	100.00

Urban Housing

Lakshadweep has three towns in three different islands. They are Minicoy, Kavaratti and Amini which has total urban population of 18,629 persons who live in 2881 residential houses. Thus per house density works out to 6.47 persons, a figure which is much lower compared to Indian standards. This is mainly because in towns and cities normally the houses are multistory structures.

While the towns of Lakshadweep are considered separately the maximum density per house is recorded in Minicoy (6.66 persons) followed by Amini (6.55 persons) and Kavaratti (6.21 persons.) Thus it is only at Kavaratti density per habited residential house is not only lowest but even lower than that of islands average. This will be clear from the Table 14.19.

TABLE 14.19: Urban Housing Density

Towns	Population	No. of residential houses	Persons per residential house
Minicoy	6,658	999	6.66
Kavarathi	6,604	1,063	6.21
Amini	5,367	819	6.55
Lakshadweep	18,629	2,881	6.47

15

THE PEOPLE AND THEIR SOCIAL LIFE

Religion and Caste

The total population of the Union Territory as classified according to religions in the Census of India 1971 was 30,019 Muslims, 1545, Hindus, 239 Christians, 4 Sikhs and 3 belonging to other religions and persuasions.

The Muhammadan religion is predominant in this Union Territory. Muslims constitute 94.37 per cent of the total population. The remaining 5.53 per cent belonging to other religions of people who are entirely temporary migrants from outside who are employed in the Union Territory. The Muslims who are natives of the islands are treated as Scheduled Tribes who constitute 37,760 out of a total population of 40,249. Thus S.T. population account for 93.82 per cent of the total population as per 1981 Census.

The Muhammadans of this Union Territory believe that there is no other God except *Allah,* as the Muslims of else where believe. According to them, Muhammad is His Prophet. Like other places in India, *Pir* (saint) worship has become a common feature with them. The *Urs of Ubaidulla* (at Androth) and Syed Muhammad Kasim (at Kavaratti) are celebrated every year. The devout Muslims keep awake for the whole night and recite the *Maulood* during the ceremony. Like the *Moplahs* of the mainland, the majority of the Muslims of the islands belong to the *Shafi* School of the *Sunni* Sect and acknowledge besides the *Koran* the authority of the *Sunnet* or customary law as interpreted by *Shafi.* The other sects among the Muslims are *Wahabis* and *Ahamadiyas* who constitute only a micro-scopic minority. The *Wahabis* have separate mosques in Agatti and Kavaratti and the *Ahamadiyas* are found only is Kalpeni. *Wahabis* are Muslim purists who reject all traditional teachings except that of the Prophet, prohibit pilgrimage to shrines, or tombs and try to restore Islam to the condition of its primitive purity.

The *Ramzan* is strictly observed. *Moiluths* are performed in the month of *Rabbil Avrul* (February-March) and three bethams or fasts are observed on the 13th, 14th and 15th of each lunar month.

On all the islands except Minicoy a curious religious exercise, the *Zikkar*, is performed in honour of the saint Seyid Ahamed every Sunday and Friday night; according to Muhammad computation (i.e. every Saturday and Thursday night) in the Moidin and Ujira Mosques. Regular bands of disciples (forty to sixty) are enrolled for these exercises and systematically trained, one of the recognised instructors being the head of the *Shoikh-indeveetil* family at Androth.

The *Ahamadiya* Movement refutes the claim that Prophet Muhammad was last of the prophets and sets up as a prophet Hazrat Mirza Ghulam Ahmad, who was born in a family of Mughal Chiefs in Quadian, a village in the Gurdaspur district of Punjab in 1835. From his childhood, Hazrat Mirza Ghulam Ahmad was devoted to the study of the *Holy Koran* and spent the greater part of his life time in prayer and contemplations. He claimed to be the recipient of revelation and announced that he was the *Messiah* mentioned in the prophecies contained in the *Bible* and *Holy Koran.* In 1889, he organised his followers in the name of *Ahamadiya* movement. It is said that its members are now sprinkled all over the world.

Different Classes of the Union Territory

Classes of Amini

In Amini the people are divided into four classes:- *1. Tarawad, 2. Tanakampranavar, 3. Kudiyatis* and *4. Melacheris.* About five per cent of the population belong to the first, 35 per cent to 40 per cent to the second, 5 per cent to the third, and the reminder to the last class. The distinction between them appears to have been based originally upon property. The *Tarawad* class consisted of the four original Tarward families, Pondambelli, Porakat, Beyumada and Thupekal (now represented by the *Porculan* family), which alone in the early days of the settlement had tenants. The *Tanakampranavar* were those possessing property of their own, but with no tenants under them. The Kudiatis were the tenant class. the Melacheris were originally the landless tree climbers.

The *Melacheris* were the original labour class of the islands form the major part of the population of Amini and Laccadive group of lands. The people of Kadmat, Kiltan, Chetlat and Bitra are all Melacheris who have migrated either from Amini or from the Malabar Coast. Their Traditional occupation is climbing coconut trees and to pluck the nuts and tap *neerah,* the sweet toddy. It appears that the name has its origin in their traditional place of residence on the western side of her island.

Classes of Minicoy

There are three different classes of inhabitants in Minicoy: *1. Manikfans, 2. Thakrus* and *3. Reveries.*

According to the spoken language *Mahls* the inhabitants of Minicoy are known as *Mahl.* The inhabitants of the Maladives are also *Mahls.* In appearance they are strikingly different from the *Malayalis* of the Laccadives. The face is round and flat and is consider to be a primitive singalise type modified to some extent by and admixture of Arab blood.

Among the class groups of Minicoy, the *Manikfans* are considered to be the highest class. They alone owned private property and were the leisured class. The *Thakrufans* were the sailors whose main function was piloting of the sailing vessels. The *Thakrus* worked in the boats during voyages, while the *Raveries* were the labourers. The women of the four classes are known as *Manikka, Beefan, Beebee,* and *Kambilo* respectively. In between the Thakrufan and Thakru, there is a sub-class known as *Bebe.*

Classes of Malabar Islands

On the Malabar group the people are divided into there classes; 1. *Koyas, 2. Malmis* and *3. Melacheris.* In the older reports the *Malmis* are also called *Urukars*, but this term is now quite unknown and never used.

The *Koya* families use the title of Koya, were the Chief land possessing class of the society. The name itself is of comparatively recent most origin and formerly they were known as *Tarawading* or the *Karnavass* class. Originally the class consisted of the principal families or *Tarawads* of the early migrants. The heads of these *Tarawads,* known as *Karnavans sat as jurors* in the Community Panchayats. They considered themselves superior to others and abhorred alliance with other sections of the population. In the earlier days, the *Karnavans* were the real masters of the land. The *Koyas* of Androth, Kavaratti and Kalpeni claim to be descended from *Nambudri* and *Nair* ancestors from the Malabar coast and hence these three islands are known as *Tarawad* island in distinction to Agatti, a *Melacherio island;* the inhabitants of which seem to have descended from *Tiyyars* and other lower castes.

The *Malmis* are the sailors. The word *Malmi* which is of Arab origin, means one who is connected with the sings of ways. The *Malmis* were the tenants of the *Koyas* and they served as sailors under them and exported their produce in the *Odam* Piloting of vessels is not, non-a-days, an exclusive privilege of this class and anybody who has acquired mastery over the nautical tables is as accomplished as a successful *Malmi*.

Religious Beliefs and Practices

Islam enjoins five duties upon its followers the recitation of the *Kalma Can* expression of faith in God and in (Mahammad), offering of *Namaz* (prayers) five times a day, *Roza* (fasting in the month of *Ramzan), Zakat* (contribution in cash or kind for charitable purposes) and *Haj* to Mecca. The people of the islands are very strict in all their religious observance. The daily prayers are said at day break, soon after midday, before sunset, after sunset and early in the night.

The *Ramzan* fast which lasts for thirty days, begins on the first day of *Ramzan*, the ninth month of *Hijira*. The fasting requires total abstinence from food and drink from Sunrise to Sunset. On the 27th day, which is regarded as most sacred day, the Muslims give *Zakat* to the poor to the tune of $2^1/_2$ per cent of their income. The *Haj* – Pilgrimage to Mecca is performed on the 9th day of *Dulhaj* 12 months of *Hijira* era). the *Haj* is not compulsory for those who can not afford to undertake the long and expensive trip. Those who have performed the *Haj* are reverentially called *Hajiar*.

The Muhammadans of the territory also follow certain ritualistic practices which do not have the sanction of Islam which is common to all islands except Minicoy. But Minicoy Island has the *Rathib*, which is performed twice a week in the name of two Shieks knowns as *Rifai Shiek* and *Moheiddin Shiek*, at the Ujira Mosque and Moheiddin Mosques respectively. But there is also the observance of special *Rathib* in special days and also by individuals. But the difference between these two groups of sacred observance of *Rathib* is negligible.

The performance of the *Rathib* is initiated by the Khalifa of the

Mosques who renders the baith. The participants sit in two rows facing each other, each holding a kind of tambourine known as *duff*. They beat the duff to the tune of the baith and perform a series of exercises. At the same time about half a dozen of them dance up and down between the rows carrying a sharp instrument known as *Labbus* and get into fits of frenzy as the pace of the faith, as well as the beating gain momentum. At the climax they leap into the air shouting and apply the *labbus* in their bodies. *Rathib* is also performed without the accompaniment of the duff and ritual of inflicting pain with *labbus* is performed only on special occasions.

The main entrances to the mosques are facing to the east. In almost all islands, there are three main mosques, the *Juma*, the *Mohiddis* is generally the largest where the *Id* congregation meets. *Rathib* is performed in *Mohiddin* and *Ujira* mosques. A part from these there are also a number of small and big size mosques. In some islands like Kavaratti, Agatti, Amini and Kiltan there are separate prayer houses (*Niskarapuras*) for woman. A mosque is in charge of a *Mukri* or *Mullah*, whose main function is to make the call for prayer five times a day and lead the *Niskaram*.

The only religious movement having some bearing on the social life of the people was the *Wahabi* movement which took root in Minicoy island during the 1940s. The movement is attributed to one Hussein Didi who was a native of Maladives. He was not in favour of the teaching of the Prophet and the practices like beating of drums, mixed clubs for men and women etc., which were un-Islamic. The reformists were leading separate way of living. In 1958, due to the above communal disturbances, the Government banned the dancing mixed clubs.

Status of Woman

The women of the Union Territory enjoy a higher social status and economic freedom than their counter parts elsewhere in the country. The matrilined system of inheritance under which the property descends through the female line saves the women from the proverbial economic dependence. The husband is obliged to make an annual payment towards the maintenance of the wife which forms a part of the marriage contract. The wife can demand a divorce on grounds of nonpayment of these customary dues. No social stigma is attached to a divorce nor is it considered a disqualification for a women to seek a fresh alliance. There is also no ban on the remarriage of a widow. The women do not wear *purda* to screen themselves from the right of strangers except for a few in Androth and Amini

In case of Minicoy Island a special feature is observed i.e. the women predominate in all walks of life. On marriage, a man passes to his wife's house and takes his wife's family name. Though the males are the bread winners of the family, the entire affairs of the family is managed by the female of the house. This is due to the absence of the male members of family who work as semen for a long period.

Social evils like prostitution are almost absent in Union Territory. Polygamy is practised in all islands except Minicoy and divorce is granted without much difficulty in the event of an unhappy alliance. Cases of adultery are, however, found not infrequently, and provide a common ground for divorce. In Minicoy, communal punishment for adulterers was imposed till recently. When in case of adultery is brought to light of the *Khatib*, the adulterers both man and women are punished by means of ginnery are hundred lashes at a public place. Then they are put together in a separate shed for three days and exposed to public sneering. Once the routine punishment is over, they are taken back into the society without any reservation.

16

MANNERS AND CUSTOMS

Except Minicoy group of Islands, there is very little difference in the social manners and customs of the people of the Lakshadweep Island. Though there is a lot of caste variation here. When a child is born, the father and his near relatives are first informed of the event. The baby is bathed and an elderly person in the family renders *Bank* (call to prayer) into its ears. The baby is usually named on the same day by the father's mother (grandmother) though this function is also sometimes performed on the third, seventh of even fourteenth day. On the 40th day by the head of the baby, whether male or female, is shaven and a feast follows. Some offerings are made to the important mosque in the island on that day. The *Markakalaanam* or the circumcision is performed for a boy between the age of 6 to 12. The responsibility of this ceremony rests with the father. In Kalpeni, the ceremony take place at the father's residence, while in other islands the father sends the articles required for the ceremony to the wife's house. Special *Moulous* (prayers) are conducted on this day. Circumcision is generally done by the family barber. Ear boring of a girl is also an important function in Kalpeni where it is done by women. The ceremony is followed by a feast. In other islands, this is not a very important function and the ceremony is performed by local goldsmith.

But Minicoy maintains its speciality even in these matters. On the day of the birth of a child, or sometimes even earlier, the father sends to his wife's house a small bed with curtains, sheet, etc. and dresses for the child. In the case of first birth beaten rice and coconuts are sent to the houses of all the relatives on the day of delivery. The child is normally taken out of the room only after six days and is immediately taken to the father's house. Silver, gold or jewels are presented to the child by the father. After 20 days, the head of the child is shaven, irrespective of the sex. The father meets the expenses connected with this function known as *Bobela.* After shaving the baby, the hair is weighed in either gold or silver and its value is given as alms to the poor. This practice is generally confined to the first birth only. The child is named on the first day itself.

Circumcision is an occasion for rejoicing and feasting the Minicoy. Groups of dancers with drums come to the house in the night and enter each room dancing to the tune of the drums and settle down to sing songs. Mean-while a group of men in fancy dress and wearing masks, enter the house. They are served with tea and eatables. If identified, they are drenched in water and booted out by the woman folk participating in the fun. They disperse quickly, but songs continue till the early hours of the morning. The festivities last for a period of eight days, which is the normal time required for the wounds to heal.

Marriage and Morals

The marriage system in the Lakshadweep is quite similar to that of the Mainland. The boys are generally married between the age of 18 and 20 and girls between 10 and 12, which are now-a-days delayed like that of the mainland because of the legal restrictions.

But as fatherless girl cannot be married until, she has attained puberty. The first match is arranged for a boy by the *Karanavarns* of both parties. Subsequent marriage is done by only his personal arrangements. The ceremony is performed as the usual *Muhammadan nikka* ceremony. It is usually performed in the bride's house if she belongs to the upper classes and in the mosques, if she is *Melacheri*. The dowry system in this Union Territory is quite interesting. The dowry is generally given to the wife by the husband, which is Rs. 30 for the first class, Rs. 12 for the 2nd class, and from Rs. 3 to Rs. 6 for Melacheris. Rich families spend very large sums on the feast which accompanies a wedding, even very rich and high status families give feast to the people of the whole island, and is to 20 *Muras* of rice, 8 to 10 cows, some 20 goats and 5 or 6 *maunds* of jaggery is usually consumed. The whole expenditure falls in the first instance upon the bride's family. After the public feasting, the relatives and friends accompany the groom to the bride's house. Among the upper classes the bridegroom is conducted to the bride's house with singing. In case of *Melacheris*, they are allowed to have singing only in their houses and not on the way. The songs (*Kettipadu*) sung on these occasions are either composed locally for the occasion or are printed *Moplah* songs brought over from the mainland. The bride's house is of course greatly decorated for the occasion. The bridegroom brings with him two companions (*Theli*) who stay with him at the bride's house for the next forty days. After the marriage, the bridegroom has to make a customary present to the bride consists of a fixed number of cloths and sares, which is in case of the higher classes is quite a costly gift. It is, however, collected by the bride-groom from among his relations and gives back to each a cloth of equal value, when their turn comes to get married.

Funeral Ceremonies and Customs

The funeral ceremonies of the islands are similar to those of the Mappilas of Malabar Coast. When a person is about to die, the *Kalima* is recited in his ears. When he dies, the body is washed and the chin and head are tied together to knee, the mouth closed. The dead body is placed on the *verandah* and the arms are tied together the right hand over the left. Camphor is applied to the eyes, ears and mouth. The body is wrapped in three pieces of cloth, one each at the head, waist and feet; cotton; wool is placed in the ears, nostrils and mouth before the cloth is tied up. A group of people recite the *Koran* sitting near the corpse. The body is removed to the mosque without delay. Generally, it is taken to the wife's house on the way. But if the death takes place at the wife's house, it is invariably taken to his own house. On reaching the mosque a special prayer known as *Mayyath Namaskaram* is offered. The dead body is then taken to the grove and placed in North-South direction with the head slanted Westwards to face Mecca. Then a passage of *Koran* is recited. The *Koran* reading continues for 3 to 7 days according the status of the decease. Sometimes it may continue till 40th day with some breaks. On the final day, a funeral feast is offered. Only males participate in this feast. But in Minicoy, neither feasting nor prayers follow funeral ceremonies at present. Recital of *Koran* at the grave is much more honoured.

Property and Inheritance

Property in the islands is either ancestral or sells acquired. Ancestral property is known as *Velliazhchas* pronounced as *Belliazhcha* in the Amindivis. Self acquired property is known as *Thinkalazhacha* in the Laccadives and *Belasha* in the Amindivis. Ancestral or *Tarward* property is governed by the *Marumak-Kothayan* law of inheritance prevalent in the Malabar Coast. But there is no specified law and the practices differ from island to island. Broadly speaking the property right descends through female line, the male members having only right for sustenance during their life time. The property is enjoyed by the joint family consisting of brother, sisters and sister's children. The children have no right. It is managed by the eldest male member known as *Karanavan*. He is responsible for all sorts of improvements of the land and plantation. He can also mortgage it for, debts and is responsible for the repayment from the household income. He has no right to sell it. It can be partitioned only by the consent of all the members. There are local variations in the criteria of partition. In Kavaratti and Agatti, for example all the members of joint family are eligible for one share. In Androth and Kalpeni it is divisible by all the branches of the family.

Self acquired or personal property is governed by Muhammadan Law of Succession. There are also variation in different islands. Under the Muslim law followed in the islands the son is eligible for two shares of the property, while the daughter gets only one share.

In Minicoy it is different. The women are the legalised head and are vested with all the properties. Males only reside there and are maintained up to their marriage.

Mehr and Customary Contributions

Mehr is the bridal price paid by the groom to the bride. It is decided between the parties before the alliance is agreed upon and is paid in cash on the day of *Nikkah* or on a subsequent day. The amount varies from island to island and depends on the economic status of the family. The minimum is fixed at Rs. 31. *Mehr* amount once paid is fixed and never taken back. A person who has not paid the *Mehr* cannot demand a divorce. In such cases the *Khasi* orders is to be paid for divorce. In Minicoy, the *Mehr* varies from class to class. The *Manikfans* pay Rs. 100 and *Thakrufans* Rs.50 while *Thakrus* and *Ravers* only Rs. 5 each. Apart from the *Mehr* the husband is obliged to make certain customary contributions like rice and dresses to the wife and children. Gifts of coconuts, rice etc. are sent when the wife is away.

Marital Age and Divorce

According to 1971 Census, 9258 persons in the Union Territory were married, of whom 4510 were males and 5348 were females. The number of persons who were not married stood at 12,217. Married males constituted 57.96 per cent and married females 43.53 per cent of their respective strength. The widowed were 5.23 per cent and divorced or separated persons were found to be 3.20 per cent only.

In the Union Territory, child marriage is very fare, although it was the rule till a few decades ago. Married males and females constitute the largest proportion in the age group 25-34. Divorced or separated males and females are found to be more in the age group of 25-34 and 15-24 respectively than in other age groups.

Petitions for divorce are received by the *Khasi* of the Island Law whose decrees are based on the *Shariat Law* and local customary laws. Generally divorces are demanded on grounds of infidelity or some quarrel between the families of the couple.

The *Khasi* attempts a compromise failing which he allows the separation. The husband renders the *Mozhi* or *Talakh* according to Muslim law and the marriage is dissolved. The Khasi takes all the charges of granting the divorce. If a husband seeks divorce, then he has to forfeit all the gift and contribution. The husband also takes all live responsibility of the children. Maternal uncle takes the general responsibility as the guardian. In Minicoy this type of practice is taking place slowly. The maintenance charge goes up to Rs.30 per month. If a wife wants a divorce from her side, she has to repay all *Mehr*, she had taken at the time of marriage.

Islam confers inheritance right on a woman to claim divorce. For a separation to be legal, the husband has to render the *Talakh.* Sometimes, the husband also takes compensation for the divorce of her wife, if the petition becomes unreasonable. In Minicoy, where most of the male population go out to work as seamen in different parts of the world, the *Kathib* allows a divorce if nothing is heard about a person for four years and one hundred and thirty days.

There are no restrictions on the remarriage of widows, which is proposed only after 130 days of the mourning. Duriong this time the widow will not wear any ornaments. A divorced woman can seek a fresh alliance only after a period of three months after the divroce.

House Type

In the Union Territory 84.60 per cent of houses have walls made of stone and 14.80 per cent have walls made of grass, leaves, burnt bricks or bamboo. House with walls made of wood, burnt bricks G.I. sheets, Cement Concrete and other materials are negligible in number.

The availability of materials and the climatic conditions are the main factors influencing the type of houses those are built. Most common material for construction of wall is the cut stone which is locally available in plenty. The only other material available in these islands i.e. the leaf of coconut tree. The leaf of coconut tree is commonly used for roof. Out of the 10,524 houses, 7170 have roofs made of coconut leaves. Next to coconut leaves, tiles are the most common material of roof.

On an average, one household has 2.99 rooms and one room accommodates 1.96 persons. If two persons per room is considered as a satisfactory norm, the overall picture of housing accommodation is fairly satisfactory. Sometimes coral stones are used in the walls. The windows are small. In Minicoy group of islands, the housing pattern is provided with verandahs. In a house, common room bedrooms, store rooms etc. are also provided.

Furniture and Decorations

The furniture in a house is almost limited to a few wooden cuts made of coconut timber and plaited with coir yarn and one or town wooden benches or stools. The well to do have of course recently stared providing chairs, dining tables, almirahs etc. the houses have very little interior decorations except on special occasions like marriage. in Minicoy, a sophisticated swing cut is very common. The coconut serpens, knives and axes are delightfully carved and painted. The bridal cot will have four or five attractive beds neatly piled up.

17

EDUCATION

From time immemorial mosques have been the centre of learning for the islander to which a school is attached. At the school going age all the boys and girls attend these schools which only enabled them to read the *Koran* written in Arabic scriptures. Of course, they used to get by heart a large portion of it without knowing its meaning. However, these mosque schools had little contribution for the mental and intellectual enlightenment of the pupils. Only in the year 1885, the British Administration, realised the need of setting up a school in Amini and sent a man from the island to the mainland to be trained as a school teacher. Generally, the *Mulla* or *Kukri* of nearby mosque would be the teacher who only got coconuts as his remuneration. Coconuts were contributed by the students on every Thursday and on the completion of each chapter of *Mushaf*, i.e. the text. The student remains in the school as long as he had the inclination or till he attained enough proficiency in the subjects. After completing their studies at *Pallidars* (Islamic schools), the students interested for higher studies leave for mainland. The system of imparting education in religious schools is continuing even now and the pupils study it along with the modern education.

Till the latter part of the 19th century no serious attempts were made for the educational development of these islands. By about 1877, the British Administration realised the need for setting schools in these islands and schools were opened in all the islands barring the island of Bitra. But poor attendance was the compelling factor for closing down the schools in Agathi and Kavaratty.

In 1878 in Androth and in 1890 in Minicoy first schools were started. But the attendance in these schools were very poor due to the conservative attitude of the people and they viewed with suspicion the introduction of modern schools and hence Grant System was introduced and inspecting officers took great interest in the educational development of the islanders. In 1888 an inspecting officer, Mir

Shujaat Ali Khan suggested the introduction of modern secular education combining with religious education. According to this system, specially trained teachers were to be attached to the mosque schools to impart secular education. Using the Arab i.e. script instruction was to be given in Malayalam or Canarese language. Thus, a man from Amini was sent to the mainland to be trained as a school teacher in the Norman School at Calicut. On his return, he was appointed in the mosque school under the patronage of most popular *Mukri*. Soon after, the *Mukri* died and the teacher (named Kadri Hazi) himself started a school independently instructing the students in *Koran*. Elementary Malayalam books were supplied to the students in which each lesson was written both in Arabic and Malayalam. In 1898, *Kadri Hazi* lost his health and gave up teaching. Island education thus reverted back to this original state. Proposals to educate the islanders in Canarese occupied the field for another a few years but were never carried out.

However, education in the island began to improve by 1905. A trained teacher from local Board Panchama School, Kasaragode, was sent to Amini. The school started with 20 boys on its role and the boys were taught up to the fourth standard. The boys were taught reading and writing in Malayalam, and arithmatic and also a little history and geography. But attempt to train some more teachers was met with disappointment as nobody was found willing to be trained in the mainland as a teacher. Canarese still was the official language of the islands and this was but natural that people preferred to learn Canarese language. A Mapila teacher was suggested to be sent to Amini to teach education in Malayalam or Canarese or both. At last, a Mapila teacher was selected and sent to Amini. Thus the first Government school in the Amindive group of islands was opened on 15th January, 1904. A great majority of students were coming to read Canarese and a few came to learn Malayalam. But in 1905, the teaching of Canarese language was discontinued. As such, enrolment in the schools began to decline. There has been a steady improvement in education only after 1912 following the governments decision to introduce the payment of Result Grants to the school masters. In 1911 an elementary school was opened in Kiltan and another in Kadmat in 1925. In 1927, a temporary school was sanctioned in Chetlat. Even then interest in education was so very poor that the higher elementary schools where standard six had been opened, in Kaipeni, Androth and Agatti had to be reduced to elementary schools.

In 1933, for the first time the scheme of scholarship was instituted as a result the students passing out from the island schools got the scholarships. The second important measure was the introduction of the *Koran* classes along with the secular education. Thus, the first measure helped the students in going over to the mainland for higher education proved very much inspiring. Sometimes at the initiative of the visiting inspecting officers, small amounts of stipends were granted to students who came to mainland for study. However, these scholarships were confined to the Malabar islands. The second measure of imparting religious education was first introduced in Kalpeni in 1938. A teacher was appointed to teach the Koran at the instance of the people. The government met half the cost and the other half was met by the people.

By 1947, each inhabited island except Bitra had a primary school. In each of the islands of the Amindivi group there was in existence a lower elementary school while in the Malabar group of islands and Minicoy has a school having from standard I to III. In Kavaratti there was a school from I to II class and I to VI in Kalpeni, Androth and Agatti. The incomplete elementary school at Minicoy was being managed by a single part time untrained teacher. Immediately after the Independence various steps were taken to help spreading of education like the supply of books, award of scholarships, mid-day meals etc. But all these did not make much progress till 1956 when the islands were declared as Union Territory.

Growth of Literacy

Till 1951, all these islands were educationally backward. It is clearly indicated from the Census reports of 1951 when the percentage of literacy was only 15.23. It is interesting to note that in 1951 out of total school age population of 2210 only 550 (24.89%) attended the schools. They consisted of 489 boys and 66 girls which accounted for 39 per cent and 7 per cent of the total school-going population of boys and girls respectively. The First Five-Year Plan had a great impact on the improvement of education in these islands. The islands became Union Territory on 1st November 1956. At that time hardly 88 per cent of the school age children attended the school. There was little incentive for education. Libraries were non-existent and the teaching staff were untrained. But the situation had improved considerably since then. In 1956, there were 9 primary schools at the rate of one for each island. By the end of the Second Five-Year Plan in 1960-61 there were sixteen schools including a High school at Aneni, which started in 1961. There were 4 primary schools for girls, four middle schools, five mixed primary schools and two feeder schools. The 1961 Census revealed that the percentage of male literacy was 35.80 while 10.98 per cent of the females were literates. The greatest handicap, for progress of female education was the old established custom of keeping women indoors.

From this stage in 1961, the island's education has now reached a very advanced position. According to 1971 Census, the percentage of literacy increased to 43.6. This was the maximum growth recorded in India during that decade which was 87.62 per cent over the 1961 rate. The male literacy was 56.48 per cent and that of female literacy was 30.56 per cent. Thus female literacy was tripled during 1961-71. Table 17.1 gives the number of literates and educated persons and the percentage of literacy as revealed by the Census of 1971[1] islandwise here Minicoy with 51.03 per cent literates tops the list while Androth with only 34.88 per cent was less literate in 1971.

TABLE 17.1: Level of Literacy in Lakshadweep Island in 1971

Union Territory	Literates in (Number)			In Percentage		
Island	Persons	Males	Females	Persons	Males	Females
Lakshadweep	13899	9081	4808	43.66	56.48	30.56
1. Minicoy	2726	1468	1258	51.03	60.34	43.25
2. Kalpeni	1499	909	590	47.56	58.23	37.08
3. Androth	1892	1388	504	34.88	52.02	18.28
4. Agatti	1362	924	438	43.17	55.86	29.18
5. Kavaratti	1961	1475	486	44.37	60.40	24.57
6. Amini	1848	1357	491	40.69	55.84	23.25
7. Kadmat	1179	683	496	48.80	57.30	40.52
8. Kiltan	856	533	323	41.84	50.67	32.49
9. Chetlat	518	315	203	43.17	53.39	33.28
10.Bitra	48	29	19	42.86	51.79	33.93

There were only 132 persons having educational level of matriculation and above in 1961, which increased to 213 degree-holder and technical personnel in 1971. There are now about 7 high schools operating in seven islands. One Junior College is also functioning at Kavaratti. Besides, each island has been provided with at least one Nursery and one Junior basic school for every 120 persons. There are

Senior Basic Schools in six of the islands. A further rise in literacy was revealed according to a survey in 1974, when there were 42 educational institutions. They are as follows:

Nursery School	9
J.B. School	18
High School	7
Higher Secondary School	1
Junior College	1
S.B. School	6

Nursery Schools

These schools are of recent growth in the Island Territory. These are intended for the children of 3 to 5 age group. The first Nursery School was established at Kavaratti in 1964. The other schools were started in quick succession in then Kalpeni, Androth, Agatti, Amini and Minicoy in 1965. During 1973-74, there were about 259 boys and 262 girls in these seven institutions. The teachers of these schools were specially trained.

Junior and Senior Basic Schools

Junior basic schools impart education from class I to IV. Children who have completed 5 years can be admitted to class 1. Arithmetic and languages are the major subjects of study at this stage. The study of languages include Malayalam, English and Hindi is also compulsory. Malayalam is the mother tongue of the people and is the medium of instruction. Gradually more lower primary schools are being opened due to the increasing demand for primary education. There were about 14 junior basic schools during 1973-74 out of which three were exclusively reserved for girls. Six feeder schools were also functioning during that year. The total enrolment in the primary classes during 1973-74 was 5380.

There were seven Senior Basic Schools which imparted education from class V to VI. Out of them three were exclusively reserved for girls.

Secondary and Higher Secondary Schools

The island of Amini had the distinction of having the first High School in the territory in 1960. There are now about 7 High Schools in the territory. These schools impart education beyond the senior basic stage upto Class-X. The other schools have been established in Kavaratti, Kalpeni, Androth, Agatti and Minicoy. The medium of instruction in these schools is Malayalam. In Kavaratti High School there is also and English Medium section. Kerala Board of Secondary Education conducts the Secondary School Leaving Certificate Examination of these schools. The headquarters island had its first High School in 1965-66.

Higher Education

Until 1972, there was no facility for University education. Students who were interested for further studies after passing the High School Certificate Examination, had to come to the mainland. Kavaratti had the distinction of having the first Junior College which was inaugurated on 15th July, 1972. The College is affiliated to the Calicut University, Trichur. There Pre-degree course is given in three groups namely Group-I Mathematics, Physics, Chemistry, Group -II: Physics Chemistry, Biology and Group-III: Indian History, World History and Economics. Till 1972 there were no facilities in the islands for further study after pre-degree education.

Interest of the Government in the Education Development of the Islands

The Government, since 1956, have taken active interest in spreading literacy in the islands. Education is free in the islands at all levels. Besides students are supplied with books and writing materials free of cost. Free mid-day meals are also given to the students in Nursery schools, J.B.Schools and S.B. Schools, Scholarships are also given to the students of High Schools and Junior College. Besides Hostel facilities, library facilities also exist in some islands. In the island of Amini and Kavaratti there are two hostels for High School boys. At Kavaratti there are separate hostels i.e. one for boys and other for girls of the Junior College. Science education in particular is being given importance. Primary schools are being supplied with science kits obtained from UNICEF. Teachers are being regularly sent to various institutions in the mainland for in-service training.

Since the beginning of the 20th Century adult education programme is functioning in the islands. A night school for adults was there at Kavaratti is early as 1909. Later other two centres were opened one at Androth and the other at Kalpeni. Since the islands are Union Territory, the government is taking active interest in spreading literacy among the adults. Government is supplying all the requirements of the adult education centres like books, writing materials, lights and kerosene oil etc. Adult Education Committees have been constituted in all the islands except Minicoy. These centres function for only five months a year during the monsoon period. In 1962-63 literacy centres were started for the first time exclusively for women.

Library facilities exist in all the islands except the island of Bitra. The government supplies books to all the libraries free of cost. Youth Clubs and Mahila Samities are functioning in all islands except Bitra. Vocationalisation of education has been receiving the attention of the administration. Typewriting and Fisheries Technology courses are being offered to the students in some high schools.

Thus educational facilities are gradually making great strides in the educational field.

Change in Literacy in 1981

Since more emphasis has been given for universal education for the children of school going age and adult education schemes have been geared up in the islands, the level of literacy has gone up from 43.66 per cent in 1971 to 55.07 per cent in 1981. This is the seventh highest in the country in 1981 preceded by Kerala, Chandigarh, Delhi, Mizoram, (Goa, Daman and Diu) and Pondicherry in order of their arrangement. The literacy level among the males has gone up from 56.48 per cent in 1971 to 65.24 per cent in 1981 recording thereby an increase of 15.50 per cent, over the past decade whereas the female literacy level has increased from only 30.56 per cent to 48.25 per cent. Thus it has witnessed a rise of 57.89 per cent over the base year of 1971. As a result the pace of literacy development is much more higher in case of females than that of males in the Lakshadweep during the decade ending in 1981.

TABLE 17.2: Literacy Rates (1981)

(*Figures in % of total of respective units*)

District/ Tahsil Island	Among Total Population			Among Rural population			Among Urban Population		
	Persons	Male	Female	Persons	Male	Female	Persons	Male	Female
1	2	3	4	5	6	7	8	9	10
MINICOY TAHSIL	61.29	71.40	59.99	—	—	—	65.29	71.40	59.99
Minicoy Island	65.29	71.40	59.99	—	—	—	65.29	71.40	59.99
ANDROTH TAHSIL	51.21	63.59	38.97	51.21	63.59	38.97	—	—	—
Kalpeni Island	55.58	67.19	43.70	55.88	67.19	43.70	—	—	—
Androth Island	48.78	61.58	36.68	48.78	61.58	36.68	—	—	—
KAVARATTI TAHSIL	58.12	68.31	46.29	54.76	64.19	44.56	60.22	70.74	47.43
Agatti island	54.76	64.19	44.56	54.76	64.19	44.56	—	—	—
Kavaratti Island	60.22	70.74	47.43	—	—	—	60.22	70.74	47.43

(*Contd.*)

TABLE 17.2 *(Contd.)*

1	2	3	4	5	6	7	8	9	10
AMINI TAHSIL	50.21	60.80	39.22	51.51	59.19	43.72	48.48	62.90	33.04
Amini Island	48.48	62.90	33.04	—	—	—	48.48	62.90	33.04
Kadmat Island	56.07	64.01	47.92	56.07	64.01	47.92	—	—	—
Kiltan Island	46.86	56.01	37.69	46.86	56.01	37.69	—	—	—
Chetlat Island	49.93	54.90	45.07	49.93	54.90	45.07	—	—	—
Bitra Island	46.96	52.48	40.00	46.96	52.48	40.00	—	—	—
Lakshadweep	55.07	65.24	44.65	51.98	65.25	41.57	58.65	68.66	48.25

Source: Lakshadweep Census of India, 1981.

When the islands are treated individually the maximum literacy level (65.29 per cent) is observed in Minicoy island and the minimum of 46.86 per cent in Kiltan island in 1981. In 1971 it was also Minicoy which has the maximum (51.03 per cent) literacy level while the minimum of 34.88 per cent was recorded in Androth island. Maximum male literacy is observed in Minicoy (71.40%) followed by Kavaratti (70.74%) whereas minimum is recorded in Bitra island (52.48%) in 1918. In female education Minicoy Island is most advanced having a total literacy of 59.99 per cent followed by Kadmat Island (47.92%). Females are least educated in Amini (33.04%).

Urban dwellers are found in Minicoy, Kavaratti and Amini Islands. Amongst these three the highest urban literacy level is met with in Minicoy (65.29%) followed by Kavaratti (60.22%) and Amini (48.48%). As usual urban males are more literate than the urban females. The maximum urban male literacy is witnessed in Minicoy (71.40%) and Minimum in Amini (62.90%). The same order followed in case of urban female literacy, maximum in Minicoy (59.99%) and minimum of 33.04 per cent in case of Amini.

Thus an inevitable conclusion is the quality of island population has gone up since 1951 and to that extent the island is advanced. This will be clear from analysis of Table 17.2.

NOTE

1. Census of India, 1971, LM & A, Islands part -II A, General Populations Tables.

18

LANGUAGE

In the Union Territory of Lakshadweep about nine languages are spoken according to the 1971 Census as specified in the Eighth Schedule of the Constitution of India. They are: Malayalam, Tamil, Hindi, Urdu, Kannada, Marathi, Telugu, Punjabi and Bengali. Of these nine languages Malayalam is predominant and is spoken as the mother tongue by 26,689(1971) persons which is 83.90 per cent of the total population. The Malayalam has been considered as the mother tongue of all the islands except the islands of Minicoy where they have their local dialect called *Mahl.* The prevalence of other languages is the result of temporary migrants who are either employed or have migrated here long ago. The Table 18.1 reveals the strength of different languages spoken as mother tongue in the lakshadweep.

TABLE 18.1: Percentage of Population Speaking different Language in Lakshadweep

Language	No.of Speakers in 1971	% to total Population
Malayalam	26,689	83.90
Tamil	113	0.36
Hindi	59	0.18
Urdu	32	0.10
Kannada	15	0.05
Marathi	8	0.02
Telugu	6	0.02
Punjabi	5	0.02
Bengali	4	0.01
	26,930	84.66

Census Centenary, 1972.Pocket Book of Population Statistics.
Language data for 1981 is not available.

Origin of the Languages

(1) *Influence of the Mainland*

The influence of the mainland on the languages of these islands is clearly evident. For example, the Archaic Malayalam script which was prevalent in the Malabar Coastal area was know as *Vatta-ezuthu* whereas this in the islands is known as *Batta-ezuthu.* In the islands the letter 'V' is being pronounced as 'B' and 'O' as 'A'. Such peculiarities in pronunciation is attributed to the long and continued isolation from the mainland.

As such, inter-island differences in speech exist. As for example, in the northern islands the pronunciation is slightly different, as certain Canarese words have found its way into their language. Thus, the influence of Mangalore of mainland is quite evident from this.

Apart from the influence of Malayalam and the Canarese, Tamil is spoken in the coastal region of the mainland has had its influence to a certain degree. The Malayalam as a spoken in these islands, has a number of Tamil words which indicate the influence of the coast of the mainland upon these islands. This proves that, in the past migration has taken place which may have been forced or voluntary.

Thus, the Malayalam language prevalent here is not in its pure form but is a modified version basically including three languages—namely the Malayalam, Tamil and Canarese. The Malayalam script which is vogue in the islands (except Minicoy) is the modern Malayalam script. This script has developed out of *Grandha* or *Arya Ezluthu,* which was popularised by *Tunchat Ezhuthachan* of Kerala, who lived in the 17th Century.

However, the *Vatta-ezuthu* script was used for navigational purposes till the end of the 19th Century and the latter for official correspondence. It was only after the British took over the administration of the islands the modern Malayalam script evolved.

(2) *Influence of the Arabic Countries*

Conversion into Islamic faith by an Arab saint has influenced the life of the people in these islands. It seems peculiar to find the usage of Arabic script in Malayalam. This was done only by a section of the people though not in these islands. Of them especially women were found using Arabic script to write Malayalam. This is known as Arabic

Malayalam. This script came into being to make the study of the *Koran*.

Amongst these islands, the island of Minicoy has a language of its own. It is known as the *Mahl* language. It has a script of its own which is written from right to left as in Alrabic. The pronounciation is exactly the same as in Arabic but the writing is different. This language has 24 letters. The influence of Arabic language has given rise to the modern *Mahl* language.

Those who have languages other than Malayalam and *Mahl* (as spoken in Minicoy) as their mother tongue are negligible in number and most of them can generally understand and speak Malayalam. Table 18.2 gives the distribution of population according to their language/mother tongue Malayalam and its percentage to total population in the Union Territory of Lakshadweep in 1971.

TABLE 18.2: Percentage of Population Speaking Malayalam in Lakshadweep in 1971

Islands	No. of people speaking Malayalam	% to total Population
Bitra	112	100.00
Agatti	3,555	100.00
Kadamat	2,414	99.92
Androth	5,410	99.72
Chetlat	1,196	99.67
Kiltan	2,035	99.46
Kalpeni	3,134	99.43
Amini	4,501	99.10
Kavaratti	4,281	96.86
Minicoy	451	8.44
Laccadive, Minicoy Amindivi Islands	26,689	83.90

It is thus, clear from the above table that except the island of Minicoy, in all the islands almost all the people speak in Malayalam. In Minicoy only 8.44 per cent of people could speak in Malayalam. Hence, one can safely conclude that Malayalam in the mothertongue in Lakshadweep Island.

19

TRANSFORMATION OF RURAL HABITAT

Rural Settlements

Out of the ten habitated islands Minicoy, Kavaratti and Amini are the three islands where no rural population is found as the entire population of these three islands live in towns. According to 1981 Census, in the entire Lakshadweep, 21,620 rural people live in seven villages having 3,439 rural residential houses.

Villages

The entire rural population of 21,620 persons live in seven villages bring the average size of a village to 3,089 persons which is quite big compared to the national average size of villages. This is mainly because the island does not have much land which can be spared for human habitation and the constraint of land is the single greatest bottleneck which has resulted in a very compact settlement. When the size of the villages is considered islands-wise, Androth Island has the largest village where 6,812 persons live. It is followed by Agati Island (4,111), Kalpeni Island (3,543) and Kadmat Island (3,114). The average size of all these are larger than the average size of a village in Lakshadweep. The smallest village is met within Bitra where only 181 persons live.

Residential Houses

Island's 21,620 rural persons live in 3,439 residential houses as per 1981 Census and thus the average density per house works out to be 6.29 persons which is also much higher than that of the national average. Thus, the rural houses are no less crowded than those of towns in the Lakshadweep where average residential house density works out to be 6.47 persons. Thus, overcrowding is as much a problem in the villages of Lakshadweep as in the towns of the island.

Islandwise, it is Androth Island which has the maximum rural residential house density of 7.07 persons against the island's average of 6.29 persons, this is followed by Kalpeni (7.04 persons), Kadmat island (5.55 persons). The rural overcrowding is the least in the Bitra Island where only 4.11 persons live in a residential house. This will be clear from Table 19.1.

TABLE 19.1: Rural Settlement Pattern, 1981

District/Tahsil/ Island	Population	No. of villagers		Residential Houses	
		Number	Average size (persons)	Number	Persons per house
Minicoy Tahsil					
Minicoy Island	Nil	—	—	—	—
Androth Tahsil	10,355	2	5,177	1,466	7.06
Kalpeni Island	3,543	1	3,543	503	7.04
Androth Island	5,812	1	6,812	963	7.07
Kavarathi Tahsil	4,111	1	4,111	584	7.04
Kavarathi Island	Nil	—	—	—	—
Agati Island	4,111	1	4,111	584	7.04
Amini Tahsil	7,154	4	1,789	1,389	5.15
Amini Island	Nil	—	—	—	—
Kadmat Island	3,114	1	3,114	561	5.55
Kiltan Island	2,375	1	2,375	431	5.51
Chetlat Island	1,484	1	1,484	353	4.20
Bitra Island	181	1	181	44	4.11
Lakshadweep	21,620	7	3,089	3,439	6.29

Transformation of Rural Habitat in Kavaratti

Lakshadweep Island (Lakshadivi the hundred thousands isles) a group of coral islands in the Arabian Sea constituting the smallest Union Territory in India, lie between 8° and 12°-30 north latitudes and between 71° and 74° east longitudes. The colloquial term Laccadives is derived from Lakshadweep which is generally interpreted as hundred thousand isles. (Laksha—one hundred thousand; Dweep islands). The word has many connotations in Sanskrit as well as in Malayalam. The word itself derived from the root 'lag' as that which is attached, carries the meaning, 'a mark or sing especially a mark to aim at' lying directly in the trade route between Africa, Arabia and Malabar, as these islands were a landmark for the navigators during the days of sailing ships and that was probably the reason why they were known as Lakshadweep. There are now in all twenty-one islands and a number of sunken banks, open reefs and sand banks. Only ten islands are inhabited which are away from Kozhikode (i.e Calicut) of Kerala by about 200-400 km.

According to the Survey of India the geographical area of Lakshadweep is 32 km while its population according to 1971 Census is 31,810.

The islands have practically no major topographic features and are largely low levelled flat-topped, generally rising to a height of a few metres (mostly 3 to 6 metres) above sea-level (Fig. 19.1). The entire group of islands lies on the prominent north-south Lakshadweep Ridge and the alignment appears to be a continuation of the Aravalli Strike of Rajasthan expect Androth island which lies in east-west directions. The lagoonal shores of the island consist of a sandy beach though at places, beach rock is exposed at the low tide mark. The depths in these lagoons vary from 1 to 2.5 m but the larger lagoons of Bitra, Minicoy and Bangaram are comparatively deep with depth of about 10-16 m. The islands do not have any rivers of creeks. Kavaratti (Latitude 10°33′30" N. and Longitude 72°6′30" E. Fig. 19.2) which lies between Androth and Agatti is perhaps the most centrally situated island of the Lakshadweep group and has rightly been chosen as the headquarters of the Union Territory. It is about 5.6 km in length and its greatest breadth is about one km and the lagoon is about 1.6 km wide.

Of all the inhabited islands Kavaratti is the most diversified and picturesque. There is a small inland like at the northern end. At this end the lagoon is shallow and provides a beautiful pool for swimming. The southern part of island is a long and narrow strip only 45.50 m wide. It would appear to have been a separate island in olden days but is now connected. On the sea side at this point sand extending round into the lagoon is a high storm beach composed of bits of coral and coraloid sand and debris. It is situated at a distance of 301 km from Kozhikode (Calicut). Its population in 1971 was 4420 distributed not uniformly in its total area of 3.50 km. Density of population per km. is 1228 which is about 1½ times its 1961 density (808).

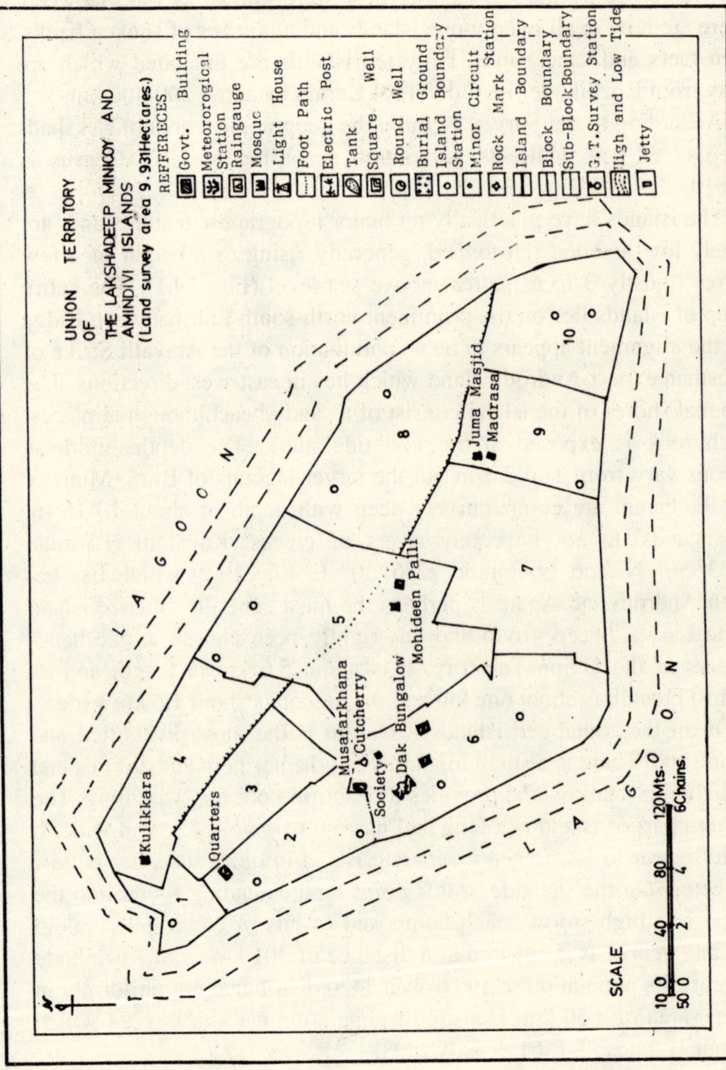

FIG. 19.1: Bitra Island: Landuse

Kavaratti can lay claim to a number of modern buildings also. By virtue of its location Kavaratti has become the headquarters of the Administration. Consequently numerous Government buildings have come up in the south of the Island. The secretariat is an imposing one which is situated near the elbow of the island. Other important buildings are the Treasury, the Wireless Station, the Police Station, the Circuit House, The Rest House and the Dak Bungalow and the Administrator's House and the High School. A godown for the co-operative stores which was founded in 1962 has been opened recently. Today Kavaratti has a College, a High School and Senior Basic School for girls. About six hundred students are attending these schools. There is a twenty-bed hospital with a Medical Officer. The Co-operative Society has about 500 members with a share capital of Rs. 21,500. Kavaratti has a poultry farm, a dairy farm and a Dish curing yard attached to the Fisheries Department. There is also a fisheries workshop here. Electricity was introduced in this island in 1963. There is an agricultural farm which gives instructions to cultivators and also it supplies manure, seeds, and instruments. It has introduced now plants and vegetables which can grow in these islands. These changes in agricultural outlook have considerable effect on the arrangement and lay-out of the dwellings since the villagers in a number of cases have introduced vegetable gardens in their shelter area.

The houses in Kavaratti are concentrated within a small area and the compounds adjoin one another. The narrow southern portion is entirely government land. This government land starts from the end of the inhabited part. The government offices and quarters for officials are located in this area in central southwest. In 1961 much of this southern part was barren and there was conspicuous absence of dwellings, private or government while by now this southern tail of island has a good number of government staff quarters in addition to some newly constructed official buildings.

Population and Dwellings

Kavaratti had a population of 2828 with a sex-ratio of 954 females per 1000 males, a good indicator of rural status insofar as male-female ratio is concerned. The population rose to 4420 in 1971 registering a spectacular rise with a sex-ratio of 810 females per 1000 males. This small female ratio is certainly not an indicator of rural population structure. It is but natural that the number of government servants has considerably increased during 1961-71 and many of them have stayed in the island without their family, thus the island registered a low female ratio against males. This is obviously a trend towards more dwellers with tertiary occupation which indicates a change towards urban characteristic in the island in the last decade.

This inference is consequently and indication of transformation in the rural habitat of the island which will be more pronounced when the type and distribution of the residential dwellings and institutional houses in the island considered both spatially and temporally. In 1961, there were 402 occupied residential houses with more than 7 persons on an average per dwelling while in 1971 it rose up to 766 with less than 6 persons per dwelling. The lower figure of per-dwelling residents has been attributed to the sudden rise in the number of government staff quarters constructed in the southern part of the island while the number of houses belonging to the islanders registered a rise of only two per cent . This has resulted in a complex population structure, registering more pressure on private residential houses while the government houses and quarters have a lower population pressure on them.

Educational Transformation and Rise in Non-Residential Houses

The island had a literacy of 15.95 per cent in 1961, the percentage of male literates being 28.06 in contrast to 3.26 for females. Such a literacy structure speaks of character of the islanders but in 1971, the position changed with 44.37 per cent literates, the male literates rising to 60.40 per cent and females to 24.57 per cent. In a strict Muslim rural settlement such astounding rise in female literacy can easily mean a changed in attitude of the islanders from a rural mentality towards an urban transition, even though the people of the mainland coming here as government servants might have appreciably contributed to such a literacy structure. Rise in educational status has been observed to have influenced the re-arrangement in the lay-out of their dwellings and improvement in their living conditions. While almost all the private dwellings in 1961 were of *kutcha* structure with thatched roofs, the houses in 1971 have made astounding improvement with more than 80 per cent of the houses having been built of *pucca* wall structure and about 40 per cent of them having improved and roofs of either tiles, slates and shingles or C.I. sheets, concrete (R.B.C./R.C.C) and asbestos sheets. At the time of field work it was seen that most of the islanders and renovated their houses and had better shelter environment than in the other islands except Minicoy.

Coming to the non-residential houses including religious shrines and structures, it is observed that back in 1961 there were only 26 such non-residential structures including 7 mosques while the number under the category jumped to 68 in 1978 which included 34 mosques, big and small. The entire island covering only 3.50 km is covered up now with such structures as mosques, barracks, agricultural store, poultry farm, handicraft society, radio station, new college campus structures, textile shop, workshop yard, furniture unit, club and godowns, etc. which would mean a considerable addition and transformation in the cultural landscape of the islands. The island though still recognised as a rural settlement has a number of urban functions peculiar to an administrative headquarters. Though the islandrs, by and large, depend even today on their traditional occupation of coconut farming and fishing supplemented by household industries associated with coconut farming and handicrafts, there has been an appreciable increase in getting employed in both secondary and tertiary activities while there has been surprising fall in employment against household industry.

Transformation in Occupational Structure

Table 19.2 shows a substantial fall in over-all employment structure from 52 per cent i.e. 1485 out of 2828 in 1961 to 24 per cent i.e. 1057 out of 4420 in 1971 while in gainful occupations of secondary and tertiary groups there has been appreciable increase. It is believed that the government subsidy to the islanders for improving their lot and literacy has effected such transformation in occupational structure and consequently it has been well reflected in transformation of the habitat and living conditions as has been observed in the foregoing while considering the transformation nature, layout and building materials of the dwellings of the islanders. It is now a matter of time to observe the already initiated transformation process in the rural habitat of Kavaratti to a substantial transformation leading to an urban transformation of this interesting rural settlement of Lakshadweep.

Conclusion

In the forgoing analysis, the criteria under consideration to assess and understand the effective transformation in rural habitat and

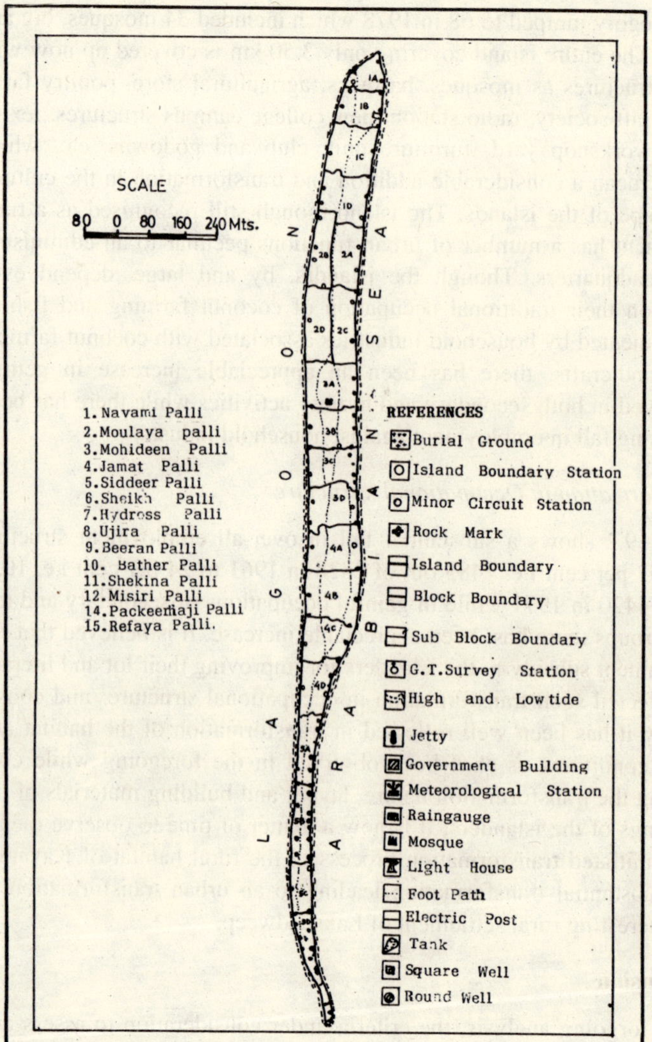

FIG. 19.2: Kadmat Island: Landuse

population structure, sex-ratio and occupation, transformation in layout and construction of living environment, nature, layout and building material of dwellings and above all the astounding rise in non-residential structures and new buildings constructed by the various government departments. It was noticed that the spatio-temporal transformation in rural habitat of Kavaratti is overwhelming and it has been a direct outcome of the rise in educational status and occupational transformation of the islanders.

TABLE 19.2: Change in Occupational Structure in Kavaratti

Year	Total Population	Total Workers	Non-Workers	Livestock fishing etc.	Manufacturing, household industry	Construction	Trade and commerce	Transport	Other services
1961	2828	1485 (52%)	1343	161	1190	45	6	11	72
1971	4420	1057 (24%)	3363	48	150	243	51	52	473

The noticeable transformation in rural landscape towards an urban landscape of the future has been some what sudden mainly due to provision of administrative infrastructure to Kavaratti as it is the headquarters of the Lakshadweep, Minicoy and Amindivi group of islands and the residential-cum-official station of the Administrator of the Union Territory of Lakshadweep. The island has a better shelter environment now that that it had only a decade back and the homogeneous and typical islanders dwellings have been changed over to a complex and heterogeneous bunch of houses striking out a contrast in the old typical shelters of the poor islanders in the north and north-east and *pucca* and semi-*pucca* with improved roofs of the well-off islanders in the central part of the island. The heterogeneity is more pronounced due to the exclusive location of the *pucca* government staff quarters and establishments in the southern part of the island in addition to non-residential houses and structures in the south-central and central locations. The substantial rise in the number of mosques from 7 to 34 in a little over one decade marks the reflection of a better economy of the island though the gap between the economic status of the rich and poor has been conspicuously wide—an indicator of a positive trend towards an urban transformation.

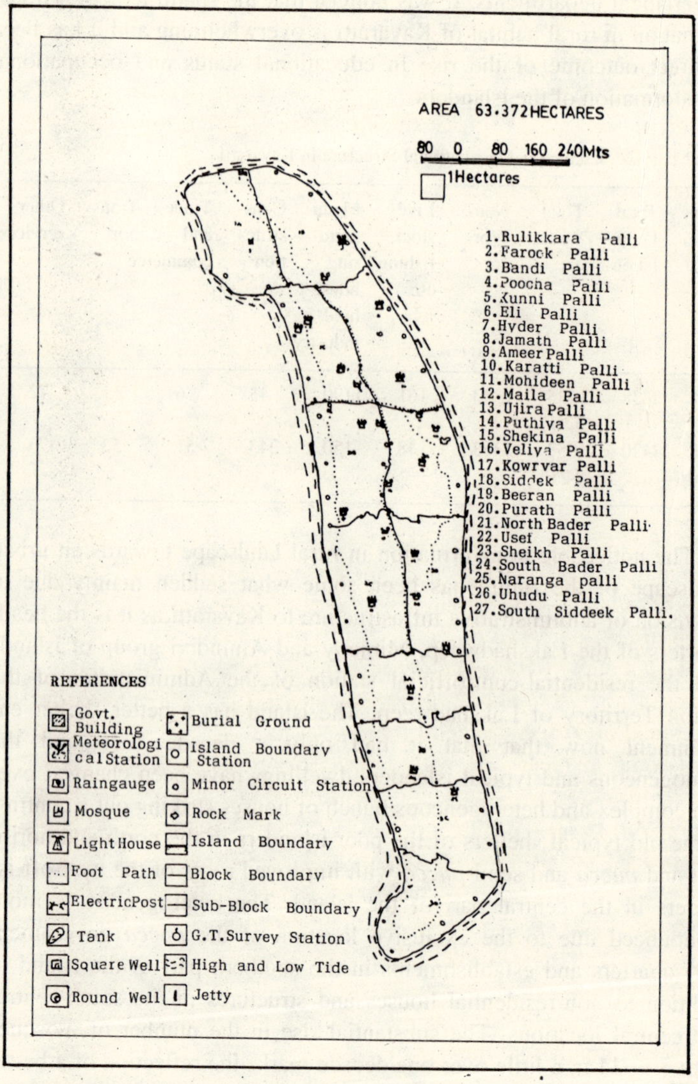

FIG. 19.3: Kiltan Island: Landuse

Transformation of Rural Habitat in Agatti

At the time of Independence, Agatti had only a tiny school functioning in a thatched house. There were also no facilities for medical aid. The Medical Officer, stationed at Kavaratti used to visit this island only once a year. The under employed population depended solely on coconut cultivation which was also not very productive.

In 1956, a dispensary was opened at Agatti which was subsequently raised into a Primary Health Centre. There is now a permanent Medical Officer stationed on this island, a Senior Basic School and a Primary School for girls. Apart from these, two feeder schools have also been opened in 1963. To provide subsidiary employment to the Islanders a Handloom Weaving Centre was organised in 1962. A small scale unit for Turn Canning has also been opened here. Agatti has a fish curing yard where Banito is prepared as is done in the Minicoy Island. In 1963, a wireless station has been opened in this island. A co-operative store has been started with nearly 400 members and a share capital of Rs. 25,000.

Population and Dwellings

Agatti had a population of 2029 with a sex ratio of 898 females per 1000 males in 1951. The population rose to 2411 in 1961 (1267 males and 1144 females getting at a sex ratio of 903 females per 1000 males) which rose to 3,155 (1654 males and 1501 females having a sex ratio of 907 females to 1000 males) by 1971. In 1981, the total population increased to 4,111 with 2,136 males and 1,975 females and the sex ratio stood at 925. In general the rate of increase of female population is quite evident. As regards the density of population it has increased from 752 persons per sq. km in 1951 to 893 persons in 1961 and 1169 in 1971. By 1981 the density of population reached 1523 persons per sq. km. Therefore, during 1951 to 1981 an increase of 771 persons per sq. km. has occurred in the island which works out to about 102.52 per cent increase in the population per sq. km within a span of 30 years against 91.34 per cent increase in respect of Lakshadweep population as a whole. Evidently the population of Agatti island has increased at a much faster rate (11.27% more) than that of the Lakshadweep population during thee last 30 years (1951-1981). This female ratio is certainly not an indicator of rural population structure as it is not natural that the number of Government servants has considerably increased during 1961-81 and many of them have stayed in the island without their family, thus the island registered a low female ratio against males. This is obviously a trend towards more dwellers with tertiary occupation which indicates a changes in urban characteristic in the island during the last decade.

This inference is consequently an indication of transformation in the rural habitat of the island which will be more pronounced when the type and distribution of the residential dwellings and institutional houses in the island is considered both spatially and temporarily. In 1971 there were 470 occupied residential houses with more than 7 persons on an average per dwelling unit. There were 473 number of households in 1971 and thus the average size of household was 6.67 persons in 1971. Thus the percentage of households to number of houses in Agatti island was 100.64 in 1971. In 1981, the number of residential houses, and the number of households which included houseless and institutional households rose to 584 and 628 respectively. The percentage of houses to households stood at 92.99 per cent and the average size of household was 6.55. The above analysis shows that the system of sharing a house by several household is not very popular in the island and the people prefer to live separately in their own houses.

Educational Transformation and Rise in Non-Residential Houses

The island had a literacy rate of 20.24 in 1961 and the percentage of male literates was 33.7 in contrast to 5.33 for females. But in 1971, the literacy percentage increased to 44.17. The percentage of male literates shoot up to 55.86 and the females to 29.18. In 1981, the literacy rate rose too 54.76 per cent with 64.19 per cent for male literacy and 44.56 per cent of female literacy. In a strict Muslim rural settlement such a phenomenal rise in female literacy can easily mean a change in attitude of the islanders from a rural outlook towards an urban transition. This might also have been partly due to the people of the mainland who have come here as government servants as well as for commercial purposes. Rise in educational status has been observed to have influenced the re-arrangement in the layout of their dwellings and improvement in their living conditions.

While almost all the private dwellings in 1961 were of *kutcha* structure with thatched roofs, in 1971 the houses have made astounding improvements with more than 18 per cent of them have tiled roofs, corrugated shouts, zinc sheets, asbestos sheets a some of the rural houses had even concrete R.B.C./R.C.C. roofs. At the time of fieldwork, it was seen that most of the islanders had renovated their houses and had better shelter environment than in the other islands except Minicoy. Coming to the non-residential houses including the religious shrines and structures, it is observed that in 1971 there were only 43 such non-residential structures including 30 mosques. The number under this category rose to 57 in 1978 while the number of mosques of 1971 remained constant.

The entire island having the area of 716 acres is now dotted with structures like mosques, barracks, agricultural store houses canning factory and handicraft society, club, godowns, etc. which presents the cultural landscape of the island. The island though still recognised as rural settlement has a number of urban functions peculiar to industrial activities. The islanders by and large although depend today on their traditional occupation of coconut farming and fishing, they are being supplemented by household industries associated with canning and handicrafts. There has been as appreciable increase in getting employed in both secondary and tertiary activities. There has also been a surprising increase in employment in household industry.

Table 19.3 reveals a substantial fall in overall employment structure i.e. from 53 per cent of the total population in 1961 to 36 per cent in 1971 while in gainful occupations of secondary and tertiary groups there has been appreciable increase. This is the result of government subsidies to the islanders for improving their lot and the improvement in literacy rate which has effected such a transformation in occupational structure. Consequently, this has been well reflected in the transformation of the habit etc. and living conditions as has been observed in the foregoing paragraphs while considering the transformation in nature, layout and building materials of the dwellings of the islanders. It is only a matter of time to observe a substantial transformation, leading to an urban transformation of this interesting rural settlement of the Agatti Island.

Conclusion

The criteria chosen to assess and understand the effective transformation in rural habitat and landscape of this tiny island of the Arabian Sea were the change in population structure, sex ratio, occupation, literacy which had effected transformation in layout construction of living environment, nature use of building materials in dwellings and above all the phenomenal rise in non residential structures and new buildings constructed by the various government departments. It has been observed that the spatio-temporal transformation in rural habitat of 'Agatti is overwhelming and it has been a direct out come of the rise in educational status and occupational transformation of the islanders. The island has a better shelter environment now than that of only a decade back and the homogeneous and typical islanders' dwellings have been changed over to a complex and heterogeneous bunch of houses striking out a contrast between the old typical settlers of the poor and modern well to do families.

The noticeable transformation is rural landscape towards an urban landscape of the future has been somewhat sudden mainly due to the springing up of Government offices and more buildings for secondary activities. The heterogeneity is more pronounced due to the location of the *pucca* government buildings in the island.

TABLE 19.3: **Transformation in Occupational Structure in Agatti**

Year	Total Population	Workers	Non-Workers	Livestock Fishing etc.	Manufacturing Household Industry	Construction
1961	2411	1281	1130	118	1074	3
1971	3155	1164	1990	350	661	22

Year	Trade and Commerce	Transport	Other
1961	13	12	58
1971	27	4	100

Transformation of Rural Habitat in Androth

Androth island, situated at N 10°-49′ and E 73°-41′ is the nearest island in the group to the mainland, and it has the maximum area (being 4.8 sq. km^2) among that of all islands.

On the north side, there is a small boat harbour. Round the harbour are built the big sheds for housing the sailing vessels. As there is no lagoon, fishing is generally poor on this island. A favourite sport is

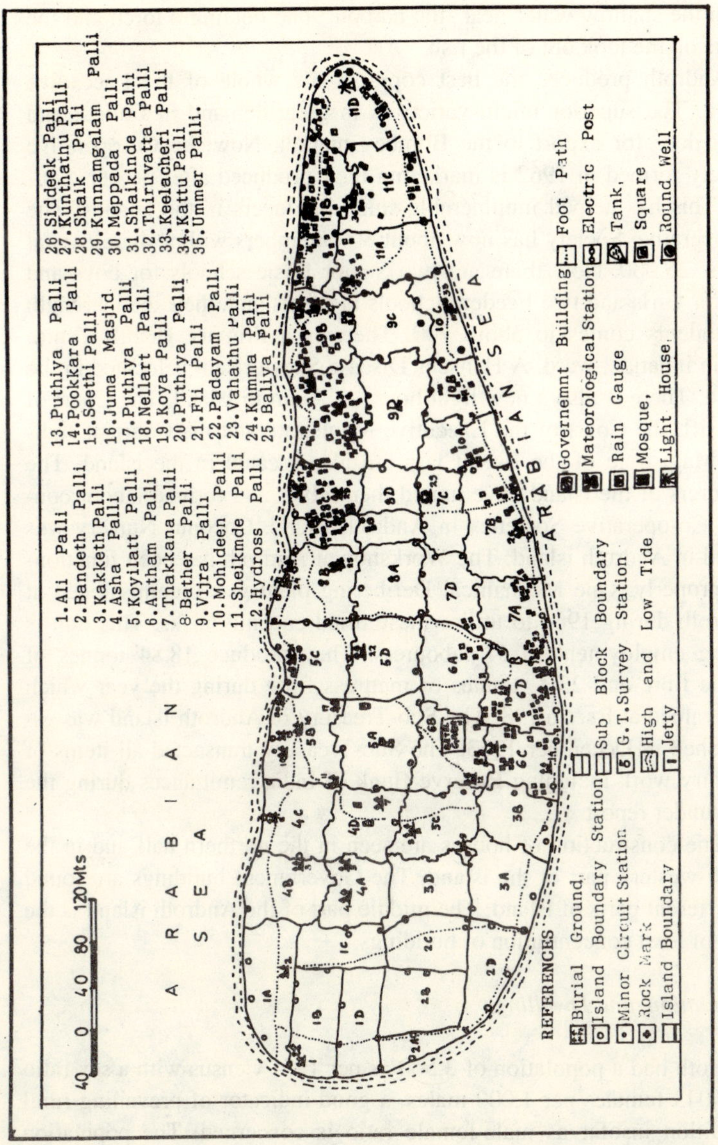

FIG. 19.4: Androth Island: Landuse

catching "Appat" a small species of octopus, which, when roasted is esteemed as a great delicacy. Every moonless night from dark till 9 or 10 p.m. men in groups of two or three are to be seen marching up and down the shallow water near the harbour, one holding a torch and the others on the look out of the fish.

Androth produces the best copra in the whole of the Laccadive Island. The superior micro-variety is in great demand in Calicut and Mangalore for export to the Bombay market. Now the Co-operative Society formed in 1962 is marketing their produced after proper grading. This has helped innumerable small producers in the Islands. The Co-operative Society has now about 800 members with a share capital of Rs. 25,000. Now there are two Senior Basic schools for boys and one for Girls and two Feeden Schools in this island, their total strength of students comes to about 700. There is a Primary Health Centre within inpatient ward. A Hansens Disease Sanatorisem is located in the island. There is also a new light house in Androth Island. The Court of Munsiff, the Court of the Executive Magistrate and the Court of Judicial Magistrate of the First Class are also located in the island. The labourers of the island have united themselves and formed labour contract Co-operative Societies in Androth island. Coconut Nursery was raised in Androth island. The Workshop at Androth has been functioning properly. One Mechanical Defibering plant was commissioned at Androth during 1964 to utilise these dried coconut husks. This unit is giving employment to 37 labourers. They produce 18.84 tonnes of bristle fibre and 23.3 tonnes of mattress fibre during the year which was valued at Rs. 56,198. The Sub-Treasury in Androth Island was established in December 1963. The Sub-Treasury transacted all items of treasury work including Reserve Bank of India remittances during the year under report.

The construction of houses are seen in the northern half and in the south-western part of the island. The Government buildings are found in different parts of island. The middle part of the Androth island is the area of least concentration of buildings.

Population and Dwellings

Androth had a population of 3,500 as per 1951 Census with a sex ratio of 1,043 females per 1,000 males, a good indicator of prevailing rural condition insofar as male-female ratio is concerned. The population has increased to 4,183 in 1961 when sex ratio changed to 1,045 females for 1,000 males. In 1971 the population increase to 5,425 where the sex ratio become 1,003 females per 1,000 males. Then gradually the female ratio has declined from 1043 to 1003 during 1951-71 which deeply indicates towards urbanisation. As regards density of population, it has been observed that while it was 729 persons per sq.km in 1951 it reached 872 in 1961 and 1,131 by 1971. And as per population projection, the density of population in Androth is likely to reach at 1307. These figures compared to the Lakshadweep as a whole are less.*

In 1971, there were 809 residential houses whereas the number of occupied households were 883. The percentage of households to number of houses is 109.15 in Androth Island. The number of institutional population in Androth was 63 having only 19 households. The average per dwelling density was more than four per cent in 1971 in case of 883 dwellings. The figure of residents per dwelling had been attributed to the sudden rise in the number of government staff quarters constructed in the island.

Educational Transformation and Rise in Non-Residential Houses

The island had a literacy ratio of 15.44 per cent in 1961 and the percentage of male literates was 29.33 in contrast to 2.15 for females. In 1971, the position changed as 34.88 per cent were literates. The male literates were 52,025 and females were 18.28 per cent. In a strict Muslim rural settlement such astounding rise in female literacy can easily indicate change in the attitude of the islanders from rural mentality towards as urban transition. Eventhough the people of the mainland who have come here as government servants might have appreciably contributed to such a rise in literacy structures. This has been observed to have influenced the re-arrangement in the lay-out of their dwelling units and improvement in their living conditions. While almost all the private dwellings in 1961 were of *Kutcha* structures with thatched roofs the houses in 1971 have made remarkable improvements with more that 80 per cent of the houses having *pucca* walls and some of them have improved roofs of either tiles, slates and shingles or C.I. sheets, concrete (R.B.C./R.C.C.) and asbestose sheets. At the time of field work it was observed that most of the islanders had renovated

* 1951—803, 1961—920, 1971—1214, 1977—1415.

their houses and had better shelter environment than in the other islands except Minicoy.

It is observed that in 1961 there were very fine non-residential structures including 39 mosques. The number of buildings under this category increased in number in 1978 but number of mosques remained as it was in 1961. The entire island is covered up now with private buildings, mosques, barracks, sanatorium, schools, agricultural demonstration unit, bungalows, workshops, godowns and sheds etc. There are also many agricultural fields and agricultural demonstration units. All theses would mean a considerable addition and transformation in the cultural landscape of the island. The island though still is recognised as a rural settlement has a number of urban functions with residential quarters. Though the island by and large depend even today on their traditional occupation of coconut farming and agricultural activities, they are supplemented by households industries associated with coconut farming and handicrafts. There has been appreciable increases in getting employment in both secondary and tertiary activities. There has been a surprising increase in employment in household industry.

An analysis of Table 19.4 reveals a substantial rise in overall employment structure from 44.8 per cent in 1961 to 99.4 per cent 1971. There has also been an increases in occupations of secondary and tertiary sectors. Consequently there has been appreciable improvement in the economic status of the islanders. Improvement position in literacy has also affected such transformation in occupational structure and consequently, it has been well reflected in transformation of the habitat and living conditions as has been discussed in the foregoing paragraphs while considering the transformation in nature of layout and use of building materials of the dwellings of the islanders. It is now a matter of time to observe the already initiated transformation process in the rural habitat of Kavaratti to substantial transformation leading to an urban transformation of this interesting rural settlement of the Lakshadweep.

Conclusion

In the above analysis, the criteria under consideration to assess and understand the effective transformation in rural habitat and landscape of this tiny island of the Arabian sea were the change in population structure, sex ratio and occupation transformation, layout and use of building materials in dwellings and above all the remarkable rise in the non-residential structures and new buildings constructed by the various government departments. It was noticed that the spatio-temporal transformation in rural habitat of Androth is over-whelming and it has been a direct outcome of the rise in educational status and occupational transformation of the islanders. This change in rural landscape towards and urban landscape of the future has been somewhat sudden mainly due to the provision of the administrative and secondary and tertiary activities in Androth. The island had a better shelter environment now than that it has only a decade back. The homogeneous and typical island dwellings had changed over to a more complex and nitrogenous cluster of houses, striking out a contrast between the old typical shelters of the poor islanders and the modern ones. The heterogeneity is more pronounced due to the exclusive location of the *pucca* government staff quarters and establishments in the island in addition to the non-residential houses and structures in the private sectors. The substantial rise in economic standard has left its imprint in the economy of the island and the gap between the haves and haves not have been conspicuously widened. All these are positive indicators towards and urban transformation.

TABLE 19.4: Transformation in Occupational Structure in Androth

Year	Total Population	Total Worker	Non-worker	Livestock, fishing etc.	Manufacturing household industry	Construction
1961	4183	1876(44.80)	2180	92	1644	6
1971	5425	5397(99.48)	27	2117	1292	389

Trade and Commerce	Transport	Other Services
11	23	100
153	55	1412

Housing

Due to lack of alluvial soil neither bricks nor tiles can be manufactured locally and these are brought from the mainland. For coarse aggregates coral reef shingles is used as other non-calcarious stones are

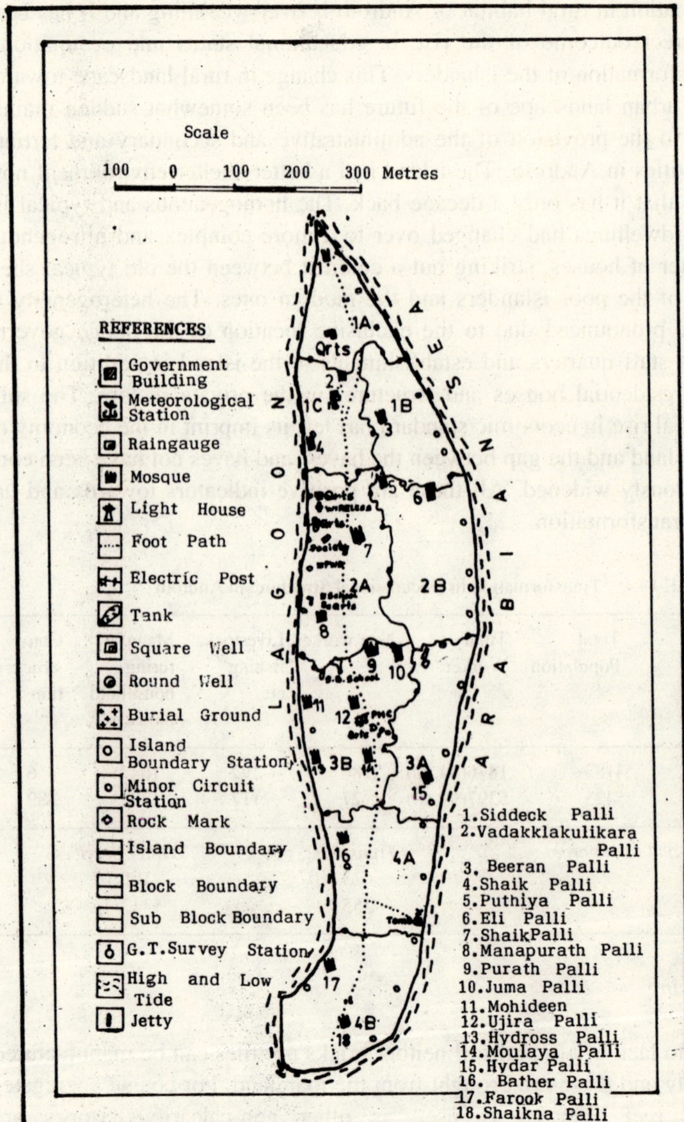

FIG. 19.5: Chetlat Island: Landuse

not available. Some lime is also manufactured from the coral shells. Consequently, coral boulders are used for foundation. The other important local building materials that are available in the island are the coconut tree trunk which is used for timber roofing skeletal system (refter/purlin), joinery and the thatch for temporary roofing which is renewed annually.

The Lakshadweep administration is setting up an institutional arrangement like an Apex Society through which financial institution loans can be raised, like from HUDCO and other agencies, for facilitating house construction activities by the beneficiaries on plots owned by them. Due to high cost of building materials transportation from the mainland, the beneficiaries demand for 3/4th of the financial assistance in kind and the rest in cash for the physical construction of the houses. Keeping in view the financial constraints, the administration at present is operating a village housing scheme up to 30 houses a year taken up as a subsidy scheme with cost upto Rs. 10,000.

Attempts have been made by the Regional Research Laboratory (RRL) as well as the Central Building Research Institute (CBRI) to produce light building materials by utilising the local resources. These include manufacture of sand-lime bricks, setting upon a small size lime kiln, the optimum utilisation of coconut trees improving the quality of coconut thatch roof, fire resistent thatch, corrugated roofing unit using coconut fibre, bricks with partial use of coconut pith and prefabricated panels from coconut palms.

Besides this, setting up of building material outlet centres, in the line of "Nirmithi Kendra" in Tamil Nadu assumes importance. These centres could manufacture and/or distribute low cost less scare building materials like hydrated lime binder, corrugated ACC/Asphaltic corrugated/Red mud plastic roofing sheets, stranut boards etc. The technology which allows less consumption of cement is relevant to the needs of the islanders. Hence, development of Ferro-Cement products would go long way in serving the housing problem of the island.

The Future

To better the existing housing conditions steps have been taken in introducing fire resistant roof, setting up a corrugated roofing unit using coconut fibre, brick with partial use of coconut pith, prefabricated panels from coconut palm have been proposed to be used for housing.

It is also proposed to manufacture bloated aggregates from Steel

Plant/foundry/waste (slag), New Sanitation units using twin soak pit pour flush water scale latrines, solar energy be used for cooking purposes and wind energy be used for electricity generation, which can be used for pumping underground water and also disalining the sea water for drinking purposes.

20

THE FUTURE

The Immediate Future by 1990

The Lakshadweep has planned for a better tomorrow through the effective implementation of its Seventh Plan by 1989-90. The total plan outlay is Rs. 438.3 million under different sectors. It is the social service which has claimed maximum outlay amounting to Rs.123.8 million which is 28.25 per cent of the total plan outlay. It is rightly followed by agriculture which claims the second position, where Rs. 120 million is planned to be invested which is 27.38 per cent of the total layout. Thus these two put together take away the lion's share of the plan outlay i.e. Rs. 243.8 million amounting to 55.63 per cent of the total plan. It is followed by transport where Rs. 92 million or 20.99 per cent of the total plan outlay is proposed to the spent. This is mainly because next to people and agriculture, the transport is the third most important problems of the Lakshadweep islands. Transport problem from the mainland to the island and inter-island transport problems are the most key problems which need to be solved during the Seventh Plan and in future plans, so that by the turn of the century inter-island transport and transport from Kavaratti of the mainland will be a lot more easier than now. In this field coastal water transport and air transport will play a vital role. Construction of all weather jetties and helipads in all the islands are desirable necessities for quick and easy transport of men and material all the year round. Since April 1988 an air-port has been opened to traffic in Agatti Island constructed at a cost of Rs.70 million. Further, Kavaratti, the capital of the Lakshadweep, should be linked by air with Cochin in the Malabar Coast. Since construction of such a runway for conventional planes is not possible due to small size of the islands either planes having vertical take-off and landing facilities or planes requiring short runways or sea planes should be introduced so that transport between the mainland and Lakshadweep will pose no problem. This is in addition to the construction of an all weather medium port at Kavaratti, capable of handling ships of 10,000-12,000 DWT. Draught will pose no problem since all the islands are coral islands. Expenditure on other items during the Seventh Plan are minor since the above three heads of planned expenditure account for 76.62 per cent of the total Seventh Plan outlay.

Energy with 9.12 per cent of the total plan outlay ranks fourth in order of importance followed by rural development (4.24%), industry and minerals (3.47%), irrigation and flood control (2.28%), communication, information and broadcasting (2.01%). It is important that the Lakshadweep should be covered by A.I.R. and Doordarshan network for the quick transmission of news and the views.

TABLE 20.1: Sector-wise Allocation for the Seventh Plan (1985-90)

Sectors	Rs. in million	In % of total
Agriculture	120.0	27.38
Rural Development	18.6	4.24
Special area programme	—	—
Irrigation and Flood Control	10.0	2.28
Energy	40.0	9.12
Industry and Minerals	15.2	3.47
Transport	92.0	20.99
Communication, Information and Broad Casting	8.8	2.01
Science and Technology	2.5	0.57
Social Services	123.8	28.25
Others	7.4	1.69
Total	438.3	100.00

Source: Seventh Five-Year Plan 1985-90 Vol.I Table 3.4(c)

A Detailed Analysis

A detailed analysis of the Seventh Plan allocation reveals many gaps. There has been no allocation of funds in some of the important sectors such as Research and Education; Soil and Water Conservation, Dairy Development; Marketing; Storage and Warehousing and Forestry all of which are under the broad heading of "Agriculture and Allied Programmes" where Rs. 120 million is stated to be spent during 1985-90.

Research as regards agriculture and educating the people on various aspects of agriculture should get priority. Improving soil for agriculture and water conservation are important aspects of the people where no finance has been provided. Attempts should be made to introduce improved breeds of cattle who can survive in the islands saline climate and stall feeding should be the rule rather than exception since saline grass may not be palatable for cattle population. Marketing the products, storage and warehousing are important aspects to better the life of the islanders. Storage includes constructing cold storage in most of the islands to conserve fish and other products. Since no funds has been provided in forestry it is an important drawback. Saline resistant plants like Cashews and Casurina can be planted which will not only solve the problem of fuel of the islanders but also provide an economic base of the islanders. In addition to all these tidal swamps like Mangroves may be planted along the coast.

Since agriculture is not an important item due to alkali soil no funds have been provided for medium and minor irrigation projects. But through lift irrigation by digging deep tubewells fresh water may be tapped which can change the landuse pattern of the islands by planting various types of fruits and vegetable. There is no provision for rural electrification which is also an important drawback. There has also been no provision for large and medium industries. Medium industries like fish canning can be introduced which have an important export potential. Coconut and Coconut products can be manufactured as is done in neighbouring Kerala State in the Malabar Coast. Activities of all India Coir Board can be extended to Lakshadweep Island. These industries will provide much needed economic base of the island people. The required amount of energy can be provided by Wind Mills for which there is a huge scope. Power thus generated can be used for domestic as well as for industrial purposes. Solar Cookers may be used extensively for domestic cooking which will ease the demand on domestic fuel (Table 20.2).

Production of Milk, Eggs and Fish

Lakshadweep Islands has got to be self-sufficient in her milk and egg requirement. She has planned to produce 1.50 thousand tonnes of milk annually by the end of 1989-90 when the Seventh Plan will come to an end. She has also planned to produce 2.5 million eggs annually. The eggs, if produced in a mass scale can find an important market in the mainland where there is a dearth of eggs. The Lakshadweep Islands also plans to produce 9.0 thousand tonnes of fish annually. This is certainly a small catch, compared to the potentialities of the islands. If fishing is done on a commercial scale it will provide as good economic base of the people (Table 20.3).

TABLE 20.2: Seventh Plan Outlay

Sectors of allocation	Rs. in millions
1. *Agriculture and Allied Programme*[a]	—
Research and Education	—
Crop husbandry	36.0
Soil and Water Conservation	—
Animal husbandry	20.0
Dairy development	—
Fisheries	52.0
Investment in Agricultural Financing Institutions	—
Marketing	—
Storage and Warehousing	—
Co-operation	12.0
Forestry	—
Total	120.0
2. Flood Control Programmes[b]	10.0
3. Minor Medium Irrigation Programme[c]	—
4. Minor Irrigation Programmes[d]	—
5. Electrification of Villages[e]	—
6. Power Sector[f]	38.5
7. Large and Medium Industries[g]	—
(a) Mining	0.5
(b) Weights and Measures	0.7
Total	1.2
8. *Health Factors*[h]	
M.N.P.	4.6
Programme other than M.N.P.	5.4
Total	10.0
9. Social Welfare	3.90

[a] Seventh Five Year Plan 1985-90 Vol.II, Govt.of India, Planning Commission Annexure-7.

[b] *Ibid.* Annexure 3.11 p.97

[c] *Ibid.* Annexure -3.5

[d] *Ibid.* Annexure -6.7 p.163

[e] *Ibid.* Annexure -6.9 p.165

[f] *Ibid.* Annexure -7.2 p.200

[g] *Ibid.* Annexure -11.2 p.289

[h] *Ibid.* Annexure-

TABLE 20.3: Targets of Production of Milk, Eggs and Fish (1989-90)

Items	Unit of Production	Production
Milk	'000 tonnes	1.50
Eggs	million	2.50
Fish	'000 tonnes	
(a) Inland	—	—
(b) Marine	-do- .	9.00
(c) Total	-do-	9.00

Source: Seventh Five Year Plan 1985-90, Vol.II, Government of India, Planning Commission Annexure-5.

Education

So far as the educational achievements are concerned by the end of the Sixth Plan in all 7000 students enrolled themselves in the primary school i.e. up to Class V, comprising of 4000 boys and 3000 girls. They constitute of the total children between the age group 1-10 years and in the Middle English School stage the drop out is 50 per cent in case of boy and 66.6 per cent in case of girls as the enrolment was 2000 in case of boys and 1000 in case of girls in VI to VIII class. Thus by 1984-85 the total enrolment of 7000 of primary stage was reduced to only 3000 in Middle English Class stage which was only 42.9 per cent of the Primary enrolment and the dropout percentage is as high as 57.1. During the Seventh Plant his trend should be checked failing which the island will remain educationally backward (Table 20.4).

The Action Plan

An action plan has been drawn up to develop Lakshadweep Islands expeditiously. To implement this, a nucleus cell has been set up and to develop industries in the islands the National Small Industries Corporation will explore the possibilities of providing marketing assistance to the industrial units in the island.[1]

The Ecology of the Lakshadweep

The delicately balanced islands ecology is seriously threatened by the interferences of men. In an area of just 32 sq. km² of a string of 36 islands of varied sizes, 40,249 people lived in 1981 bringing the density per sq.km to 1258 persons. This is quite high by any standard as the average Indian density is only 216 as per 1981 Census. Thus, the population density in the island is 5.8 times higher than that of the Indian average and this is the root cause which is threatening the fragile ecological balance of the islands. Thus the human interferences on the ecology is very intense and significant.

TABLE 20.4: Likely Achievement of Enrolment in 1984-85

Students	Enrolment	(in '000)	Enrolment in Percentage	
	I to V	VI to VIII	I to V	VI to VIII
Boys	4	2	177.0	127.0
Girls	3	1	150.0	94.0
Total	7	3	168.0	111.0

Source: Seventh Five year Plan 1985-90, Vol.I, Planning Commission, Annexure 10.2.

The quarrying of the corals for the private house construction is seriously destroying the coral reef fringing the islands. As a result coastal erosion is eroding the atolls and there is a danger of toilet wastes polluting the high ground-water table which is the only source of water supply of the islands.

Thus the key-note of development should be the development of the island without ruining its ecology. The principal vegetation of the island is coconut and almost every item of food and building material has to come from the Mainland. Electricity is generated at Rs.4.47 per unit by burning diesel and fishing and copra making are the only industries.

Since land is scarce, the grandiose plan for setting up a one Megawatt Ocean Thermal electric conversion plant in Kavaratti in a four hectare area should be abandoned. Instead it is proposed to augment the existing diesel generation from half to one megawatt. A 20 kW aerogenerator imported from Denmark is already under installation.

Bitra, the smallest of the islands, will soon have a photo voltaic system for generating five kilowatts of power from sunlight and the administration is seriously considering solar power for all the islands particularly replacing diesel power. Soon the Vayudoot Planes will land in Agatti Island from where helicopters will transport people and material to different islands.

Pitti Island is to be developed as a bird sanctuary and one or two lagoons will be declared Marine Park to prevent extraction of corals. But the Plan for mining of lime stones from the lagoons for steel and cement industries should not be implemented as it will seriously disturb the marine ecology. The Lagoons of Lakshadweep have an estimated 2000 M. Tonnes of calcarious sand, an industrial raw material sufficient for a mini Cement Plant at Kavaratti. But this when implemented will seriously affect the ecological balance, but this proposed factory will solve the unemployment problems of the islands to a great extent.[2]

Lakshadweep by 2001

There is no doubt that the present pessimistic scenario of the islands would change for better in all fields of activities by A.D. 2001. As per the present trend of population growth, the islands must have been covered almost fully with houses and buildings belonging to Government and public by the end of this century.

While drawing the future of Lakshadweep by A.D. 2001 one should keep in view the cases of failure and success of the islands. There should not be delay in implementation of development programme and there should be proper co-ordination among different implementing agencies, departments and Ministries. Though the people in Lakshadweep have been living for centuries without much scientific and technological inputs, their aspirations for improved quality of life are increasing day by day. Based on the aspirations of the people there may be some desirable and likely changes in the islands in future. The Table 20.5 presents an optimum scenario for certain sectors of Lakshadweep Islands by A.D.2001.

TABLE 20.5: Optimum Scenario for Certain Sectors of Lakshadweep Islands

Sector	1981 (base)	1986	1991	1996	2001
Population	40,249	43,848	47,070	50,064	52,872
Houses	6,320	6,775	7,273	7,780	8,281
Fisheries output (Tonnes/annum)	3,300	4,335	5,668	7,407	9,682
Educated employed	1,200	1,743	2,570	3,622	4,847
Educated unemployed	970	3,292	5,110	6,538	7,655

Source: Summary Report of "Futurology workshop on Identification of S&T Inputs Towards Long range Socio-economic prospective of Lakshadweep Islands, Trivandrum 21-23, July, 1986, Table-1.

Resources

Marine Resources

(a) *Fisheries*

Due to an extensive EEZ area surrounding the Lakshadweep Islands, development of fisheries should be considered an integral part of marine fisheries development of India as a whole. It has been estimated that the potential tuna fish catch in Lakshadweep would be 50,000 tonnes per annum. As against this potential catch the actual catch is only 3,500 tonnes per annum in 1985-86. Bait Fish is an important input in the pole-and-line fishery. But the limitations on the availability of live-baits is hindering the growth of Tuna fishery. Research studies prove that undue exploitation of live and dead corals and dradging of lagoons for navigational purposes contribute to the destruction of live corals which ultimately lead to the decline of bait-fish and consequently Tuna fish. For the development of fishery, conservation of coral ecosystem is urgently called for. Development of new methods of fish catching, processing storage and product diversification is necessary for upliftment of Lakshadweep economy. Conservation of turtles by intensive farming cultivation and harvesting of marine algae and development of live-bait resources for Tuna fishing are some of the suggestions which must be implemented by A.D.2001.

(b) *Ocean Thermal Energy*

Development of Lakshadweep Islands is conditioned by adequate supply of energy. Energy requirement in the islands is at present met by 2,000 kW capacity diesel power generator. This is quite insufficient to meet the present demand and the cost of power generation is very high which is nearly 10 times higher than that of the mainland because of the transportation of diesel from the mainland. In view of this, an alternate system of power generation should be devised depending on the utilisation of ocean resources which covers an area of 7,00,000 sq.km^2 although islands have an area of only 32 sq. kms. Ocean Thermal Energy Conversion (OTEC) is though to be most suitable source of energy for the islands. The OTEC plant of one MW capacity requires Rs.95.35 million towards fixed capital investment. Besides this, exploitation of tide, wave and wind for generation of energy could be made to enhance the supply. Particular emphasis should be given on renewable energy sources like solar energy and wind. Wind mills if set up can supply a large amount of energy to the island.

Island's only source of power generation is diesel generators. Present installed capacity is 2790 kW Power consumption in the islands is increasing steadily from 1785 kW in 1982-83 to 3193 KW in 1984-85. It is envisaged to add another 302 kW generating capacity during Seventh Five Year Plan. Sixty per cent of power is consumed by household sectors mainly for lighting purposes.

Fresh Water Resources

Main source of limited sweet water in the Lakshadweep Islands is the rain water the percolates through porous sand soil to from sweet water lens above of groundwater estimated at Kavaratti if 0.33×10^6 cu.m. The estimated annual rainfall is 5.4×10^6 cu.m. The estimated recharge of fresh water lens per annum is 0.51×10^6 cu.m. The estimated annual requirement of drinking water in Kavaratti during the years 1998 and 2013 A.D. are 0.232×10^6 cu.m. and 0.346×19^6 cu.m. respectively. There are more than 165 Govt. wells and many private wells. The groundwater is available at a depth of 1.5 metre.

Information so far available indicates that groundwater resources alone are inadequate to meet all the demands of water supply. But the groundwater that is available in most of the times in not suitable for human consumption. The close proximity of sea water introduce saline water into fresh groundwater even without overdrafts. The sewage disposal by means of septic tank and numerous burial grounds scattered all over islands cause pollution to the sweet water. Even community wells are also unhygienically maintained. However, in Bitra the requirements of sweet water are met by a solar desalination plant. A plan for tapping groundwater in Kavaratti by under ground tank supplemented by feeder tanks is undertaken to meet the need for adequate supply of water in the islands. Installation of plants for disalination of sea water by reverse Osmosis techniques and/or electrodialysis technique to ensure adequate water supply to the island be attempted.

Agriculture

The land utilisation pattern of the Lakshadweep Islands shows that only 47 hectares of land is available for growing crops. The ecology and soil fertility of the islands are generally hostile to intensive agriculture. But the demand for food is ever growing with the growth of population which is about 2.65 per cent per annum. With this growth rate, it is estimated that the population would reach 68,000 by 2000 A.D. would be as shown in Table 20.6.

TABLE 20.6: Estimated Demand for Food Items for the Population of Lakshadweep Islands in 2,000 A.D.

Food item	Per capita requirement	Total Requirement
Rice	125 kg.	8500 tonnes
Pulses	18.5 kg.	1250 tonnes
Meat	20 kg.	1360 tonnes
Egg	100 nos.	6.8 million nos.
Milk	18.25 kg.	1240 tonnes
Vegetables	90 kg.	6000 tonnes
Fruits	75 kg.	5000 tonnes

Source: Ibid., Table 20.3

Hence, efforts should be made towards effective and efficient utilisation of land.

Although rice constitutes staple food of the islanders, coconut is the most important crop of the islands. Coconut plantation covers an area of 2,780 hectares. The principal source of agricultural economy of Lakshadweep islands is based on sale of copra and coir products to the mainland. It helps them to obtain necessary articles including rice from the mainland. It is suggested that tuber crops like tapioca be intercropped in coconut gardens, high yielding varieties of coconut which require less water be introduced. The landuse is proposed as per Table 20.7.

Establishment of coconut processing units to produce quality fibres, coir ropes, coconut oil, derivated coconut powder partially difatted coconut gratings, coconut cream and bottling of coconut water for soft drink purposes be attempted.

Industry and Environment

According to the Government of India's declaration, Lakshadweep is a no industry island. There is no medium and large scale industry in the islands. About 35 small industries are engaged in saw milling, bakeries, soda making, fibre retting and extraction, flour mills, book binding etc. Causes attributed for such a situation are lack of infrastructure like land, transport, power and market, lack of technical knowledge and skilled manpower, high cost of power generation and lack of entrepreneurship of the people.

TABLE 20.7: Proposed Landuse by 2000 A.D. in Cultivable Land

Crops	Area	
	In hectares	In % of total cultivable land
(a) Fruit crops (Banana, Popaya Bread fruit)	120	4.61
(b) Vegetables: (Tomato, Potato egg Plant,beans and chillies)	104	4.00
(c) Oil seeds (castor)	25	0.96
Total cultivable land	2600	100.00

It is observed by experts that there is 2000 million tonnes of calcarious sand reserves of which 712 m. tonnes of phosphate reserve in the island. These can be exploited for industrializing and developing the economy of the islands.

Coconut cultivation followed by fishing are the main economic activity of the people in the islands. Coconut cultivation which comprises of 6,00,000 coconut trees occupies 85 per cent of land of the islands. Coconut trees yield 23.6 million nuts per annum. Coir production is declining over the years due to coir monopoly scheme leading to non-remunerative prices earned by the coir producers. Coir procurement which stood at 1210 quintals in 1971-72 come down to only 160 quintals in 1984-85. Like-wise the exploitation of marine wealth is about 0.1 million tonnes of which only 6 per cent have been exploited.

Establishment of mechanised units for fibre extraction and manufacture of coir yarn, ropes, mats and mattings and development of communication, transport and power generation systems to widen the market scope for industrial products will go a long way to industrialise the islands.

Education

Development of education in Lakshadweep islands is of a recent origin and can be traced back only to 1960-61 when a High School was established in Amini. Progress of education in terms of schools, pupils and teachers as on June 1986 is shown in Table 20.8.

TABLE 20.8: Status of Education in the Lakshadweep as on June 1986

	Number of schools
Primary Schools	20
J.B. Schools	18
S.B. Schools	4
High Schools	9
Junior Colleges	2
Pupils	12,696
Teachers	640
Teacher-Pupil Ratio	1:20

Source: *Ibid*, Table-4.

Arrangements are made for higher studies of students from the islands in the colleges and professional institutions of mainland. A sum of Rs. 23.370 million was spent on education in the islands during Sixth Plan. The Seventh Plan outlay for education stands at Rs. 40.5 million. Twenty Centres for National Adult Education Programme have been established to cover the entire illiterate population in the age groups of 15-35 by 1990. Decade-wise percentage of literacy achieved in the islands is shown in the Table 20.9.

TABLE 20.9: Decade-wise Achievement of Literacy in the Lakshadweep Islands

Year	Percentage of Literacy achieve
1951	15.50
1961	23.57
1971	43.66
1981	55.04
2005	By neutral forecast, should exceed 80

Source: *Ibid*, Table -5.

Health

After the formation of Union Territory, the health care came under the perview of Lakshadweep Administrator. In April 1972, the Director of Medical Health Service tookover the charge of health care. Many diseases like cholera, small pox, leprosy, tuberculosis, malaria and filariasis which were very much common in the early days are now controlled to a large extent and considerable advancement have been made in the health service facility in the recent years.

At present there are 2 hospitals, 7 Primary Health Centres and one First-aid centre. At Kavaratti there is a 50-bed referral hospital with facilities for dental, maternal and paediatric care. Minicoy has a 920-bed hospital. There are two Ayurvedic Dispensaries, one at Kavaratti and another at Androth. One Homeopathic Dispensary was started in Amini during April, 1986. A Health Education Bureau was started in Kavaratti in 1983 and one Centre in each island was established in 1984-85. Medical stores from Cochin supply medicines to the island hospitals.

Buildings

With the increase in Government offices and increase in population, there has been a steep rise in building activities in Lakshadweep Islands recently. But the great hurdles faced in this regard are land which is very much scare and the building materials which are obtained at a very high cost from the mainland. However, Lakshadweep Administration alone built residential houses covering plinth area of 50,000 sq.m. and non-residential buildings covering plinth area of 105,000 sq.m. It has completed construction of 1,085 quarters during Sixth Five Year Plan period though the requirement is for 3,102 quarters. It is envisaged to construct 2,700 additional quarters of different categories during Seventh Five Year Plan period.

In view of the limitations referred to earlier, there is a great need for development of newer materials and newer designs. Design of double storey buildings with high strength and light structure materials would be more suitable for the coral islands. Till now about 0.55 million cu.m. of singles, 0.3 million cu.m. of sand has already been quarried for construction purposes. It is found that any further quarrying will disturb adversely the island ecology. Attempts should be made to use prefabricated panels made out coconut leaves, roofing structure made out of trunks of coconut and palm trees, cement bonded coconut fibre boards, hallow clay block etc. be made. Awareness towards the need for adopting newer design systems of houses be created by educating the people in this regard.

Transport and Tourism

Lakshadweep Islands is suitable for promotion of both domestic and international tourism. Kavaratti is the main disposal centre for the tourists. Bangaram, an uninhabited island is good for beach resort. Foreign tourists are permitted to visit Bangaram provided they get permits from the Ministry of Home Affairs. The liaison offices of Union Territory at New Delhi and Cochin also issue permits to the foreign tourists. Table 20.10 shows the current inflow of turists to the islands and projected inflow by A.D. 2001.

TABLE 20.10: Tourist Inflow to Lakshadweep Islands

Year	Domestic	Foreign	Total
1982-83	490	470	960
1983-84	930	160	1090
1984-85	1200	41	1241
2000-01	*5000	10,000	15,000

* Estimated on the assumption that requisite infrastructure including airport is developed.

Source: Ibid, Table 20.7.

The infrastructural facility available in the island puts a bottleneck for the development of tourism. There is only 153 km. of road available in the islands of which 37 kms. are surfaced. Most of these roads are only cycle tracts and whatever little road is available for vehicular traffic are having 3 metres width without shoulder. Inter-island transportation is only through uses of *Odams*, speed boats and ships. Passenger traffic between mainland and islands and *vice versa* is increasing year after year. Table 20.11 shows the current growth of passenger traffic into and out of the islands.

All essential commodities needed for survival are obtained from the mainland. It was recorded that 7636 tonnes of goods traffic moves to the islands from the mainland and during 1985 of which 65 per cent was rice alone. It is expected that the cargo movement from mainland to island is likely to increase to 15,516 tonnes by A.D. 2005.

TABLE 20.11: Volume of Passenger Traffic into and out of Lakshadweep Islands

Year	Mainland to Islands (person trips)	Inter Islands (person trips)	Islands to Mainland (person trips)	Total (person trips)
1982-83	12,244	13,341	13,057	38,642
1983-84	15,541	15,690	17,674	48,905
1984-85	16,011	15,372	17,808	49,191
2005 A.D.	30,000	29,000	—	59,000

Source: Ibid. Table 20.8.

Thus, in view of the increasing trends in tourists, passenger traffic and cargo movement it is essential that there should be development of roads tourist huts and Dak-Bunglows in the islands. Besides the air port which has recently been opened in Agatti the member of ships should be increases to facilities inter and intra movement of passengers and cargo traffic.

NOTES

1. *Statesman*, Calcutta, edition 23rd May, 1986.
2. *Statesman*, Calcutta, edition of 8th November, 1986.

BIBLIOGRAPHY

Bavappa, K.V.A. and Biddappa, C.C., "Agricultural Production Strategy for Lakshadweep upto 2000 A.D."

CBRI, "Immediate and long-term S & T Inputs: Building."

Jacob, T.V., "Note on water Resources in Lakshadweep".

James, P.S.B.R. and Jacob, T., "Scope for marine fisheries research in Lakshadweep".

Lakshadweep Administration, "Building."

Lakshadweep Administration, "Water".

Lakshadweep Administration, "Industry".

Lakshadweep Administration, " Education".

Muthuswamy, S., "Lakshadweep Future Transport".

Narayanan, C.S., "Product Diversification Strategy for Coconut".

Prabhu, G.N., "Coir Industry in Lakshadweep".

Ragavendran, P., "Computer modelling studies of Lakshadweep Futures".

Ranoti, M.V., Balusu, K.R. and Rao, C.S.G., "Water Resources and Quality of Lakshadweep".

Ravindran, M., "Ocean Thermal Energy for Lakshadweep".

Sagar, J., "The Future of Lakshadweep.

Sastry, P., "Lakshadweep -A Tourist Paradise by 2000 A.D.".

Sen Gupta, R., Anand, N.M., Nailk, C.G., Chauhan, Y.S., "Study of Oceanography in Lakshadweep".

Suresh, V., "Building needs in Lakshadweep".

Udayavarma, P., Panicker P., Sivadas, P. and Krishnankutty, M., "Role of marine sector in the long-term development of the Lakshadweep Islands".

All the following papers were presented in the "Futurology Workshop on Identification of S & T Inputs towards Long-Range Socio-Economic Perspective of Lakshadweep Island" held during 21-23 July, 1986 at Trivandrum.

Alcock, A, 1894, An Account of a recent collection of bathybial fishes from the Bay of Bengal and from the Laccadive Sea, *J. Asiat, Soc. Beng.*, 63,115-137.

Ali, D.M. 1983, "Fish Catching Methods in Minicoy Island, MSc. Thesis, C.I.F.E. Bombay (Unpub.).

Anon, 1979, " A Report of Survey of Marine algal resources of Lakshadweep-1977-79. Cent. Salt & Mar. Ch.Res. Instt. 48 p.

Anon, 1984, " The Coral Paradise. Planning Secretariat, Kavaratti, Govt. Press, Kavaratti: 51 p.

Ansari, Z.A., 1980 "Benthic micro- and macro-fauna of seagrass (*Thalassia hemprichii*) bed at Minicoy. Lakshadweep. *Indian J. Mar. Sci.* 13 (3): 126-127.

Appukuttan, K.K., P.N. Radhakrishnan Nair and K.K. Kunhikoya 1977. Studies on the fishery and growth rate of oceanic skipjack Katsuwonus pelamis (Linnaeus) at Minicoy Island from 1966-1969. *Indian J. Fish.* 24 (1&2): 33-47.

Ayyangar, S.R. 1922, Notes on the fauna and fishing Industries of the Laccadives, *Madras Fish, Bull.* 15:45-69.

Balan, V. 1958, Notes on a visit to certain islands of the Laccadive Archipelago, with special reference to fisheries. *J. Bombay Nat. Hist. Soc.* 55(2): 297-306.

Bell, F.J. 1903, The actinogonidiate echinoderms of the Maldive and Laccadive islands. In: J.S. Gardiner (Ed.) *The Fauna and Geography of the Maldive and Laccadive Archipelagoes,* 1:223-233, Cambridge University, Press Cambridge.

Betts, F.N. 1938, The Birds of the Laccadive Islands. *J. Bombay Nat. Hist. Soc.* 40 (3), 382-387.

Bhattathiri, P.M. and V.P. Devassy, 1979, Biological characteristics of the Laccadive Sea, In: *The Laccadive Sea (Lakshadweep)* NIO, Technical Reports: 182 p.

Borradaile, L.A. 1903, A Marine crustaceans.II. Portunidae in J.S. Gardiner, (ed) *The Fauna and Geography of the Maldive and Laccadive Archipelagoes,* 1:199-208, Cambridge Univ. Press, Cambridge.

Burton, R.W. 1940. A visit to the Laccadive Islands. *J. Bombay Nat. Hist. Soc.* 41(3) : 489-513.

Census of India, 1961—L.M. & A Islands Vol. XXI.

Census of India, 1971—Establishment Reports and Tables and Housing Report and Tables, Part III & IV, Series, 29

Census of India, 1971—L.M. & A Islands Economic Tables, Part-IIB, Series-29.

Census of India, 1981—Lakshadweep, Series, 30.

Chandran, E.T. 1980. Handling and Processing of Sharks in India (Lakshadweep), M.Sc. Thesis, C.I.F.E. Bombay, 100 pp. (Unpub.).

Chapman, F.C. 1895. One some Foraminifera obtained by the Royal Indian Marine Survey's S.S. Investigator from the Arabian Sea near the Laccadive Islands. *Proc. Zool. Soc. London:* 4-55.

Cooper, C.F. 1903. Cephalochorde.I. Systematic and anatomical account. In: J.S. Gardiner (Ed.), *The Fauna and Geography of the Maldive and Laccadive Archipelagoes,* 1:347-360, Cambridge Univ. Press, Cambridge.

Coutiere, H., 1903. Note Surquelques Alpheidaedes Maldives et Laquedives. *Bulletin de la Societe Philomathique de Paris,* 9(5); 72-90.

Coutiere, H., 1905. Sur les Alpheidae de Laquedives et des Maldives. Competes Rendus hedomadarie: des Seances de I, *Academic des Science*, 140; 736-738.

Coutiere, H., 1960, Les Alpheidae, In: J.S. Gardiner (ed.), The *Fauna and Geography of the Maldive and Laccadive Archipelagoes,* 2; 852-921, Cambridge Univ., Press, Cambridge.

Davies, P.S., Stoddart, D.R., and Sigee, D.C. In regional variation in Indian Ocean Coral reefs. Symposia of the Zoological Society of London, No. 28, Edited by Stoddest, D.R. and Yonge, M (Academic Press) 1971-217.

Elliot, C. 1960, Nudibranchiata, with some remarks on the families and genera and description of a new genus, Doridomorpha, In: J. S. Gardiner (Ed.), *The Fauna and Geography of the Maldive and Laccadive Archipelagoes,* 2: 540-573 Cambridge Univ. Press, Cambridge.

Ellis, R.H. 1924, A Short Account of the Laccadive Islands and Minicoy Govt. Press. Madras; IV + 122 p.

Ellish, R.H. "A Short Account of the Laccadive Islands and Minicoy, 1924".

Gardiner J.S. 1900, The Atoll of Minicoy *Proc. Camb. Phil. Soc. Biol. Sci.*, 11(1) : 22-26.

Gardiner J.S. 1930, The Fauna and Geography of the Maldive and Laccadive Archipelagoes, Vol.I, (Cambridge Univ., Press),471 p.

Gardiner, J.S. 1903(a), Introduction. In: J.S. Gardiner (ed.). The *Fauna and Geõgraphy of the Maldive and Laccadive Archipelagoes* 1: 1-11, Cambridge Univ. Press, Cambridge.

Gardiner, J.S. 1903(b), the Maldive and Laccadive groups with notes on other coral formations in the Indian Ocean. *Ibid*: 12-50, 146-183, 313-346, 376-423.

Gazetteer of India — Lakshadweep, 1977.

George, K.C., P.A Thomas, K.K. Appukuttan and G. Gopakumar 1986. Ancillary living marine resources of Lakshadweep. *Mar. Fish. Infor. Serv. T & E. Ser.,* 68: 45-50.

Glennie, A.A. 1936, A Report on the values of gravity in the Maldive and Laccadive Island. *Scient. Rep. John Murrary Exped.* 1:95-106.

Goswamy, S.C. 1973. Observations on some Planktonic groups of Kavaratti Atoll (Laccadives). *Indian Nat. Sci. Acad.* 391 (6) : 676-686.

Goswamy, S.C. 1983. Production and Zooplankton community structure in the lagoon and surrounding sea at Kavaratti Atoll (Lakshadweep) *Indian J. Mar Sci.*, 12:31-34.

Govt. of India, "Union Territory of Lakshadweep, 1976".

Haneefakoya, C.L. 1982. Ray fishing of the Kalpeni Island of the Lakshadweep group of islands. M.Sc. Thesis, C.I.F.E., Bombay. (Unpub.).

Hornell, J., 1910, Report on the results of the fishery cruise along the Malabar Coast and the Laccadive Islands in 1908. *Madras Fish Bull* 4:71-126.

Hoyle, W.E. 1906. The Cephalopoda. In: J.S. Gardiner (ed) *The Fauna and Geography of the Maldive and Laccadive Archipelagoes,* 2:975-988, Cambridge Univ. Press, Cambridge.

Jagtap, T.G. and A.G. Untawale 1984. Chemical composition of marine macrophytes and their surrounding water and sediment from Minicoy, Lakshadweep. *Indian J. Mar. Sci* 13(3): 123-125.

James, P.S.B.R. and Jacob, T. "Scope for Marine fisheries research in Lakshadweep".

James, P.S.B.R., C.S. Gopinadha Pillai, P.O. Pillai, P. Linvingston and Madan Mohan 1986. Marine Fisheries Research in Lakshadweep—A historical resume. *Mar. Fish. Inform. Serv. T & E Ser.* 68:7-9.

James, P.S.B.R.,T. Jacob, C.S. Gopinadha Pillai and P.P. Pillai 1986. Prospects of development of marine fisheries resources in Lakshadweep. *Mar. Fish. Inform. Serv. T & E Ser.*, 68:51-54.

Jayaraman, R., C.P. Ramamirtham and K.V. Sundararaman 1959. The vertical distribution of dissolved oxygen in the deeper waters of the Arabian Sea in the neighbourhood of the Laccadives during the summer, 1959, *J. Mar. Biol. Ass. India,* 2 (1): 24-34.

Jayaraman, R., C.P. Ramamirtham, K.V. Sundaraman and Aravindakshan Nair, 1960. Hydrography of the Laccadive off shore waters. *Ibid.* 2(1): 24-35.

Jones, S. 1914a. A Preliminary Survey of the common tuna bait fishes of Minicoy and their distribution in the Laccadive Archipelago. *Proc. Symp. Scomb. fishes, Mar. Biol. Ass. India, Mandapam Camp.* 2:643-680.

Jones, S. 1958b. Tuna live bait fishery of Minicoy Island Ibid;, 5(2): 300-307.

Jones, S. 1961b. Spratelloides delicatulus (Bennett) as a potential live biat for tuna in the Laccadives, *J. Mar. Biol. Ass. India* 2(1); 103-104.

Jones, S. 1964b. On the introduction of *Tilapia mossambica* (Peters) as a tuna live bait in the island of Minicoy in the Indian ocean, *Ibid:* 691-692.

Jones, S. 1961c. On the snake mackerel, Gempylus serpens Cuvier from the Laccadive Sea. *Ibid,* 2(1) 85-88.

Jones, S. 1959d. On a juvenile sailfish Istiophorus gladius (Broussonet) from the Laccadive Sea, *Ibid.*, 1:225.

Jones, S. 1966. Lakshadweep General features and some considerations. *Mar.Fish. Infor. Serv. T & E. Ser.* 68: 3-6.

Jones, S. 1968. The fishery resources of the Laccadive Archipelago. Proc. Symp. Living resources of the seas around India. *Cent. Mar. Fish. Res. Inst.*, Cochin, Abstracts; 10(1968).

Jones, S. 1969. Catalogue of fishes from the Laccadive Archipelago in the reference collections of the the CMFR Institute, *Bull. Cent. Mar. Fish. Res. Inst.* 8:1-32.

Jones, S. and M,. Kumaran, 1971. Biogeography of the ichthyofauna of the Laccadive Archipelago. Symp. Indian Ocean and adjacent seas. *Mar. Biol. Ass. India.* Cochin, Abstracts:128

Jones, S. and M. Kumaran and M. Ali Manikfan, 1970. The ichthyofauna of the intertidal zone in the atolls of the Laccadive Archipelago. *Symp. Marine Intertidal Ecoloyg Andhra University,* Waltair, Abstracts : 7.

Jones, S. and M. Kumaran, 1959. The fishing industry of Minicoy Island with special reference to the fishery. *Indian J. Fish.,* 6(1); 30-54.

Jones, S. and M. Kumaran, 1980. Fishes of the Laccadive Archipelago, Nature Conservation and Aquatic Sciences Service, Trivandrum: 760 p.

Jones, S., E.G. Silas and M. Kumaran, 1969. The resident ichthyofauna of the atolls and reefs of the Laccadive Archipelago. Symp. Corals and coral reefs. *Mar. Biol. Asst. India.* Mandapam Camp, Abstracts: 26(1969).

Koya, K.P.S. 1984. Crafts and Gears of Androth, Lakshadweep, M.Sc. Thesis C.I.F.E., Bombay, (Unpub.).

Kumaran, M. and G. Gopakumar 1986. Potential resources of fishes other than tuna in Lakshadweep. *Mar. Fish Infor. Serv.T & E. Ser.,* 68: 41-45.

Laidlaw, F.F. 1903. The marine Turbellaria, with an account of the anatomy of some of the species. In: J.S. Gardiner (ed.). *The Fauna and Geography of the Maldive and Laccadive Archipelagoes,* 1: 282-312, Cambridge Univ. Press, Cambridge.

Lakhar, S.K. "A Portrait of Population L.M. & A. Islands", Census of India, 1971.

Lakshadweep Admn. "Lakshadweep at a (Statistical Wing) Glance-1975-76".

Lakshadweep Admn. (Planning Dept.) "Lakshadweep at a Glance, 1977-78".

Lakshadweep Admn. (Planning Dept.) "Kavaratti at a Glance, 1978".

Madan Mohan 1986. Observations on the tuna schools associated with flotsam in the offshore waters of Minicoy Island during 1932-83 season. *Bull. Cent. Mar. Fish Res. Inst.* 36:196-200.

Madan Mohan and K.K. Kunhikoya. 1986a. Length-weight relationship of skipjack Katsuwonus pelamis and yellowfin tuna Thunnus albacares from Minicoy waters. *Ibid.,* 143-148.

Madan Mohan and K.K. Kunhikoya. 1986b. Spawning biology of skipjack tuna, *Katsuwonus pelamis* (Linn.) from Minicoy waters *Ibid.* 149-154.

Madan Mohan and K.K. Kunhikoya. 1986c. Biology of the bait fishes, *Spratelloides delicatulus* (Bennett) and *S. Japonicus* (Houttuyn) from Minicoy waters, *Ibid.,* 164-172.

Madan Mohan, C.S. Gopinadha Pillai and K.K. Kunhikoya. The biology of the blue-puller Chromis caeruleus (Pomacentridae; pisces) from Minicoy Atoll. *Indian J. Fish.*

Madhupratap, M., M.V.M. Wafar, P. Haridas, B. Narayanan, P. Gopala Menon and P. Sivadas, 1977. Comparative studies in the abundance of zooplankton in the surrounding sea and lagoons in the Lakshadweep. *Indian J. Mar. Sci.* 6:138-141.

Mallik, T.K. 1976. Grain size variation in the Kavaratti lagoon sediments, Lakshadweep, *Arabian Sea Mar. Geology,* 20(1): 57-75.

Mamman, T.A. 1963. On a collection of hydroids from south India, including Andamans, Laccadives and Maldives. *J. Mar. Biol. Ass. India.* 5(1): 27-61.

Mannadiar, N.S. (ed.) 1977. *Lakshadweep Gazetteer of India,* Administration of Union Territory of Lakshadweep, Kavaratti, 375 p.

Mannadiar, N.S. 1973. Laccadive and Aminidive Islands-27 years in retrospect.

Mascarenhas, A., H.N. Siddiquie, and R.S. Togpi 1989. Distribution of strontium in sediments of the Minicoy Atoll, Lakshadweep. *Indian J. Mar. Sci.,* 9(4): 281-282.

Matthew, K.J. 1969. Report on the R.V. Varuna Cruise No. 134 of the Laccadives. CMFRI, Research Cruise Rept. No. 1:18-28.

Matthew, M.J. and T.B. Ramachandran, 1956. Notes on a survey of the fishing industry of Laccadive and Amindivi Islands. *Fisheries Station Reports and Year Book 1954-55.* Govt. Press, Madras: 12-137.

Mc. Eachern J. & Towle, F.L., 1974. Ecological Guidelines for Island Development. ICUN Publications New Series, No. 30.

Meiyappan, M.M. and M. Kathirvel 1987. On some new records of crabs and lobsters from Minicoy, Lakshadweep (Laccadives) *J. Mar. Biol. India,* 20 (1&2): 116-119.

Mukhopadhyay, S.K. and Samanta, T.K. 1933. On a collection of shallow water holothurians from Lakshadweep. *Rec. Zool. Surv. India.,* 81:299-314.

Mukundan, T.K. "Lakshadweep—A hundred thousand Islands", The Academic Press, 1979.

Murty, A.V.S., C.S. Gopinadha Pillai, G. Subbaraju and V. Josanto. 1980. On the Occurrence of *Acanthaster Planci* (the Crown of Thorns) at Minicoy Atoll. *Mar. Fish. Infor. Serv.,* T & E. Ser. 13: 10-13.

Muthukoya, M.C. 1978. Problems and prospects of fisheries development in Lakshadweep. M.Sc. Thesis, C.I.F.E. Bombay, 82 pp (Unpub.).

Nagabhushanam, A.K. and G.C. Rao 1972. An ecological survey of the marine fauna of the Minicoy Atoll (Laccadive Archipelago,) *Arabian sea. Mitt. Zool, Mus, Berl.* 48(2): 265-324.

Nair, K.S. 1986. Fisheries development in Lakshadweep. *Fishing Chimes,* 6(2): 20-25.

Nair, N. Balakrishnan and K. Dharmaraj 1983. Marine wood boring Molluscs of the Lakshadweep Arichpelago. *Indian J, Mar. Sci.,* 12(2) 96-99.

Nair, P.V.R., A.V.S. Murty, C.P. Ramamirtham, D.S.Rao and V.K. Pillai. 1986. Environmental features in the sea around Lakshadweep. *Mar. Fish. Inform. Serv. T & E. Ser. 68:* 10-13.

Nair, P.V.R., G. Subbaraju, K.J. Mathew, V.K. Pillai and V.K. Balachandran 1986. Productivity of the seas around Lakshadweep. *India.* 68:13-15.

Nair, V.R., and T.S. Rao 1973. Chaetognaths from the Laccadives with the new record of *Spadella angulata* (Tokioka,1951) In: *The Biology of Indian Ocean,* Bernt Zeitschel (ed.) 319-327. Springer-Verlag, New York.

Namboodiri, P.N. and P. Sivadas 1979. Zonation of molluscan assembllage at Kavaratti Atoll (Laccadives). *Mahasagar,* 12(4): 239-246.

Panicker, K.C. 1987. Marine gastropod shells of Lakshadweep. M. Sc. Thesis C.I.F.E. Bombay (Unpub.).

Patil, M.R. and C.P. Ramamirtham 1963. Hydrography of Laccadive offshore waters. A study of the winter conditions. *J. Mar. Biol. Ass. India.* 5(2): 159-169.

Pillai, C.S. Gopinadha 1971a. Distribution of shallow-waterstony corals at Minicoy Atoll in the Indian Ocean. *Atoll Rs. Bull. Wash.* 141: 1-12.

Pillai, C.S. Gopinadha, 1971b. Composition of the coral fauna of the southeastern coast of India and the Laccadives. In: *Regional Variation in Indian Ocean Coral Reefs.* C.M. Yonge and D.R. Stoddart (eds.), *Symp. Zool. Soc. Lond.* 28:301-327. Academic Press.

Pillai, C.S. Gopinadha 1983. The endangered marine and terrestrial habitats of Minicoy Atoll in Lakshadweep. Proc. Seminar, World Conservation Developing Countries, Bombay Nat. Hist. Soc. (In press).

Pillai, C.S. Gopinadha 1986. Status of coral reefs in Lakshadweep. *Mar. Fish. Infor. Serv. T&E. Ser.* 68: 34-41.

Pillai, C.S. Gopinadha and Madan Mohan 1986a. Ecological Stress in Minicoy lagoon and its impact on tuna baits. *Mar. Fish. Infor. Serv. T&E Ser.* 68:33-37.

Pillai, C.S. Gopinadha, Madan Mohan and K.K. Kunhikoya 1984a. Observation on the lobsters of Minicoy Atoll. *Indian J. Fish.* 30(2): 112-122.

Pillai, C.S. Gopinadha, Madan Mohan and K.K. Kunhikoya 1984b. On an unusual massive recruitment of the reef fish *Ctenochaetus strigosus* (Bennett) (Perciformis) Acanthuridae to the Minicoy Atoll and its significance. *Ibid.* 261-268.

Pillai, P.P., M. Kumaran, C.S.G. Pillai, Madan Mohan, G., Gopakumar, P. Livingston and M. Srinath 1986. Exploited and potential resources of live bait fishes of Lakshadweep. *Mar. Fish. Infor. Serv. T & E Ser*, 68: 25-32.

Prain, D. 1892. Botany of the Laccadives. *J. Bombay Nat. Hist. Soc.* 7: 268-295, 460-486, 8:57-86.

Prasad, R. Reghu and P.R.S. Tampi 1959. On a collection of palinurid phyllosomas from the Laccadive seas. *J. Mar. Biol Ass. India.* 1(2): 143-164.

Punnet, R.C. 1903. Namertines, In: J.S. Gardiner (ed.). *The Fauna and Geography of Maldive and Laccadive Archipelagoes* 1: 101-118 Cambridge Univ. Press, Cambridge.

Qasim, S.Z. 1970. Some characteristics of Trichodesmium bloom in the Laccadives. *Deep Sea Res.*, 17: 655-660.

Qasim, S.Z. and P.M.A. Bhattathiri 1971. Primary Productivity of seagrass bed on Kavaratti Atoll (Laccadives) *Bydrobiol,* 38: 29-38.

Qasim, S.Z. and V. Sankaranaryanan 1980. Production of particulate organic matter by the reef on Kavaratti Atoll (Laccadives). *Limnol. Oceanogr.* 15: 574-578.

Qasim, S.Z. *et al.* 1979. Energy pathways in the Laccadive Sea (Lakshadweep). *Indian J. Mr. Sci.* 8; 242-246.

Raghavendran, P. Computer Modelling Studies of Lakshadweep Futures.

Rajagopalan, M. and M.M. Meiyappan 1976. Redescription of the sand shark *Negaprion odontaspis* (Fowler) obtained from Minicoy Atoll, Lakshadweep, *J. Mar. Biol. Ass. India* 18(1): 162-164.

Raju, G. 1963. Spawning of the oceanic skipjack *Katsuwonus pelamis* (Linnaeus) in the Laccadive Sea. *FAO Fish Rep.* (6) 3: 1669-1682

Raju, G. 1964 a. Studies on the spawning of the oceanic skipjack *Katsuwonus pelamis* (Linnaeus) in Lakshadweep waters. *Proc. Symp. Scomb. Fishes. Mar. Biol. Ass. India* 1: 744-768.

Raju, G. 1964 b. Observations on the food and feeding habits of the oceanic skipjack *Katsuwonus pelamis* (Linn.) of the Lakshadweep Sea during the year 1958-59. *Ibid* 1: 607-630.

Raju, G. 1964c. Fecundity of the oceanic skipjack, *Katsuwonus pelamis* (Linnaeus) of Minicoy. *Ibid.* 2: 725-732.

Ramunni, M. 1965. *Atlas of the Laccadive Minicoy and Aminidive Islands:* 92 p.

Sankaranarayanan, V.N. 1973. Chemical characteristics of waters around Kavaratti Atoll (Laccadives). *Indian J. Mar. Sci.* 2: 23-26.

Sankarankutty, C. 1961. On some crabs (Decapoda-Brachyura) from the Laccadive Archipelago. *J. Mar. Biol Ass. India.* 3 (1&2) : 121-150.

Sen Gupta, R. Caroline Moraes, T.N. Kureshy, V.N. Sankaranaryanan, T.K. Jana, S.W.A. Naqvi and M.D. Rajagopal 1979. Chemical oceanography of Arabian Sea. Part-IV-Laccadive Sea. *Indian J. Mar. Sci.* 8: 215-221.

Shilpley, A.E. 1903a. Echiuroidea In: J.S. Gardiner (ed.) *The Fauna and Geography of the Maldive and Laccadive Archipelagoes,* 1: 127-130. Cambridge Univ. Press, Cambridge.

Silas, E.G. 1968. Oceanic and demersal fishery resources of the west coast of India and the Laccadive Sea based on exploratory fishing from R.V. Varuna Symp. Living resources of the seas around India, *Cent. Mar. Fish. Res. Inst. Cochin Abstracts:* 8-9.

Silas, E.G. 1972. Investigations on the deep scattering layers in the Laccadive Sea. In: Proc. Symp. corals and coral reefs. 1969. *Mar. Biol. Ass. India:* 257-274. (Ed.C. Mukundan and C.S.G. Pillai).

Silas, E.G. and K.C. George 1970. On the larval and postlarval development and distribution of the mesopelagic fish *Vinciguerria nimbaria* (Jordan and Williams) (Family Gonostomatidae) off the west coast of India and the Laccadive *Sea. J. Mar. Biol. Ass. India* 11 (1&2) : 218-250.

Silas, E.G., K.V.N. Rao, P.P. Pillai, Madan Mohan, G. Gopakumar, P. Livingston and M. Srinath 1986. Exploited and potential resources of tunas of Lakshadweep. *Mar. Fish. Infor. Serv.* T&E Ser. 68; 15-25.

Sivadas, P. 1977. Report on the occurrence of Acanthaster sp. in Lakshadweep waters. *Mahasagar,* 10(3-4) 179-180.

Sivadas, P.B. Narayana and K. Sivaprasad 1983. An account of the vegetation of Kavaratti Island, Laccadives Atoll. *Res. Bull. Wash.,* 299:1-9.

Smith, E.A. 1906. Marine mollusca. In: J.S.Gardiner (Ed.), *The Fauna and Geography of the Maldive and Laccadive Archipelagoes,* 2:589-630. Cambridge Univ. Press, Cambridge.

Thomas, P.A. 1979. Demospongiae of Minicoy Island (Indian Ocean) part-I. Orders Keratosida and Haploscleride. *Ibid.*21 (1&2); 10-16.

Thomas, P.T. 1964a. Food of *Katsuwonus pelamis* (Linnaeus) *Neothunns macropterus* (Temminck and Schegel) from Minicoy waters during the season 1960-61. Proc. Symp. Scomb. Fishes. Pt.2:626-630, *Mar. Biol Ass. India.*

Thomas, P.T. 1967. Size compositions of the oceanic skipjack *Katsuwonus pelamis* (Linnacus) and the yellowfin tuna *Neothunnus macropterus* (Temminck and schlegel) from the Laccadive seas around Minicoy during the season 1960-61 *Ibid*, Pt.3:1146-1153.

Thomas, P.T., 1964b. A study on the fluctuations in the occurrence of the major tuna live-bait fishes of Minicoy. *Ibid.* 681-690.

Tranter. D.J. and Jacob George 1972. Zoplankton abundance at Kavaratti and Kalpeni Atolls in the Laccadive Sea. In: Proc. Symp. corals and coral reefs; 239-256. *Mar. Biol. Ass. India.*

Udayavarma, P., Panicker, P.A., Sivadas, P. Krishnankutty, M. "Role of marine sector in the long term Development of the Lakshadweep island".

Untawale, A.G. and T.W. Jagtap 1984. Marine microphytes of Minicoy (Lakshadweep) coral Atoll of the Arabian Sea. *Aquatic Botany,* 19: 97-103

Varghese, T.J. 1974. Shark resources of the Laccadive waters. *Seafood Export Journal,* 6(1) : 65-68.

Varma, P.V., Panicker, P.A. *et al.* Role of the marine sector in the long Tuna Development of the Lakshadweep Island.

Walker, A.O. 1906. Marine crustaceans. XIV Amphipoda In: J.S. Gardiner (Ed.) *The Fauna and Geography of the Maldive and Laccadive Archipelagoes,* 2:923-932, Cambridge Univ. Press, Cambridge.

INDEX